MISSION FOR THE 21ST CENTURY

Papers from the Symposium and Consultation

Celebrating

The 100th Anniversary of the Foundation of Techny

and

The 125th Anniversary of the Foundation of the

Society of the Divine Word

Stephen B. Bevans, SVD

Roger Schroeder, SVD

editors

CCGM Publications
Chicago, IL
2001

The Chicago Center for Global Ministries (CCGM) is an ecumenical venture of Catholic Theological Union (CTU), Lutheran School of Theology at Chicago (LSTC) and McCormick (Presbyterian Church, USA) Theological Seminary (MTS).

Its mission is to provide an ecumenical context for theological education and scholarly research from the perspective of the church's catholicity in an increasingly globalized world. CCGM coordinates and seeks to develop the faculty, student and curricular resources of the three schools in the areas of

      *world mission
      *cross-cultural studies
      *study of and dialogue with the world's religions
      *urban ministry
      *justice, peace and the integrity of creation

CCGM Publications aims to disseminate the results of scholarly collaboration among faculty and students of the CCGM schools and to make more available the proceedings of lectures and conferences sponsored by the Center.

© 2001, Stephen B. Bevans, SVD and Roger Schroeder, SVD
ISBN: 0-9677245-2-X

TABLE OF CONTENTS

ABBREVIATIONS

AG -- Vatican Council II, *Ad Gentes*, Decree on the Church's Missionary Activity

DH -- Vatican Council II, *Dignitatis Humanae*, Declaration on Religious Freedom

DI -- Congregation for the Doctrine of the Faith, "Dominus Iesus"

DV -- Vatican Council II, *Dei Verbum*, Dogmatic Constitution on Divine Revelation

EA -- Pope John Paul II, Apostolic Exhortation, *Ecclesia in Asia*

EAf -- Pope John Paul II, Apostolic Exhortation, *Ecclesia in Africa*

EN -- Pope Paul VI, Apostolic Exhortation, *Evangelii Nuntiandi*, Evangelization in the Modern World

FABC -- Federation of Asian Bishops' Conferences

GS -- ` Vatican Council II, *Gaudium et Spes*, Pastoral Constitution on the Church in the Modern World

LG -- Vatican Council II, *Lumen Gentium*, Dogmatic Constitution on the Church

MD -- Earlier version of the decree on the church's missionary activity, Second Vatican Council, Third Session

NA -- Vatican Council II, *Nostra Aetate*, Declaration on the Relationship of the Church to Non-Christian Religions

OE -- Vatican Council II, *Orientalium Ecclesiarum*, Decree on Eastern Catholic Churches

PC -- Vatican Council II, *Perfectae Caritatis*, Decree on the Appropriate Renewal of the Religious Life

RM -- Pope John Paul II, Encyclical Letter, *Redemptoris Missio*, On the Permanent Validity of the Church's Missionary Mandate

SC --   Vatican Council II, *Sacrosanctum Concilium*, Constitution on the Sacred Liturgy

UR --   Vatican Council II, *Unitatis Redintegratio*, Decree on Ecumenism

VC --   Pope John Paul II, Apostolic Exhortation, *Vita Consecrata*

INTRODUCTION

In the Fall of 1998 we received a letter from Fr. John Donaghey, SVD in the name of the committee that was planning the one hundredth anniversary of the foundation of Techny (the motherhouse of Divine Word Missionaries in North America). The letter was an invitation to us to organize a symposium during the centennial year 2000--a year that would also be the one hundred twenty-fifth anniversary of the Society of the Divine Word--that would focus on the issue of missionary work in the first years of the new century and new millennium. To be perfectly honest, neither of us were thrilled at the prospect of organizing another symposium on mission. We had organized a wonderful symposium as part of the centennial celebration of the Society of the Divine Word in North America in 1995, and had edited a volume which had incorporated similar symposia held in every North American SVD province.[1] In addition, there had already been planned for the year 2000 a number of missiological conferences, including a major gathering in Chicago sponsored by a number of national organizations, including the Mission Committee of the National Conference of Catholic Bishops (as it was then called) and the United States Catholic Mission Association. Would *another* conference on mission in the year 2000 simply be too much of a good thing?

As we began to discuss the possibilities of such a symposium, however, our excitement began to grow. Here was an opportunity, we realized, to gather together SVD missiologists and mission theologians from around the world to reflect on our future together. As far as we knew--and this has been borne out as true--there had never been such a gathering in the whole of SVD history. In addition, we would be able to invite a number of other important missiologists to help us reflect from various perspectives.

Our reflections on possibilities led us to conceive of a two-part gathering. A first part would be a symposium open to all SVDs and to the public in general, and would have as its theme "Mission in the 21st Century." At this symposium we would have a member of the SVD General Council, and both a Catholic and Protestant missiologist, to reflect on the future of mission both from the perspective of the three major Catholic mission documents of the twentieth century (*Ad Gentes, Evangelii Nuntiandi*, and *Redemptoris Missio*) and the statement of the Fifteenth SVD General Chapter. (The Chapter was to be held in June-July, 2000; the final document was eventually entitled *Listening to the Spirit: Our Missionary Response Today*.)[2] In addition, the afternoon of the symposium would offer workshops by (mostly) SVD missiologists working in the contexts of Africa, Asia, Europe, Latin America and North America, together with a summary session from a variety of viewpoints (that of a bishop, an Asian, a woman and the mission secretary of the SVD).

Then, in the two days following the symposium, there would be a "consultation," open only to invited scholars, which would attempt to issue a statement in the light of contemporary missiological thought and what had been presented at the symposium. For this consultation we would invite representative SVD missiologists from every part of the world, along with a number of other key thinkers about mission.

And so we accepted Fr. Donaghey's and the committee's invitation. The date was set for December 8 and 9, 2000 for the symposium, and December 10 and 11 for the consultation. The committee graciously and generously supported our plan, and, without exception, every scholar that we invited to participate in the symposium and consultation accepted. Fr. Tom Krosnicki at the Chicago Province Mission Office graciously allowed us to employ Ms. Carmie Linden to design a brochure; Fr. Frank Kamp and Fr. Mark Schramm just as graciously volunteered to plan and organize the closing Eucharistic liturgy on the day of the symposium; Cardinal Jozef Tomko, Prefect of the Congregation for the Evangelization of Peoples in Rome, accepted the committee's invitation to preside at the closing liturgy-- as well as to deliver an address at the symposium and be present for the consultation. We were most fortunate that Fr. Antonio Pernia, who had been invited to speak at the symposium from the SVD perspective, was elected Superior General at the Fifteenth General Chapter. Steve Bevans was a delegate to the Chapter, and the first thing he said to the new General was that he hoped he could still speak at the Symposium--and Fr. Pernia assured him that he would!

Both the symposium and the consultation were overwhelmingly successful. Attendance at the symposium on both the evening of December 8 and the day of December 9 was well over 200. The talks and workshops were all quite thought-provoking; the concluding liturgy, particularly because of the choirs and the marvelous offertory procession with representatives from every nation, was a perfect end to the symposium and the entire Techny centennial year. The consultation was an amazing event. Under the able facilitation of Fr. Gary Riebe-Estrella, SVD, the twenty-five participants worked hard and well to produce a short but meaningful statement which outlined the *status questionis* of mission today, and offered an agenda for further and future discussion and research. Very gratifying to all was the presence--and participation--of both Cardinal Tomko and Fr. General Pernia during the entire consultation.

***

This volume contains the proceedings of the symposium of December 8 and 9, 2000, as well as the statement on "Mission for the Twenty-first Century" produced by the consultation. In addition, we have included two additional articles. The first, by SVD Indian missiologist Jacob Kavunkal, was written specifically for the event as part of Fr. Kavunkal's process of applying for a U.S. visa. The second, by SVD general councillor Leo Kleden, was written originally for the 2001 annual meeting of the Catholic Theological Society of America in Milwaukee, Wisconsin. Unfortunately, because of visa problems, Fr. Kleden was not able to attend the meeting and deliver his paper in person. We thought it appropriate, therefore, to publish it along with these other groundbreaking reflections on the future of mission--both of the church in general and the SVD in particular.

In presenting these papers for publication, we are grateful first of all to Fr. Donaghey for his challenging invitation back in the Fall of 1998. Over the years, if we have learned one thing, it is that one grows both physically and spiritually by being stretched beyond one's comfort zone. We were stretched, and we did grow. High on the list of our gratitude is Fr. Casimir Garbacz, the rector of the Techny community, and his house council. Fr. Garbacz and the council generously provided the funding both for the symposium/consultation *and* for the publication of this book. Among many others to whom we owe thanks are Fr. Paul Connors, Fr. Frank Kamp, Brother Pat Hogan, Ms. Marian Anetsberger (these last two especially for making the accommodations at Techny so comfortable), and Chicago Province Provincial Fr. Stanley Uroda. We are extremely grateful to Fr. Tom Krosnicki in the Mission Office at Techny--and in particular to Ms. Carmie Linden--for the beautiful brochure she designed for publicizing the symposium. The design of the brochure is the basis of the cover--also designed by Ms. Linden--which graces this volume. To all our symposium presenters, especially Cardinal Tomko, Fr. Pernia, and Bishop Curtis Guillory, SVD, and to the twenty-five participants in the consultation, goes a specially deserved word of thanks. And among them Dr. Wilbert Shenk, Dr. William Burrows and Sr. Margaret Guider are to be particularly singled out as the only Protestant, only lay person and only woman in the group respectively.

What will mission look like in the twenty-first century? We hope that this volume will provide some glimpse, although we are sure--and we hope!--that the Spirit has some surprises in store. But from what we have discerned from this symposium and this consultation, mission will be--as always, but perhaps in the future more consciously so--grounded in the dialogical and salvation-seeking nature of the triune God (see the contributions of Pernia, Tomko, Shenk, Schreiter and Gittins). Mission in this new century will be lived out in the confidence that, as Anthony Gittins says in his contribution, God is taking the church to the world rather than the church taking God. And, as so many of the contributors to this volume insist, God is taking the church to the world through the practice and spirit of dialogue. Fr. Superior General Pernia puts it trenchantly: "Somehow one gets a feeling that women and men in the twenty-first century need dialogue in order to ensure their--and the world's--very survival" (p. 18). Dialogue will be *how* mission witnesses and proclaims God's salvation. As we see now, it has everything to do as well with the *content* of that salvation, for, in the words of Robert J. Schreiter in this volume, "one of the most compelling forms the Good News of Jesus Christ takes on today is the possibility of reconciliation" (p. 35)--that is, people truly able to *talk* with one another, *communicate* with one another, *learn* from one another. To do this, of course, mission needs to be motivated by a new spirit of vulnerability and powerlessness (Pernia; Kleden); it needs to be done out of authentic solidarity with the poor and the marginalized (see the contributions of Prior, Valle and Kavunkal), and with an appreciation--albeit at times critical--of local cultures (Afagbegee). We must pass, says Edênio Valle, "from life conceived as our own conquest," to conceiving "*life as gift.*" We must never shrink from working for justice, but we need to realize that justice comes "through the intrinsic power of the good news, sown in patience and in hope" (p. 140). Whether mission is lived out in what have been traditionally called "mission countries," or in the more-recently recognized "mission fields" of Europe and North America (Bettscheider and Gittins), mission in our new century will not proceed from a strong political or economic power base, but from genuine relationship with Jesus of Nazareth on the one hand and the local people on the other.

The mission is not our own, but God's; it is lived out in prophetic dialogue and confident vulnerability. There is much more to ponder in this rich collection of committed mission theologians and practitioners, but perhaps these three ideas sum up best the exciting vision that the participants in the symposium and colloquium put before us. The stimulating ideas expressed in these pages are not just *ideas*; they come out of a deep commitment on the part of all the participants to God's work in the world.

May they not *remain* ideas for those who read them, but bear fruit in creative and faithful practice in those readers' lives.

Catholic Theological Union
July 1, 2001

Stephen B. Bevans, SVD
Louis J. Luzbetak, SVD Professor of Mission and Culture

Roger Schroeder, SVD
Associate Professor of Cross Cultural Ministry

Notes

1. Stephen Bevans and Roger Schroeder, eds., *Word Remembered, Word Proclaimed: Selected Papers from Symposia Celebrating the SVD Centennial in North America*. Studia Instituti Missiologici Societatis Verbi Divini 65 (Nettetal: Steyler Verlag, 1997).

2. The statement was officially published in *Dialogue with the Word*, 1 (Rome: SVD Generalate, 2000), 13-47.

MISSION FOR THE TWENTY-FIRST CENTURY:
An SVD Perspective

Antonio M. Pernia, SVD[*]

Introduction

I'd like to begin by thanking the organizers of this symposium for choosing the topic, "Mission for the Twenty-First Century," which will engage us in a re-reading of the three major documents on Mission of the Twentieth Century--*Ad Gentes* (AG--1965), *Evangelii Nuntiandi* (EN--1975), and *Redemptoris Missio* (RM--1990). My own re-reading of these documents in preparation for this symposium has made me appreciate their immense importance not only in shaping our understanding and practice of mission during the last thirty-five years, but also in indicating the direction of mission at the beginning of the twenty-first century. I do think these documents deserve to be read and re-read, indeed from different perspectives, as this symposium will attempt to do.

I am pleased to offer tonight one particular re-reading, from one particular perspective, of the three documents. Knowing that tomorrow experts will be doing a fuller re-reading of the documents, tonight I will limit myself to picking out what I consider, from the perspective of the Society of the Divine Word (SVD), to have been the central idea of each document. My presentation tonight, then, is divided into three parts: *first,* the central ideas of each of the documents; *second,* the echo that these ideas have had in the SVD; and *third,* some reflections on mission for the twenty-first century from the SVD perspective.

I. *The Central Ideas of the Three Documents*

It should be stated at the outset that each of the three documents contains a wealth of ideas or themes and that, in each case, it would be a

---

[*]*Antonio M. Pernia, SVD is Superior General of the Society of the Divine Word. He holds a doctorate from the Pontifical Gregorian University, and is the author of* **God's Kingdom and Human Liberation** *(Manila: Divine Word Publications, 1990).*

dangerous proposition to pick out one idea as the central theme and subsume all other ideas under it. Having said that, it should also be stated that, seen from a particular perspective, each document could be identified closely with one of its major ideas. I believe this is the case when the documents are read from the SVD perspective. And seen from the perspective of the SVD penchant for culture, I believe we can say that the main ideas of the three documents are the following:

AG: inculturation and the local church,
EN: the evangelization of cultures and integral evangelization
RM: new cultural settings or the new Areopagus

Seen in this framework, the three documents yield three differing but complementary notions of mission:

AG: Mission as building up a truly local church through the inculturation of the Gospel;

EN: Mission as giving witness to God's Kingdom by renewing the whole of humanity through integral evangelization or the evangelization of . cultures;

RM: Mission as proclaiming Christ in those "geographical areas" and "cultural settings" which still remain uninfluenced by the gospel.

Allow me now to say a few words on each of the documents under this framework.

Ad Gentes (1965): **Inculturation and the Local Church**

No. 6 of AG states that:

> The proper purpose of . . . [this] . . . missionary activity is evangelization, and the planting of the Church among those peoples and groups where it has not yet taken root. Thus from the seed which is the Word of God, particular autochthonous Churches should be sufficiently established and should grow up all over the world, endowed with their own maturity and vital forces.

No. 10 which is the paragraph that opens Chapter II, entitled "Mission Work Itself," adds that:

> The Church, in order to be able to offer all human beings the mystery of salvation and the life brought by God, must implant herself into these groups for the same motive which led Christ to bind Himself, in virtue of His incarnation, to certain social and cultural conditions of those human beings among whom He dwelt.

From here on, inculturation becomes a recurring theme in the whole of the document. Local churches should be "deeply rooted in the people" (15); the national formation program for priests should be in touch "with their own particular national way of thinking and acting" (16); religious institutes should strive to give expression to the mystical tradition of the Church and "hand them on according to the nature and genius of each nation" (18); institutes of the contemplative life should "live out their lives in a way accommodated to the truly religious traditions of the people" (40); the lay faithful should give witness to the newness of life in Christ "in the social and cultural framework of their homeland, according to their own national traditions" (21).

I believe there is no need to multiply similar quotations from AG. It is quite clear that inculturation is a dominant idea in the document. Naturally, the term as such is not yet used. Instead the document still uses such terms as "accommodation" and "adaptation" (22). Similarly, the language employed in reference to the local church is still the "implanting of the Church" (*plantatio ecclesiae*) rather than the "building up of the local church." In any case, the term "implanting" serves to highlight the need to "inculturate" the Church or root it in the cultural and religious traditions of the local people.

The context for this emphasis in AG on inculturation and the local church is the whole direction of the Second Vatican Council. On the one hand, both *Lumen Gentium* (the Dogmatic Constitution on the church) and *Christus Dominus* (the Decree on the pastoral office of bishops in the church) contain, as we know, a renewed understanding of the "particular churches" and of the role of bishops in the church. A particular church is not just a sector of the universal church but the presence of the universal church in a particular time and space. The authority of the bishop does not simply come from papal delegation but is based on the sacrament of ordination. On the other hand, the idea of inculturation–or adaptation and accommodation--

had already been introduced by *Sacrosanctum Concilium* (SC–the Constitution on the Sacred Liturgy) two years before it found its way into AG. SC contains a whole section dedicated to the "Norms for Adapting the Liturgy to the Temperament and Traditions of Peoples" (37-40). In fact, the use of the vernacular in the liturgy became the first and most visible expression of the complex process of inculturation.

Thus, I believe we can say that AG understands mission as primarily the task of implanting the church in a particular people and culture, or in more familiar terms, the task of building up the local church through the inculturation of the gospel among a particular people. This is an understanding of mission which, obviously, is largely ecclesiocentric or church-centered.

Evangelii Nuntiandi (1975):
Evangelization of Cultures or Integral Evangelization

Ten years after AG, the "questio disputata," so to say, had shifted to liberation theology and the whole question of human and social development, especially in the so-called Third World. By the time of the Synod of Bishops in 1974, liberation theology and the phenomenon of the base ecclesial communities had reached Asia and Africa from Latin America where they had originated. The "option for the poor" was the order of the day. All this formed part of the context for the 1974 Synod of Bishops and subsequently for Pope Paul VI's Apostolic Exhortation, *Evangelii Nuntiandi*, which came out the following year. Paragraph 30 of EN puts it in this way:

> It is well known in what terms numerous Bishops from all the continents spoke of this [i.e., the message of liberation] at the last Synod, especially the Bishops from the Third World, with a pastoral accent resonant with the voice of millions of sons and daughters of the Church who make up those peoples.

It is no surprise, then, that one of the main themes of EN is "integral evangelization," or an evangelization that proclaims both the message of salvation and the message of liberation. Thus, paragraph 31 speaks of the "profound links" between evangelization and liberation--links of an anthropological order, in the theological order, and of the evangelical order. In the same vein, paragraph 9 speaks of the salvation proclaimed by Christ as the "great gift of God which is liberation from everything that oppresses the human being but which is above all liberation from sin and the Evil One."

This notion of integral evangelization and of integral salvation is placed in the framework of a "global vision" which sees evangelization as a "complex process made up of varied elements" (24) and defines it as "bringing the Good News into all strata of humanity, and through its influence transforming humanity from within and making it new" (18). Paragraph 19 explains what transforming the strata of humanity means:

> . . . it is a question not only of preaching the Gospel in ever wider geographic areas or to ever greater numbers of people, but also of affecting and as it were upsetting, through the power of the Gospel, humankind's criteria of judgment, determining values, points of interest, lines of thought, sources of inspiration and models of life, which are in contrast with the Word of God and the plan of salvation.

Paragraph 20 sums up the whole matter by speaking of the "evangelization of cultures."

> The split between the Gospel and culture is without a doubt the drama of our time, just as it was of other times. Therefore every effort must be made to ensure a full evangelization of culture, or more correctly of cultures. They have to be regenerated by an encounter with the Gospel.

The horizon for this global vision of evangelization is the Kingdom of God. It is interesting to note that EN opens its first chapter, entitled "From Christ the Evangelizer to the Evangelizing Church," with two references to chapter 4 of Luke's Gospel which are both favorite biblical texts of liberation theology. "I must proclaim the Good News of the kingdom of God. This is what I was sent to do" (Lk 4:43)--this for EN sums up the whole mission of Jesus. And these words, says EN, take on their full significance when linked the words of the Prophet Isaiah which Jesus applies to himself: "The Spirit of the Lord has been given to me, for he has anointed. He has sent me to bring the good news to the poor" (6).

In Paragraph 23, EN describes the Kingdom as "the new world, the new state of things, the new manner of being, of living, of living in community, which the Gospel inaugurates." In light of this, I believe we can say that for EN, mission is giving witness to God's Kingdom by renewing humanity through integral evangelization or the evangelization of cultures. In this sense, we can say that EN's understanding of mission is one that is basically Kingdom-centered.

Redemptoris Missio (1990):
New Cultural Settings or the New Areopagus.

Chapter I of RM carries the title, "Jesus Christ, the Only Savior," and sets the tone of what I consider to be a strongly Christo-centric understanding of mission. It should be noted though that a chapter each is also devoted to "The Kingdom of God" (Chapter II) and "The Holy Spirit, the Principal Agent of Mission" (Chapter III). However, despite the many beautiful statements about both the Kingdom and the Spirit, one gets the impression that the main purpose of these chapters is a Christo-centric one, i.e., to underline the fact that the Kingdom and the Spirit cannot and must not be separated from Christ and the Church. Paragraph 18 states: "The Kingdom cannot be detached either from Christ or from the Church." And paragraphs 28 and 29 take pains to show that the "Spirit who sows the seeds of the Word present in various customs and cultures" (28) is the "same Spirit who was at work in the Incarnation and in the life, death and Resurrection of Jesus, and who is at work in the Church. He (i.e., the Spirit) is not an alternative to Christ" (29).

I believe it is safe to say that part of the context for the emergence of RM were the various theologies of religions originating from Asia, particularly from India. In a sense, the "questio disputata" had shifted once more, this time to the question of interreligious dialogue and the discourse on the uniqueness of Jesus Christ. One can indeed sense in RM the concern over theologies of religions which do not give proper place to the uniqueness of Jesus Christ. Paragraph 6 explicitly states that "to introduce any sort of separation between the Word and Jesus Christ is contrary to the Christian faith." And paragraph 36 lists among the difficulties of mission *ad gentes* the "widespread indifferentism which is based on incorrect theological perspectives and is characterized by a religious relativism which leads to the belief that 'one religion is as good as another.'"

Taking the encyclical as a whole, however, I believe that it will be chiefly remembered for the expression "the New Areopagus." This expression comes in the context of RM's discussion on the "Parameters of Mission *Ad Gentes*" (37-38) and is connected with the broadening of the ambit of mission *ad gentes* to include not just "territorial limits" but also "new worlds and new social phenomena" and "cultural sectors." This last sector is what RM calls "the modern equivalents of the Areopagus." In a sense, then, RM projects an understanding of mission that is no longer exclusively geographic but also situational, or an understanding of mission that is no longer tied solely to the notion of "mission territories" but also incorporates the idea of "missionary situations." Donal Dorr, in his book *Mission in Today's World*, calls these missionary situations or cultural settings the new frontiers of mission *ad gentes*.[1]

Perhaps it can be said, even at the risk of oversimplification, that there are two movements in RM, namely, the movement to recapture or re-emphasize the centrality of Jesus Christ as the only Savior and the movement to extend the borders of mission to include not just "mission territories" but also "missionary situations." And so what emerges as an understanding of mission in RM is the idea of proclaiming Christ in those "geographical areas" and "cultural settings" which still remain uninfluenced by the Gospel (40).

II. *Echoes in the SVD*

I believe it can be said that the central ideas of the three documents have found an echo in the SVD in three or four of our own documents. I refer to, *first,* our revised Constitutions; *second,* the General Chapter documents of 1982 and 1988; and *third,* the Statement of the recently concluded General Chapter of 2000.

The SVD Constitutions

Although the final revision of our Constitutions came only in the General Chapter of 1982, the basic direction of this revision was set already in the General Chapter of 1967/68, the first of the so-called "renewal chapters" of the Society, and in the General Chapters immediately following.[2]

It is evident that the revision of the "100s" section of our Constitutions, the section which presents an understanding of our missionary service, was greatly influenced by AG. While other ideas of AG have also entered into this revision, the theme of inculturation and the local church, in particular, has a strong echo in this section of the Constitutions. Indeed, this theme is mentioned directly or indirectly in so many places that, as a consequence, one gets the impression that our missionary service is to be organized around the building up of, and collaboration with, the local church.

Const. 113, which deals explicitly with this theme, deserves to be quoted in full:

> The universal church lives and finds expression in many and diverse local churches. For a local church to be truly a living church, it must be rooted in the cultural and social milieu of its own people. It is our task to work with the local church in its efforts to express the gospel message without distortion in the thought patterns, languages and symbols of its culture. In this way Christian and indigenous values complement and mutually enrich each other.

Directory 113.2 is a classic expression of our commitment to the promotion of the process of inculturation:

> In line with a tradition of our founder, one of the basic tasks of our scholarly institutes should be to promote reflection on our mission work and research into the interaction of gospel, culture and religion.

The 1982 and 1988 General Chapters

The 1982 General Chapter is important not only for having finalized the revision of our Constitutions but also for having introduced Constitution 112 and its directories which speak of our option for the poor. In addition, and along the same vein, the Chapter also produced two major documents-- the first, entitled "The Promotion of Justice and Peace in Solidarity with the Poor in the Light of Constitution 112," and the second, "Directives on Poverty and Finance." These documents were ranked by the capitulars as the number one and number two priorities of the Society after the Chapter.[3]

From this one can see how much this Chapter was influenced by the concerns of EN, namely, the questions of justice and peace and the theme of evangelization as the proclamation of the message of liberating salvation. As the first document puts it:

> The Church on various occasions and at all levels has seriously reflected on the situation of the world today in the light of sacred scripture. More and more the Church has come to realize that faithfulness to Jesus' Kingdom message

and his preferential love for the poor entails an active involvement in transforming unjust structures and promoting justice and peace. Consequently the Church's mission of proclaiming the Gospel today implies participation in creating a new world order that better reflects the Kingdom of God already present in the world (see EN 8 and 30).[4]

The 1988 General Chapter, on the other hand, will be remembered for having introduced the theme of "Passing Over" which runs through its threefold document on SVD mission, spirituality and formation.[5] While the concerns of this Chapter go beyond those of EN, still we hear echoes of the concerns of EN in its document. For instance, SVD mission is treated under five headings--the local church, dialogue, inculturation, secularization and integral liberation. Or, SVD spirituality is seen as a threefold process of passing over to other cultures, to the poor, and to people of other religions. Or still, one of the seven principles of SVD formation is openness to the world, especially to the non-evangelized, the marginalized, the poor and the oppressed.

The 2000 General Chapter

About four months after the conclusion of the Fifteenth General Chapter, we are still in the process of studying and assimilating the content of its statement, "Listening to the Spirit: Our Missionary Response Today."[6] Even so, I believe it is not difficult to hear echoes of RM in the statement. Aside from the six explicit references to RM, two other elements in the statement reflect major ideas of the encyclical.

The first is the view of mission as no longer tied exclusively to "geographical areas" but includes "cultural settings." No. 27 of the statement explicitly adverts to this idea. But beyond that, the whole notion of mission as prophetic dialogue with four different groups of people is a concrete example of the identification of particular "cultural settings" or of "new frontiers" of mission. No. 52, which introduces the section on the "fourfold prophetic dialogue," says it explicitly: "Our discussions in the Chapter have confirmed that our understanding of mission has shifted from an exclusively geographical orientation to one that includes missionary situations."

And the second element is the choice of "dialogue" as the key term expressing the kind of approach which we ought to take toward these four groups of people. This also is an echo of RM. In fact, nos. 53 and 54 of the statement explicitly refer to RM in talking about the fourfold prophetic dialogue. One characteristic of RM, of course, is that it undertakes a longer and fuller treatment of interreligious dialogue (as it does with other similar themes) than AG or EN. Reflecting the spirit of RM's treatment of interreligious dialogue, no. 53 of the statement says:

> . . . already in the Vatican II documents, the term "dialogue," in all its richness, is used in a wider meaning to describe our proper attitude toward and relationship with all people. Dialogue is an attitude of "solidarity, respect, and love" (*Gaudium et Spes* [GS] 3) that is to permeate all of our activities. Limited as we are by our personal and cultural viewpoints, none of us has attained the whole truth contained in God and revealed fully in Christ. In dialogue we search together for this truth.

III. *Some Reflections on SVD Mission for the Twenty-First Century*

From all that has been said so far, what reflections can we make for mission for the twenty-first century? Allow me to share just two reflections:

First, from our re-reading of the three documents, I believe we can say that each of these documents was a response to questions arising from the concrete situation of mission--the growth of the local church in the case of AG, the question of social justice and human promotion in the case of EN, and the emergence of new worlds or cultural settings in the case of RM. And so, the major issues taken up by these documents were inculturation in the case of AG, integral liberation in the case of EN, and proclamation in the New Areopagus in the case of RM.

And so it is that our theory of mission is often determined by our praxis of mission. A new concept of mission emerges from new mission engagements. I believe we need to be more daring in the twenty-first century in discovering and responding to new challenges in mission. What amazes me in the three documents is the courage to enlarge our understanding of mission in response to concrete mission situations--inculturation: enlarging the *expressions of the faith*; integral liberation: enlarging the *content of evangelization*; new cultural settings or the New Areopagus: enlarging the *field of mission*.

For us, SVDs, a number of possibilities for new mission engagements are indicated in statement of the last General Chapter--all organized around the notion of prophetic dialogue. It still remains to be seen in what way our engagement in prophetic dialogue will enlarge our understanding of mission. Will prophetic dialogue perhaps lead to enlarging our notion of the "communion of faith"? Or the "oikoumene"? Or the "ekklesia"?

Second, the great themes of the three major documents on mission will continue to be valid in the twenty-first century--inculturation, integral liberation, new cultural settings, interreligious dialogue. AG, EN, RM do not supersede each other. Rather, each one contributes lasting insights to the overall theology of mission. However, as far as SVD Mission for the twenty-first century is concerned, the last General Chapter has proposed "the fourfold prophetic dialogue" as the key concept. The Chapter Statement explains this concept rather well and I do not wish to repeat that here. But I do wish to state here that I believe the choice of the term "dialogue" is a happy one, for at least three reasons:

In the first place, "dialogue" seems to be a very "twenty-first century" word. For the twenty-first century is and needs to be an age of dialogue--both in the sense of the urgent need for dialogue in our deeply divided world and in the sense of the tremendous possibilities for dialogue offered by our globalized world. Somehow one gets a feeling that women and men in the twenty-first century need to dialogue in order to ensure their--and the world's--very survival.

Secondly, understanding mission as dialogue corrects a one-sided view of mission which puts the emphasis almost entirely on the great work done by missionaries and the great gift brought by them, with little attention paid to the recipients of this gift. Dialogue underlines the fact that the Spirit is at work in the people being evangelized as well as in the evangelizers, and that mission is a two-way exchange of gifts between missionaries and the people with whom they work.[7]

Third, SVD mission in the twenty-first century will be carried out largely by missionaries originating from the third world, or more particularly, from Asia. I believe some of the problems that we have encountered with missionaries originating from these countries are due to the fact that they may find it difficult or impossible to conform to an older model of mission. I believe dialogue as a model of mission is one that better accords with their cultural characteristics or dispositions. Let me mention just three examples:

Powerlessness. Much of Asia, as we know, is characterized by the historical experience of colonization, a socio-economic condition of poverty, and a religious situation where Christianity is a minority. So, the Asian missionary cannot, or ought not, evangelize from a position of power or superiority. He or she must approach mission from a position of powerlessness and humility.

Contemplation – Another distinctive characteristic of Asia is its religiosity and contemplative spirit, and the priority given to being over doing. And so, the Asian missionary will not, or ought not, evangelize by doing things for the people but by being with them and enabling them to do things themselves. His or her approach to mission will be marked not so much by frenetic activity but by contemplative presence among God's people.

Stewardship – Still another characteristic of Asia is that the Christian faith has come to it as something imported or even imposed from outside. And despite the enormous efforts at inculturation, the Christian faith in much of Asia has not really become its own yet. Thus, the Asian missionary will not, or ought not, share the faith as if he or she owned it, dictating thereby the terms by which it must be understood, lived and celebrated. His or her approach to mission will be to share the faith as a gift received from God through others, conscious of himself or herself as merely its steward or servant and never its owner or master.

Powerlessness, contemplation, stewardship--all these, I believe, are requirements of genuine dialogue. For how can one dialogue from a position of power? Or how can one dialogue without listening in contemplative silence? And how can one dialogue if one already possesses all?

My dear confreres and friends, it is exciting to be standing on the threshold of the twenty-first century. The challenges to mission are many. The number of our missionaries seems to be sufficient (for now at least). The vision of mission given us by the Fifteenth General Chapter appears to be appropriate. It is therefore my hope that, under the guidance of the Spirit, through dialogue we will be able to meet the challenges with our resources.

NOTES

1. Donal Dorr, *Mission in Today's World* (Dublin: Columba Press, 2000), 202 ff.

2. See *Nuntius SVD* VIII (1964-1968), 641-643; *Nuntius SVD* IX (1969-1973), 157-162; 416-438.

3. *Nuntius SVD* XI (1979-1983), English Edition, 575.

4. Ibid, 578.

5. See *Nuntius SVD* XII (1984-1988), English Edition, 668-708.

6. See *In Dialogue with the Word*, No. 1, Sept 2000.

7. See Dorr, 16.

MISSION FOR THE TWENTY-FIRST CENTURY:
The Perspective of the Magisterium

Jozef Cardinal Tomko[*]

I wish to thank the Rector, Fr. Casimir Garbacz, and the community of the Divine Word Missionaries in Techny for the invitation to take part in this Symposium. I would also like to offer my congratulations on the occasion of the closing of Techny's centenary celebration.

This Symposium honors the Society of the Divine Word because it manifests your ecclesial as well as your missionary sensitivity and your desire to study in depth the directions that come from the three most important missionary documents of the church. In fact, *Redemptoris Missio* has the date of 7th December 1990 "on the 25th anniversary of the Conciliar Decree *Ad Gentes*," while the Apostolic Exhortation *"Evangelii Nuntiandi"* of Paul VI was published on 8th December 1975. With this Symposium you anticipate a similar celebration of the 10th anniversary of *Redemptoris Missio* which the Congregation for Evangelization of Peoples, together with the Pontifical Urban University, will organize in Rome on the 19-20th January, 2001, the date that corresponds with the actual publication of the Encyclical.

Allow me, in the short time available, to present for your reflection a few observations. Inevitably they will be short and incomplete. I trust that the two addresses that follow will have sufficient space to deal with topics in a scientific manner.

I. *Short History*

Up to Vatican Council II

From the outset, the church has been carrying out its mission of evangelization in response to the solemn commandment, beginning with the Jerusalem community and continuing in the work of the Apostles and their successors, and also through the witness of the faithful. The steps are well-known: Jerusalem, Samaria, Antioch, Rome, Asia Minor, Athens, the

---

[*]*Jozef Cardinal Tomko has recently retired from his position as Prefect of the Congregation of the Evangelization of Peoples in Rome.*

Mediterranean, Gaul, Britain, Germanic tribes, Slavic peoples, the "New World" of the two Americas, right up to the evangelization in the 19th and 20th century of Africa, Oceania and Asia. The Church carried out her missionary activity mainly through missionaries, almost through a form of delegation. The "established" particular churches did not participate directly, and the missionary imperative was not very widespread among the masses of the faithful.

Missiology as a theological science is a very late development. Gustav Warneck published his work between 1892 and 1903 and he died in 1919. Joseph Schmidlin, who died in 1944, was the founder of Catholic missiology. Theology for missionary clergy was being taught in the Urban College "De Propaganda Fide," which was founded in the year 1627 (1st August). But the first chair of missiology only came in 1919-1920, and this set the seeds for the erection of the Pontifical Scientific Missionary Institute in 1933. My predecessor, Cardinal Fumasoni-Biondi, wrote on that occasion: "Missiology has now assumed the dignity of a scientific discipline." The Gregorian University only began a modest course of missiology in 1929. In the 1920s and 1930s at the University of Louvain, Fr. Pierre Charles founded, first the "*Collana Xaveriana*," and then two chairs of missiological studies which went to form a school, out of which emerged A. Seumois, OMI, J. Masson, J. Philips and other missiologists. Fr. Charles proposed the "*plantatio Ecclesiae visibilis*" as the aim of mission, while the School of Münster, which was linked to the Schmidlin, proposed instead the model of *conversion*.

Vatican Council II

The Second Vatican Council arrived at a moment of crisis and doctrinal tension. We were at the beginning of the movement for independence in various Third World countries, with the end of colonization that had provided protection for missionaries in some regions, while in others it was an obstacle to evangelization. Missiological and theological discussions did not in general seem to offer a united base for a missiology at a conciliar level. But as the work of the Council progressed, certain important documents began to mature, and these eventually helped in the formulation of the Decree on the Church's Missionary Activity -- *Ad Gentes Divinitus*, which was published on 7 December 1965. This made use of important texts such as the Dogmatic Constitution on the Church *Lumen Gentium* (21 November 1964) whose principal drafter, Gerard Philips, also collaborated in the preparation of *Ad Gentes*. We should not forget that the Prefect of the Congregation "de Propaganda Fide" was at that time the Armenian (and therefore Oriental) Cardinal Agagianian, also a fine theologian. In order to understand the missiological thought of the Council, one also needs to know the theology of other documents, such as *Dei Verbum* (18 November 1965), *Gaudium et Spes* (7 December 1965) and *Nostra aetate* (28 October 1965).

The Decree *Ad Gentes* gathers into six chapters the whole theological problematic and the praxis linked to mission, which came to be referred to more and more by the Pauline term "*ad gentes*": 1. doctrinal principles, 2. missionary work in itself, 3. particular churches, 4. missionaries, 5. organization of missionary activity, 6. cooperation. It is a theological, pastoral and practical synthesis, with some intuitions that receive the backing of the highest conciliar Magisterium. The doctrinal principles of mission have their origins in the trinitarian source, in other words in the source of love that is God the Father, in the mission of the Son and in the mission of the Holy Spirit, who was sent by Christ and continues to act in the church, the very nature of which is missionary from birth. Missionary activity therefore concerns the whole church and is the "epiphany and realization of God's plan in the world and in history; that by which God, through mission, clearly brings to a conclusion the history of salvation . . . and tends towards eschatological fullness" (AG 9). In the denseness of number 9, this activity is described in profound and inspirational terms, with the vision of salvation that "purges of evil associations those elements of truth and grace which are found among peoples, and which are, as it were, a secret presence of God; and it restores them to Christ their source who overthrows the rule of the devil and limits the manifold malice of evil. So whatever goodness is found in people's minds and hearts, or in the particular customs and cultures of peoples, far from being lost is purified, raised to a higher level and reaches its perfection . . . ."

Missionary work is described as "the witness of life and dialogue," "the presence of charity," "the preaching of the Gospel and assembling the People of God" (evangelization and conversion, catechumenate and Christian initiation), "forming of the Christian community" (community, indigenous clergy, catechesis, religious life, laity).

From these few references it is already clear that the Decree is the point of arrival of a missionary era, but it is also the point of departure for other developments. The trinitarian base, the continuity of the mission of the Church--defined by her very nature as missionary--the importance of proclamation and the foundation of Christian communities, are by now permanent acquisitions, while the positive appreciation of religions and cultures, of the seeds of the Word hidden therein (AG 11) together with the recognition of "limits" and of "malice" are the first steps towards a future theology of religions, while there are also some bases for a critical evaluation of the theology of liberation (AG 12).

After the Council

The post-Conciliar period is marked in its first twenty years by a fervor of research and of changes, but also of violent unrest and deep crises. This is true in particular in the field of mission. The achievement of independence on a massive scale led to the quick rejection in many countries of everything that came from outside. Some then launched accusations of colonialism against missionaries. The too swift transfer of responsibility into the hands of the young indigenous forces created uncertainty in many missionaries, but also in the indigenous pastoral agents. The drop in vocations in the West reduced not only the number of missionaries but also their morale. At the same time the mission was widening out its field of action and facing new demands such as development, justice and peace, liberation, inter-religious dialogue and inculturation. Theology was unable to channel the new realities or new aspects of mission into an organic vision, and it easily insisted blindly on one aspect to the detriment of others, especially the classical ways of mission.

In this situation the new collegial institute of the Synod of Bishops has been a great help. After the first steps (1967, 1971), the theme of "evangelization" was taken up by the representatives of the world's bishops in the third general assembly in 1974. The bishops had to face new realities but also new theologies, such as political theology (J.B. Metz), theology of development and theology of liberation (G. Gutiérrez), as well as the new interpretations of the theology of salvation with an orientation more directed towards the world, towards the person and the "humanum," towards justice and poverty. After a rich discussion the two special secretaries (D. Grasso and D. S. Amalorpavadass) were unable to harmonize their positions or to propose a single project of a final document on which to vote. For this reason the bishops presented all the material to Pope Paul VI, asking him to use it for a document of his own. A year later, Paul VI published the Apostolic Exhortation *Evangelii Nuntiandi* which immediately found a wide consensus.

Without doubt the exhortation introduced and underlined new and important elements. It used the term "evangelization," but yet "mission" and "missionary" appear eleven times and the Decree *Ad Gentes* was quoted fourteen times. The point of departure was directly "From Christ the Evangelizer to the Evangelizing Church" (Ch. I). The reality of evangelization is highlighted in all its "richness, complexity and dynamism" (EN 17); it is composed of various elements (witness of life, inculturation, integral human development, liberation, conversion, liturgy, catechetics; see Ch. III on "Contents" and Ch. IV on the "Methods of Evangelization"), culminating in the vigorous reminder of the necessity of an explicit proclamation of Jesus Christ: "The Good News proclaimed by the witness of life sooner or later has to be proclaimed by the word of life" (22). What is also clear is its warning against the temptation "to reduce her mission to the dimensions of a simply temporal project; they would reduce her aims to a man-centered goal; salvation . . . would be reduced to material well-being; her activity . . . would become initiatives of the political or social order" (32). Nevertheless, "the Church is certainly not willing to restrict her mission only to the religious field and dissociate herself from man's temporal problems. Nevertheless she reaffirms the primacy of her spiritual vocation and refuses to replace the proclamation of the Kingdom by the proclamation of forms of human liberation...'(34). The approach towards non-Christian religions is positive, because they are seen to possess many "seeds of the Word" and can constitute a true preparation for the Gospel." They are like "arms stretched out towards heaven," but only the religion of Jesus "objectively places man in relation with the plan of God" (53). The exhortation also faces the phenomenon of the "dechristianized world," of the non-believers and of those who do not practice, and in the final chapter VII it mentions the "action of the Holy Spirit" (75), which is necessary for evangelization.

The exhortation has contributed in redirecting the specific mission *"ad gentes"* to the riverbed of evangelization or the general mission of the Church. It has also definitively clarified the relationship between liberation, human development and salvation. But in the eighties (1980-1990), further changes came in, such as massive migration, the presence of adherents of the great ancient religions and oriental cultures in Europe, growing globalization through the mass media, the process of inculturation and further evaluation of the non-Christian religions and the search for the "seeds of the Word." In missionary theology and activity, we see in some regions the abandonment of a Christocentric approach in favor of a Kingdom-centered one; we see proclamation substituted by dialogue (effectively reduced to dialogue of life); but above all we see the radical tendency to consider all religions as valid ways of salvation. This all creates great confusion among missionaries who launch themselves into social works or go in search of faith among the non-Christians, rather than bring the faith in Jesus Christ to them. The conviction also spreads among Christians that all religions are equally good ways of salvation. Missionaries obviously suffer from this. The international missiological Congress organized in 1988 by the Pontifical Urban University on the theme "Salvation Today" spoke explicitly of this problem.

And then John Paul II decided to intervene with his own personal magisterial document: the encyclical *Redemptoris Missio*.

The Encyclical "Redemptoris Missio"

A missionary encyclical was part of a logical progression in the Pontificate of John Paul II, not only in the sense of complementing his other documents linked to the Redeemer (*Redemptor Hominis, Redemptoris Mater, Redemptoris Custos*), but as a response of the supreme Pastor of the Church to the experiences lived during his numerous journeys. It is an act of faith in the "permanent validity of the Church's missionary mandate," as the Pauline "cry" for the urgency of the missionary activity and the need to "clear up doubts and ambiguities regarding missionary activity *ad gentes.*" Our own times, affirmed John Paul II, offer the Church new opportunities: the collapse of oppressive ideologies and political systems, not only in Central and Eastern Europe, but also in some countries in Asia (Cambodia, Mongolia, Central Asia) and in Africa (Angola, Ethiopia, Mozambique, Benin, Congo); the affirmation among peoples of the gospel values which Jesus made incarnate in his own life (peace, justice, brotherhood, concern for the poor "*anawim Yahweh*" and for the little people, etc.); a kind of soulless economic and technological development which only stimulates the search for the truth about God, about humanity, about the meaning of life itself (see RM 3). The Gulf War, which exploded in January, 1991, just a few days before the publication of *Redemptoris Missio,* was a sign of the latent unrest in the political situation at an international level.

The reason why such a propelling force emanates from the encyclical is perhaps found in the harmonious unity of the various theological tendencies and concrete initiatives that quickly grew in the field of mission in the post-conciliar period. *Redemptoris Missio* presents itself in fact as a symphony of aspects that were in harmonious tension. In this sense we could talk of the theological re-foundation of mission, or at least of a well-expressed *aggiornamento* on the part of the Petrine office, in the sense of "distinguishing in order to unite" ("distinguer pour unir," as Jacques Maritain would say) rather than uniting opposites. I will give a few examples:

Regarding Universal Mission and Specific Mission

"The Church received a *universal mission*--one which knows no boundaries--which involves the communication of salvation in its integrity . . . . This mission is one and undivided, having one origin and one final purpose; but within it, there are different tasks and kinds of activity. First, there is the missionary activity which we call *mission ad gentes"* (31).

The mission *ad gentes* is addressed to "peoples, groups and socio-cultural contexts in which Christ and his Gospel are not known, or which lacks Christian communities sufficiently mature to be able to incarnate the faith in their own environment and proclaim it to other groups" (33).

The mission *ad gentes* is therefore to be distinguished from *other* situations and activities within the one mission of the Church, in other words from the normal *pastoral* care of the well-established ecclesial communities, and from the *new evangelization* or *re-evangelization.*

So the mission *ad gentes* fits within the one universal mission, but must not lose its *specific* character:
"Nevertheless," insists the Holy Father, "care must be taken to avoid the risk of putting very different situations on the same level and of reducing, or even eliminating, the Church's mission and missionaries *ad gentes"* (32).

Jesus Christ the Only Saviour and Participated Forms of Mediation

This is one of the three doctrinal themes that are an authoritative response to the new theological ideas discussed.

The Church's universal mission is born of faith in Jesus Christ . . . . (4).

Christ is the only Savior of all, the only one able to reveal God and lead to God . . . there is salvation in no one else, for there is no other name . . . . The universality of this salvation in Christ is asserted throughout the New

Testament: (1 Cor 8, 5-6; Jn 1,9; Heb 1,1-2) . . . . Christ is
the one mediator between God and mankind: 1 Tim 2, 5-7.
. . . (See paragraph 5).

After these unequivocal biblical reaffirmations the pope applies them
to the present-clay theories of religious pluralism that propose a plurality of
saviours and mediators:

> No one, therefore, can enter into communion with God
> except through Christ, by the working of the Holy Spirit.
> Christ's one, universal mediation, far from being an
> obstacle on the journey towards God, is the way established
> by God himself, a fact of which Christ is fully aware.
> Although participated forms of mediation of different kinds
> and degrees are not excluded, they acquire meaning and
> value *only* from Christ's own mediation, and they cannot be
> understood as parallel or complementary to his (5).

Equally clear is the position assumed in regard to the attempts to
separate the Logos and the historical Jesus:

> To introduce any sort of separation between the Word and
> Jesus Christ is contrary to the Christian faith. Saint John
> clearly states that the Word, who 'was in the beginning with
> God', is the very one who "became flesh" (Jn 1:2, 14).
> Jesus is the incarnate Word--a single and indivisible person.
> One cannot separate Jesus from the Christ or speak of a
> "Jesus of history" who would differ from the "Christ of
> faith" . . . It is precisely this uniqueness of Christ which
> gives him an *absolute* and *universal* significance, whereby,
> while belonging to history, he remains history's center and
> goal (6).

The Holy Spirit as the Principal Agent of Mission with Christ

There is no counter-position between the Holy Spirit and Jesus
Christ, as if the Holy Spirit acted before the coming of the historical Jesus
and outside the church, and therefore without reference to Christ; according

to this line of thinking, people would be saved by the Spirit who is present everywhere, without needing the mediation of the historical Christ.

The encyclical responds to this danger with two clear affirmations:

> This is the same Spirit who was at work in the Incarnation and in the life, death and Resurrection of Jesus, and who is at work in the Church. He is therefore not an alternative to Christ, nor does he fill a sort of void which is sometimes suggested as existing between (Jesus) Christ and the Logos (29).

And the second follows immediately:

> Whatever the Spirit brings about in human hearts and in the history of peoples, in cultures and religions, serves as a preparation for the Gospel (LG 16) and can only be understood in reference to Christ, the Word who took flesh by the power of the Spirit 'so that as perfectly human he would save all human beings and sum up all things (GS 45) (29).

Kingdom Inseparable from the King

The whole second chapter of the encyclical is dedicated to clearing the misunderstandings that have developed concerning the Kingdom of God as the ultimate end of mission, creating a conflict between "Kingdom-centeredness," "Christocentrism" and "ecclesiocentrism".

After a prolonged scriptural analysis of the meaning of the Kingdom of God, John Paul II comes to the first historical-theological conclusion:

> The disciples recognize that the Kingdom is already present in the person of Jesus and is slowly being established within man and the world through a mysterious connection with him . . . . The first Christians also proclaim "the Kingdom of Christ and of God" (Eph 5:5; see Rev 11:15; 12: 10) . . . . Now, as then, there is a need to *unite* the proclamation of the Kingdom of God (the content of Jesus' own

"kerygma") and the proclamation of the Christ-event (the "kerygma" of the Apostles) (16).

The Pope thus considers it important to concretely point out some negative aspects of the conceptions that could be termed "anthropocentric," "kingdom-centered" and "theocentric" that are taken in a reductive sense because they "are focused on man's earthly needs," or "are silent about Christ," or "put great stress on the mystery, of creation, but they keep silent about the mystery of redemption . . . leaving very little room for the Church or undervaluing the Church" (17). The tendency to reduce the Kingdom to "values," separated from Jesus Christ and from the church as the beginning, sacrament and instrument of the Kingdom, renders it an anthropological project, and Christian mission is no longer a divine project for salvation. Perhaps this is an implicit reference to some of the exaggerations of the so-called "Copernican Revolution."

The Holy Father then concludes:

This is not the Kingdom of God as we know it from Revelation. The Kingdom cannot be detached either from Christ or from the Church (18).

Contrasting Views in the Concrete Situation

In the field of missionary activity, many misunderstandings or contrasting views are also clarified. Within the rich and complex concept of evangelization certain doubts emerged about its essential element, and on the other hand there developed a certain tendency to insist on one aspect to the detriment of the others. In the fifth chapter on the "Paths of Mission," John Paul II lists nine paths, giving to each one its due importance without exclusiveness nor undue forcefulness.

This can be applied when considering the relationship between *proclamation* and *inter-religious dialogue*, between *conversion, baptism* and *the foundation of the new ecclesial communities*; between *development* and *evangelization*, which is considered "the best service we can offer to our brother" (58).

But I cannot develop these aspects because I must conclude.

Conclusion

It would be very interesting to analyze how the encyclical was received in the various continents and how it influenced the other documents of the pope and of the Synods of Bishops, and then on missionary activity. The fact is that it is being continually quoted and it has had its own impact in the Apostolic Letter *Tertio Millenio Adveniente* and in the Declaration of the Congregation for the Doctrine of the Faith, "Dominus Jesus."

Beginning with Asia, where there have been attempts to oppose this magisterial document with an "alternative" theology, it was warmly received by the FABC from the mouth of its Secretary General, Archbishop Henry De Souza and from Cardinal Kim at the Asian Congress on Evangelization in Manila, in November 1992.

For Africa it is sufficient to take the words of Cardinal Arinze, President of the Pontifical Council for Inter-Religious Dialogue: "This Encyclical is a blessing." In the ecumenical field, the comment of Gerald Anderson, former editor of the *International Bulletin of Missionary Research* and former director of the Overseas Ministries Study Center, greets it as the most important document of the Catholic Church on its universal mission since Vatican II.

The encyclical was enthusiastically welcomed at the Latin-American Missionary Congress COMLA VI in Lima, and at successive Congresses, as also at the Conference of Bishops at Santo Domingo.

In Europe, Cardinal Danneels affirmed: "There is no doubt that the encyclical *Redemptoris Missio* is one of the most important pontifical writings in the latter part of the century. The first three chapters especially are of capital importance. This is not only true for the countries where the mission *ad gentes* is carried out . . . . But everything said in it is equally valid for evangelization in the first world" ("Two years after *Redemptoris Missio*," 5).

And John Paul II himself, through his presence and in the address he gave during the solemn academic act of the Pontifical Urban University on the 11th April 1991, wished to reaffirm its fundamental concepts, concluding: "In joyfully receiving your gratitude for the recent Encyclical on mission *ad gentes,* I invite you to consider it as a commitment for yourselves, and as an appeal addressed to the all the Churches, to all missionary institutes, to individual believers." After ten years, we feel ever more grateful and our commitment is all the stronger.

MISSION FOR THE TWENTY-FIRST CENTURY:
A Catholic Perspective

Robert J. Schreiter, CPPS[*]

Introduction

As we look to how we might undertake mission in the twenty-first century, we have a great foundation upon which to build. The second half of the twentieth century left us three important magisterial documents which not only bring together the best of missiological thinking and direction from that period, but serve as life-giving vectors to move us into the future. I speak, of course, of the Decree on Missionary Activity of the Church from the Second Vatican Council, *Ad Gentes* (AG), the Apostolic Exhortation of Pope Paul VI, *Evangelii Nuntiandi* (EN), and the Encyclical Letter on the Permanent Validity of the Church's Missionary Mandate, *Redemptoris Missio* (RM). These documents are magisterial in two senses of that word: they are magisterial, first of all, in the traditional theological sense of being issued from the highest levels of authority within the Roman Catholic Church, as the decree of a Council, and from the papal teaching office. But they are also magisterial in the more ordinary usage of that word, namely, authoritative guides to thinking and practice. Together, they have provided impulses for rethinking missionary activity that have been widely and wholeheartedly received throughout the Catholic Church, and thus have had a profound impact upon how mission work is being undertaken in the world today.

It was therefore a natural move for the organizers of this conference to take these three documents as a point of departure for thinking about how a major missionary actor in the church, the Society of the Divine Word, should think about its future. For not only has this missionary society been nurtured by the teaching found in these documents, its Superior General at

---

[*]*Robert J. Schreiter is Professor of Doctrinal Theology at Catholic Theological Union and the current holder of the Chair of Religion and Culture-- instituted to honor Edward Schillebeeckx--at the University of Nijmegen, The Netherlands. Past president of the Catholic Theological Society of America and the American Society of Missiology, Fr. Schreiter is the author of numerous articles and books, among which are* **Constructing Local Theologies** *(1985),* **The New Catholicity** *(1997), and* **The Ministry of Reconciliation: Spirituality and Strategies** *(1998).*

the time of the Second Vatican Council, Fr. Johannes Schütte, had a major hand in the drafting of the Decree *Ad Gentes*.

I have been asked to reflect upon these three documents in order to suggest what elements and ideas from them continue in a special way to move mission forward, as well as what aspects of them perhaps need to be rethought in light of changed circumstances. I have taken the liberty to add to these reflections something of my own reading of the statement "Listening to the Spirit: Our Missionary Response Today," issued at the conclusion of the Fifteenth General Chapter of the SVD.

It is of course impossible to follow out all the impulses which these three documents have given to missionary activity, or to evaluate all the changes that might be envisioned in light of changed circumstances over a period of nearly four decades. These magisterial documents do present the enduring teaching of the Church, but necessarily also reflect the times in which in they were written.

I would like to focus these remarks around four key ideas found in these three documents and explore how they continue to sustain missionary activity, but also invite us to think differently about the challenges before us as we enter the twenty-first century. Each of these ideas calls us in a special way to reflect upon major issues facing missionary activity today, the outcome of which still remains unclear. Together, these documents provide us a framework and a series of vectors which can move us into a more faithful exercise of mission and, with God's help, a prophetic pattern of missionary activity.

The four ideas which I would like to explore here are the following: (1) mission is first and foremost the work of God; (2) the trinitarian character of the mission of God; (3) the centrality of dialogue; and (4) the multiple aspects of evangelization.

Mission As the Work of God

Lying at the basis of all the magisterial thinking about mission is chapter one of AG. dealing with the doctrinal principles of mission. By presenting a coherent theological account of the meaning of mission, this opening section of the decree has provided a continuing source of reflection for all subsequent missiological thought.

A prominent feature of this theological account is that mission is first and foremost the work of God. This idea is framed in the language of "God's plan": "Missionary activity is nothing else, and nothing less, than the manifestation of God's plan, its epiphany and realization in the world and in history; that by which God, through mission, clearly brings to its conclusion the history of salvation" (9). Missiological thinking since the beginning of the twentieth century, but especially in the decade immediately preceding the Second Vatican Council, had been focusing on the *missio Dei*, the mission of God. This idea emphasizes that mission first and foremost belongs to God, and that the Church but participates in God's mission. The decree goes into great detail about precisely what God's plan is for the world, more about which will be said in the next section. Here I wish to reflect upon this idea of the primacy of God in mission.

Such an idea has important theological and practical consequences. If mission is first and foremost God's work, it has consequences for how the church thinks of itself. As AG makes so clear, this means that the church does not have missions but is, by its very nature, missionary. The church to be church must participate in God's saving plan. Mission is not ultimately about the self-aggrandizement of the church. The church, as sacrament to the world, looks to the fulfillment of God's plan of bringing together and reconciling all peoples in Christ.

Why is this idea of the primacy of God in mission so important as we enter the twenty-first century? It seems to me important because of the place the world finds itself at century's turn. A combination of factors has made us deeply aware of the paradoxical character of human efforts. Humankind has made stunning advances in science and medicine and the potential for human communication and interaction in the last several decades. At the same time, there are whole segments of the human population--and these segments are very large--who are actually worse off economically than they were twenty years ago. Communications technologies may be there for greater human interaction and communion, but a majority of the world is excluded from this possibility, and the gap between rich and poor grows ever wider. Humankind has made great advances in understanding and promoting human rights, but we have just finished what the philosopher Isaiah Berlin called "the most terrible of centuries" stained by war, bloodshed, and repeated efforts at genocide. A mastery of nature has gone hand in hand with threats of the collapse of that very ecosphere which makes life possible at all. We map the human genome but cannot control the devastating spread of HIV/AIDS in Africa.

The West sees in all of this the collapse of the grand narrative of modernity into a bevy of smaller rationalities of postmodernity. Much of the rest of the world sees it as the ultimate product of the West's hubris and greed. In either reading, we are brought back to a fundamental tenet of Christian faith, namely, that we do not and cannot save ourselves. God and who God is and can be for us looms largely once again, after the confidence of an western Enlightenment view of the perfectibility of humanity and human society. Saving work is, and will be, ultimately God's work.

There are two important consequences of this view for the conduct of mission as we enter the twenty-first century. First of all, by centering on the idea of the primacy of God in missionary activity, it becomes imperative that we attend especially to the quality of our communion with God. Missionary spirituality, then, becomes more than finding and sustaining motivation for engaging in mission. It becomes a means of hearing where God is calling us, and what God is asking us to do in sometimes apparently hopeless situations. In view of this, contemplation becomes once again an essential element of missionary spirituality.

An example might be helpful here. I have said on a number of occasions that one of the most compelling forms the Good News of Jesus Christ takes on today is the possibility of reconciliation. The worldwide interest in and hunger for reconciliation we are experiencing at this moment in history suggests that this might indeed be one of the ways God is being sought today. Anyone who has engaged in reconciliation work knows how arduous and often unsuccessful this kind of work can be. The burnout rate among those who do this work is very high. What has become increasingly apparent to both religious and secular persons in reconciliation work is the need for some kind of sustaining spirituality or interiority, lest the overwhelming character of the task simply consumes those working to change the situation. Christians name this spirituality or interiority as communion with God, because ultimately God is the one who effects reconciliation. Contemplative prayer, which allows one at once to acknowledge one's own wounds (upon which the insidious nature of evil will play to wear down reconciliation efforts), and to learn to wait, watch, and listen, becomes a prime way of sustaining persons involved in reconciliation work.

The second consequence of the primacy of God in mission is this: methods of mission typically follow other, larger patterns of human activity operative at the time. Focusing upon God creates a critical space out of which one can evaluate and change the negative aspects of this symbiosis between mission methods and larger patterns of social activity. Out of that critical space one can affirm that God's ways may not be our ways.

Mission methods have always followed the patterns of the world in which they are found. St. Paul's preaching and founding of communities followed the highways of the eastern Roman Empire. Much reflection has been given to how mission and European colonialism went hand in hand in the second half of the second millennium. We in turn need to reflect today how we conduct mission in a period of economic globalization. To be sure, mission has never conformed itself utterly to the larger social patterns in which it takes place, but given especially powerful social trends--such as colonialism in the recent past and globalization in the present--we need to be especially reflective upon how mission is helped and hindered by its relation to the social configurations of its time. Maintaining the primacy of God creates the social space that provides critical distance for looking at such things.

The Trinitarian Character of Mission

Keeping our focus on God bring us to the second point, namely the trinitarian character of mission. AG, and the magisterial documents on mission subsequent to it, reaffirm that God's action in the world is trinitarian. It begins in the "fountain-like love" of God the Father which leads to the sending of the Son and the Spirit into the world. Indeed, it is present already in the very creation of the world, when the Spirit hovers over the formless void, and God's Word forms the world. The Spirit, who spoke through the prophets, prepares the way for Word becoming flesh in Jesus of Nazareth. In his passion, death, and resurrection, Jesus begins the process of reconciliation of the world, freeing the world from sin and death, that it might be taken up into the eternal love of God, manifested for us in the Trinity. The sending forth of the Spirit at Pentecost both strengthens and sustains the church as the Body of Christ, and prepares the way throughout the world for God's reconciling action.

What are consequences of this trinitarian character of mission for mission in the twenty-first century? Let me focus here on two. First of all, thinking of God's plan for the world in terms of God as triune provides an important avenue for dealing with what might be the most challenging issue facing mission--and indeed, the entirety of theology today--namely, pluralism.

Pluralism poses a challenge in many ways today. There is, first of all, the great diversity of human cultures and societies, of which we have become even more aware today as means of social communication inform more and more of our lives. How will we as a church maintain unity and exhibit genuine catholicity all at once? Even more challenging is the place of Christianity amid the world's great religious traditions? How are we to interpret and communicate the central tenets of Christian faith about the finality of Jesus Christ and the salvation which he offers? And, indeed, how do we engage in mission in such a pluralistic world?

Much has been, and continues to be, written about this issue. Relativism is not an acceptable option, nor is an uncritical pluralism which does not evaluate and engage difference. It is easier to speak of what is not acceptable than to create a more positive interpretation of these phenomena.

I do not think that it is accidental that precisely in this time when we are grappling with issues which pluralism raises there has also been a much increased interest in a theology of the Trinity. The Trinity itself holds within it the paradox plurality and unity, with the three Persons in one God. While not exactly retrieving the social theories of the Trinity found in Anglican theology in the early part of the twentieth century, one can begin to think what a trinitarian view of the world might mean for, say, a non-monistic metaphysics, or for encounter with Asian religious traditions who find the absoluteness of western claims incompatible with ideas of harmony and harmonious unity.

A second consequence for mission which its trinitarian character suggests has to do with a critical stance toward how Christians speak of the pluralist challenge. In speaking of these things, there is sometimes a tendency to focus almost entirely on the Second Person of the Trinity and not recall the roles of the Father and the Spirit. The story of salvation does not begin with the Incarnation, but with the Creation of the world by God. One has to account for what role the other religions play in the order of creation. Nor can one collapse the work of the Holy Spirit entirely into that of the Logos. The Holy Spirit and the Logos do not work at odds with each other, to be sure, but the communion and unity they enjoy does not mean that they can be utterly identified with each either. The trinitarian character of mission should help us avoid a christomonistic theology of mission. A rereading of Chapter III of RM on the Holy Spirit as the principal agent of mission is instructive in this regard.

We are still in the early stages of understanding just what more extensive reflection on the Trinity will mean for understanding the various challenges raised by pluralism. Such thinking as the potential, it seems to me, to move us beyond monistic proposals which do not get us further.

Dialogue

Paragraph 56 of RM gives an eloquent description of the qualities of dialogue in mission. Dialogue, the encyclical says, "is demanded by deep respect for everything that has been brought about in human beings by the Spirit who blows where he wills." This deep respect for the work of the Spirit "gives rise to the spirit which must enliven dialogue in the context of mission. Those engaged in this dialogue must be consistent with their own religious traditions and convictions, and be open to understanding those of the other party without pretence or close-mindedness, but with truth, humility and frankness, knowing that dialogue can enrich each side."

The importance of dialogue for mission has continued to grow since the Second Vatican Council, where it was first proposed as a way of engaging the world. In the SVD General Chapter Statement, the primary missionary commitments of the Society are summed up in a "fourfold prophetic dialogue" (nos. 52-71).

Dialogue has been important for two of its dimensions. One is for the basic stance it entails. Rooted theologically in the dialogue of persons in the Holy Trinity, dialogue acknowledges and respects the other, but also says at the same time that relationality is constitutive of our very being. Dialogue is not simply something we choose to do, but flows out of the processes by which we become who we are. Dialogue is thus a way of understanding the very structure of the world and of human beings.

Dialogue is also a mode of communication. It involves the hearer as well as the speaker in non-dominative discourse. It is a way of acknowledging difference which does not resort to violence. For that reason, dialogue is also a discipline which assures peaceful communication among parties.

Dialogue seems deceptively simple, but we know from experience how difficult it can be and how misunderstood it has been. When used wrongly, as a way of relativizing views rather than presenting them, dialogue can foster false communication.

Dialogue in mission has involved the full spectrum of understandings and misunderstandings about this important concept. There has been concern in some quarters that dialogue was being substituted for proclamation or even for evangelization altogether. RM reviews this range of understandings and practices, and reassert both the intimate connection of proclamation and dialogue, and also their distinctiveness, and as notes that "they should not be confused, manipulated or regarded as identical, as though they were interchangeable" (RM 55).

What are some consequences of the importance of dialogue for mission in the twenty-first century? Again, let me name but two. The first has to do with the careful linking of dialogue as a theological stance and dialogue as a mode of communication. For dialogue not to go awry, it must be rooted in this trinitarian theology. When that happens, one can understand better and support more effectively the repeated call we have heard from bishops and theologians in Asia for dialogue and dialogical action as the best mode of the church's presence in Asia. This call from bishops and theologians has often been hard for westerners to understand. To them, such thoroughgoing commitment to dialogue sounds "soft" and not entirely faithful to call for Christian proclamation and witness. Asians respond by saying that this is not an adequate characterization of what they mean by dialogue. Perhaps also something of the critical stance toward mission history might be useful for westerners. Assertive witness may connote commitment for westerners, but for a part of the world which suffered at the hands of western empire, assertive witness smacks of arrogance and domination. It simply does not convey the message westerners hope they are communicating. A challenge to mission in the twenty-first century is a deepening of both the theology and the discipline of dialogue.

A second consequence for mission in the twenty-first century is the role of dialogue in countering interreligious violence. Most of the armed conflicts in the world today happen within states rather than between them. And an alarming number of conflicts use religion as a motivation or a legitimation for those conflicts. More often than not, religion is not at the basis of the conflict, but is used to fuel the fires of hatred. Nonetheless, religion can be used in this manner. That is partially due to the fact that, while all the great religious traditions see peace as an ideal, they also contain passages in their sacred texts which legitimate violence against their enemies.

Dialogue between religions, especially at local levels, can help stem local interreligious violence, either preventing the engagement of religious feelings in situation of violence, or by getting religious leaders to stand together when violence threatens to break out. Along with the church assuming a dialogical posture (and not just in Asia), there must be the practice of dialogue as well, especially what has been called the dialogue of life and the dialogue of action.

Evangelization

The doctrinal base of evangelization was worked out in that same first chapter of AG referred to earlier. But it was in the Apostolic Exhortation on Evangelization in the Modern World, *Evangelii Nuntiandi*, that the understanding of evangelization was both deepened and broadened. Especially significant in this document is the sensitivity to the complexity of evangelizing action (EN 17). Evangelization is about the renewal of humanity in all its strata and forms. "The purpose of evangelization is therefore precisely this interior change [i.e., the renewal of humanity], and if it had to be expressed in one sentence the best way of stating it would be to say that the Church evangelizes when she seeks to convert, solely through the divine power of the Message she proclaims, both the personal and collective consciences of people, the activities in which they engage, and the lives and concrete milieux which are theirs" (EN 18).

Moreover, EN not only marked an advance in our understanding of evangelization, it also interwove the developing thought of the church on culture. It introduces what it calls the evangelization of cultures. Cultures are, of course, not living subjects. What Pope Paul intended here was a renewal of those human processes by which cultures are developed. In other words, he was trying to get to the very heart of the humanization (and dehumanization) process as an indispensable part of the evangelization process.

Pope John Paul II has made evangelization a central theme in his papacy, and has carried through the motif of culture in much of his writing and teaching. What was a relatively new idea for much of mission thought in the middle of the twentieth century has become nearly a commonplace at its end. He has also made much of "New Evangelization," that is, a renewal of Christian life where it has grown tepid or disappeared altogether.

What are some consequences of the theme of evangelization for the twenty-first century? Again, let me name two.

First of all, evangelization, and evangelization of cultures, has focused upon local (and often rural) cultures. What does the evangelization of cultures mean in an age of globalization, when nearly every culture is invaded by powerful global cultural forces, which at once homogenize local cultures into a large hyperculture, and exaggerate local cultural characteristics through the acts of resistance people undertake? Globalization has both blurred cultural distinctiveness by pushing aside local aspects, and heightened senses of ethnicity, often to the point of violence. Can a hybrid, hyperculture be evangelized along the lines EN envisions? What does inculturation mean when local and global forces are in constant (and often conflictual) interaction? Theologies of liberation tried to respond to these questions at an earlier stage, but the dynamics of globalization, while similar to those of colonialism, operate differently, principally because they frequently have no definable subject. This has special importance for ministry in megacities and among migrants and refugees, where these forces come together in a very strong way.

Second, how will methods of evangelization interact, on the one hand, with increasingly secularized societies such as those of Europe, and on the other hand, with the growing religiosity of movements such as fundamentalism and Pentecostalism? The Second Vatican Council positioned itself to deal with a secularizing world, one could say. What are the elements which have changed the situation today? In parts of Western Europe, secularization has gone from a sometimes anti-theistic or anti-church approach to utter indifference, as a whole generation is come of age with very little religious socialization. At the same time, inchoate, noninstitutional streams of religiosity criss-cross the same landscape. How should one proceed? This is especially acute, I believe, for missionary institutes who began in Europe, and may find themselves comfortable in everywhere except Europe.

If we say that we have a primary commitment to the poor, then we must engage the fastest growing form of religiosity among the poor, Pentecostalism. Fundamentalism, on the other hand, is often found more in middle classes. What does the rapid spread of Pentecostalism tell us about the world today, and what is being heard of the Good News of Jesus Christ? The answers to both questions are not simple. The spread of Pentecostalism is tied up with urban dislocation, and access to religious power without the usual institutional mediation for many. The "Good News" of Pentecostal faith for some is a Prosperity Gospel of getting rich. But the phenomenon cannot be reduced to either. Some estimates put Pentecostalism as growing to the size of Roman Catholicism within two decades, if current rates continue, making it a movement larger than mainline Protestant and Orthodox forms of Christianity combined. What does all of this mean for evangelization?

Conclusion

AG, EN and AG, issued thirty-five, twenty-five, and ten years ago, respectively, shaped the missiological landscape for the Catholic Church in the second half of the twentieth century. Their potential is far from exhausted, as I hope this presentation has shown. In the course of this period, and now in our own time, the circumstances in which we carry out missionary activity have continued to change. The teaching of these three documents have stood well the test of time. Yet we must continue also, in order to be faithful to the best elements of these documents, to engage them with these changing contexts.

As stated so well in the conclusion to the SVD Chapter Document, "we need to continue to listen to the Spirit so as to know and do the will of the Triune God" (no. 109). The document goes on to reaffirm that mission is ultimately the work of God, and that dialogue is essential to the meaning of mission today. I hope that these remarks in this present, which parallel in significant ways the thinking in that document, will help the Society take the next steps to responding to its missionary calling in the twenty-first century.

MISSION FOR THE TWENTY-FIRST CENTURY:
A Protestant Perspective

Wilbert R. Shenk[*]

One of the noteworthy features of the Christian mission over the past two millennia is that it has not progressed in a straight line. Rather it has moved in ebbs and flows. The final twenty-five years of the twentieth century have been a time of disorientation and adjustment. During this period nearly five centuries of European colonialism have ended and the Cold War between the Soviet and Western Blocs collapsed in 1989. Long-established western-based missionary orders and agencies have experienced decline in the number of missioners and financial resources. These programs seem to have become increasingly ineffective. New ministries are needed. At the same time the churches in Asia, Africa, and Latin America have grown to the point where they are now in the majority and it is from these churches that fresh energy and enthusiasm are flowing.

The Christian mission depends on a combination of fundamental continuities and strategic new departures. Teaching documents of the church, including *Ad Gentes* ([AG]Flannery 1988), *Evangelii Nuntiandi* ([EN] Paul VI 1975) and *Redemptoris Missio* ([RM] John Paul II 1990) can play an important role in clarifying and reaffirming fundamental perspectives on mission, including the *Missio Dei* of the Triune God, Jesus Christ as the prototypical missionary (EN 7) and savior of the world (RM 5), the Holy Spirit as the primary agent and enabler (EN 75; RM Chapt. III), the Kingdom of God as the essential message as indicated by Jesus at the inauguration of his public ministry (Matt 4:17; Mk 1:14-15; Lk 4:18-19) (EN 6, 8; RM Chapt. II), that the church exists for mission and the whole people are called to missionary witness (AG 2, EN 15), and the church herself is called to continual conversion by the gospel (EN 15). It is more difficult to speak with any degree of confidence as to what the future holds.

---

*Wilbert R. Shenk is Professor of Mission History and Contemporary Culture at the School of World Mission at Fuller Theological Seminary, Pasadena, CA, USA. A past president of the American Society of Missiology, he is one of the world's most eminent missiologists. He is the author of numerous books and articles, the most recent of which is **Changing Frontiers of Mission** (Maryknoll, NY: Orbis Books, 1999).*

Yet it is useful to identify broad trends and seek to discern their significance for the church in mission. I propose to reflect on the future of mission in the next several decades in terms of three overlapping circles: World, Word and Church. My object is to identify representative themes and suggest an interactive process by which we can clarify the implications of all this for the future of Christian mission.

I. *World*

The first circle represents the world to which mission is directed. The modern world has been marked by unprecedented dynamism. This dynamism will continue to define the context in which mission will be carried out in the twenty-first century. A basic characteristic of the modern world is the *pace* of change that sets this culture apart from all previous cultures.

WORLD

A. *Modernity*

Today social theorists are debating how to name the present moment. Is *postmodernity* the most accurate term or should it be called *radicalized modernity* or *hyper-modernity*? The intricacies of this debate need not detain us here. What we do know is that strong continuities bind us to modernity and modern culture will not disappear any time soon. Many of the issues we are facing stem from the modern period, not least the marginalization of religion in society.

One of the most important features of the past three decades is the emergence of multiple global systems--communications, transportation, financial, and commercial, to name the more visible. These systems put faces on important dimensions of the new systems of power and influence but do not explain the deep cultural and spiritual significance of these developments for humankind. Borrowing a line from Robert W. Jenson (1993), we can say that over the past several centuries "the world has lost its story." It is important to try to understand how this has come about. What are the consequences for people who are facing a future that lacks a narrative structure?

The processes by which this loss has occurred have been centered in the modern West and to all appearances it is in its most advanced form there. But the same processes are at work the world over. The resurgence of local and regional cultural, religious, and political forces are signs that they intend to resist these waves of global influences that threaten their existence. Our purpose here is to analyze how this loss of story occurred in modern culture and what this entails for Christian mission.

Modernity has been constructed on the foundation of instrumental and critical reason. The result has been a culture of unprecedented power measured in terms of its *intensiveness* and *extensiveness*. But the processes of modernity have eroded these foundation stones and modernity itself is crumbling. We turn now to an examination of the dynamics of modernity in order to understand the world today. The dynamics of modernity can be analyzed in terms of three themes: (1) the separation of time and space; (2) the disembedding of social systems; and (3) reflexive ordering and reordering (Giddens 1990: 14-54).

(1) **The separation of time and space.** Every people has had their way of marking time and these methods of time-keeping reflected the culture and environment in which a people lived. Traditional time is linked to a place and the people who inhabit it; it is always "local." "When" and "where" form a unity. The invention of the mechanical clock permanently altered this traditional understanding of time. Time and space could now be dealt with separately. Calendars were introduced and time zones established, bringing the entire globe under a common definition of time. "Traditional" time had been superseded. Although various peoples still follow their traditional calendars, these are used for cultural and religious purposes. The Gregorian calendar is accepted as the basis for conducting international commerce and political affairs, not the Muslim or Chinese. More important is the fundamental change in the meaning of time and space. In the modern period human activities have been increasingly conducted without reference to place. Unseen or unknown forces now act upon the local without any relationship to it. Time and space are routinely manipulated for instrumental purposes; they are treated as factors of production.

The collapse of time and space has affected the way people experience God. Richard Sennett (1990: 10-19) has shown the evolution that has taken place in the theory that guided the construction of church buildings in Europe prior to the nineteenth century and since. Within traditional church buildings worshipers found space that contrasted with their world--a place of chaotic disorder. The church building was a major statement about a space where God was at the center. After 1800, amid the growing industrialization of the modern city, architects added spires to church buildings that were out-of-scale with the rest of the structure and that focused attention on the external. This coincided with the beginning of a general decline in attendance that has marked Christian practice in the twentieth century. The secularization of all space meant people no longer knew where to meet God.

(2) The disembedding of social systems. Traditional society is based on face-to-face relationships. All transactions--whether economic, legal, or political--in traditional society carry social meaning. Sociologists have usually interpreted the shift from traditional to modern society in terms of increased *differentiation* and *specialization*. In this view modernity has taken traditional values and intensified them. But this obscures the degree to which the changed meaning of time and space relationship has affected social relations. This shift can be illustrated by examining two mechanisms that have been used to "dis-embed" social systems: the "symbolic token" and "expert systems." Money is the symbolic token that has become the universal medium of exchange without reference to the socio-cultural particularities of those who use it. In traditional societies the exchange of goods and services takes place by the process of barter. In modern society money has become the impersonal standard for buying and selling goods and services. In late modernity money has become ever more abstract since vast sums of money can be moved electronically and instantaneously worldwide. Such a transaction does not depend on who knows whom. Similarly, expert systems function anonymously and independently of those being served. Indeed, to live in modern society requires that we entrust matters of life and death to "experts" and "systems" that the vast majority of people do not understand and could never master, including modern means of transportation and health care. All of these systems operate without reference to social relations. Whereas in traditional societies social relations are fundamental to the functioning of society, such "socializing" is regarded as an impediment to the carrying out of expert duties in modern society. This is expressed in most professions in terms of codes of professional conduct that govern the relationship between the expert and the client.

(3) Reflexive ordering and reordering. Since humans are capable of reflecting on their actions and gleaning insight from their experiences, they can apply these learnings to future decisions. In traditional society the past is valued over the present. Authority is vested in tradition so that decisions are validated in the light of tradition. In modern society authority resides in the future. Decisions are made in the light of the probabilities that change will enhance profits or bring happiness or some other desired benefit. Modernity demands continual re-examination of what *is* in order to promote progress. Anthony Giddens (1990: 39) observes: "What is characteristic of modernity is not an embracing of the new for its own sake, but the

presumption of wholesale reflexivity." It is assumed that everything must continually be challenged and changed--for the better. Only in this way can progress be ensured. The effect on society is unsettling for nothing remains secure. The more knowledge we acquire the more we become aware of what we do not know; the quest for knowledge is endless.

To summarize: In modernity the future has replaced tradition as the focal point of human effort; skepticism and doubt have been institutionalized and dogmatic certainty is suspect. Modernity is antagonistic to tradition. Knowledge develops in a circular--not cumulative--fashion; all knowing is subject to revision and grows by continually incorporating new information. Even though there is no *telos*, the dynamics of modernity demand growth and are inherently globalizing. Modernity's appetite for innovation is insatiable even though it has no overarching purpose or destination.

B. *"McDonaldization"*

Sociologist George Ritzer (1996) has demonstrated that "McDonaldization" is a defining feature of contemporary society. The rationalization that has been the hallmark of modernity has resulted in a process that continues to spread around the world. The four essential elements of rationalization are *efficiency, calculability, predictability*, and *control*--increasingly achieved by replacing humans with technology. Tom Friedman (1999) gives a telling example of the latter characteristic in his best-selling book on globalization, *The Lexus and the Olive Tree*. Friedman visited the Lexus car factory in Toyota City, Japan where he observed a system that produces 300 Lexus sedans each day. The work force consists of 66 workers and 310 robots. For Friedman "Lexus" is the symbol of the global system based on technology. The "olive tree" represents traditional society rooted in the local (Ibid.: 30). The McDonald Company has used rationalization to the maximum to devise a system for selling fast food. The entire McDonald's operation rests on these four features. Max Weber predicted that a society based on radical rationalization and bureaucracy ultimately would land in the iron cage.

In addition to the fact McDonald's has been one of the great commercial success stories of the twentieth century, it has had an extraordinary impact on contemporary culture. "McDonald's" has become a cultural icon. Furthermore, the McDonald's idea has been applied to a wide range of enterprises. Although George Ritzer is at pains to point out that not all of society has come under the sway of McDonaldization, yet he says "McDonaldization has an inexorable quality, multiplying and extending itself continuously" (Ritzer 1996: 161). Ritzer documents the way McDonald's methodology is being applied across the life cycle--from the birth of babies to the way funerals are conducted. Even churches have found ways to adopt the principles of rationalization to Christian ministry (Ibid.: 119). At its worst it can become a numbing routinization that results in the dehumanization of people. This underscores the ambiguous nature of modernity.

C. *The Loss of a Narrative*

The stunning success of modernity is undeniable. Yet it has carried within itself the seeds of its own undoing. Ultimately, instrumental and critical reason was self-destructive. Radical skepticism inevitably leads to a process that undermines itself. Modernity's success was made possible by the moral and intellectual capital it inherited from the Christian faith, but modernity has not had its own means of replenishing that capital. Indeed, it could only have done so by repudiating the very foundation on which it was built (Jenson 1993).

Hans Frei distinguished between "realistic narrative" and other forms. Two things characterize realistic narrative: (1) the sequence of events is understood as a coherent depiction of life, and (2) this drama could "really" have happened. This is the world of biblical faith. Modernity assumed that we do live in such a "narratable world" since this was inherent in its inheritance from the Judeo-Christian faith tradition. But it insisted on secularizing the narrative by eliminating God as the narrator. In the absence of the narrator modernity has been unable to sustain a master narrative. Consequently, the West has lost faith in a narratable world. To reiterate: the world of the Enlightenment wanted a realistic faith, but it insisted that it be a faith without God. As Robert Jenson says, "The story of the Bible is asserted to be the story of God with His creatures . . . . Modernity was defined by the attempt to live in a universal story without a universal storyteller" (Ibid: 21).

The evidence for the loss of a narratable world can readily be found in modern art and literature. For example, "realistic modernism" in literature and art reproduces pieces of the world but in such a way that no story is told. In his paintings Magritte incorporates items of everyday life; but he does so in such a way that no coherent meaning is conveyed. He does not intend to tell a story. Rather he focuses attention on the pieces and the fragments (ibid). One can find parallel examples in other art forms. Popular culture increasingly reflects a culture that has no realistic narrative and, therefore, a culture without *telos*.

D. *Summary*

Our contemporary world presents Christian mission with major challenges and new opportunities. The self-confidence that marked western culture for several centuries is gone. The secularism of the past several generations has given way to a quest for spirituality and meaning. While the present pervasive relativist-pluralist outlook presents its own problems, we must take account of the shift.

2. *Word*

The second circle represents the Word. The goal of *Missio Dei* is that the Word as God's revelation encounters the world, showing to the world its need of God. We will consider three aspects of the Word in relation to the future of mission.

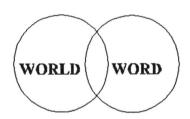

A. *The Word in the Modern World*

A significant, but seldom discussed, theme of Christian history is the role of the Scriptures in cultural development. Stephen Neill (1957: 98-102) pointed out that there have been only two brief periods in English history when it could be said that something approaching a *Christian* culture had been realized: the early seventeenth century and mid-nineteenth century. In both instances an important factor was the rise in biblical literacy among the masses. The upsurge in the seventeenth century may be correlated with the publication of the Authorized Version in 1611 that had great popular appeal, and in the nineteenth century the evangelical revivals stimulated church attendance so that many people were regularly hearing the Bible read and expounded.

The story of western civilization is inextricably linked to the Christian scriptures. At the start of the twenty-first century the indicators tell us that we are in a period of sharp decline in the level of biblical literacy in the wider society as well as among the Christian faithful. Many observers link this trend to a more general pattern in modern culture, i.e., a shift away from reading and toward television and movies. But this entails more than simply a reallocation of personal time. Jacques Ellul (1985: 228) noted that we are bombarded with artificial images. We live in "a visible universe of proliferating images produced by all sorts of techniques. No longer are we surrounded by fields, woods, and rivers, but by signs, signals, billboards, screens, labels, and trademarks: this is our universe . . . . Modern people thus are deprived of reference to truth at the same time they lose their situation in lived reality." This new universe of "virtual reality"--and all its variants: virtual faith, virtual relationships, etc.--is qualitatively different from what we inhabited prior to the advent of the mass media. This datum is an important element in our search for greater missionary effectiveness in the future.

B. *Incarnate Word*

Traditionally, Protestant evangelicals have looked to the Great Commission as given in Matt 28:18-20 and Mk 16:15-16 as the authoritative basis of mission. Samuel Escobar has drawn attention recently to a shift in evangelical sensibility. Evangelicals are increasingly turning to Jn 20:19-23 as the foundational text for the missionary mandate. This is a salutary development. The modern missionary movement reached its high point at the same time that western imperialism was imposing its control over many non-western nations. In that atmosphere advocates of mission mis-read the Great Commission by making "go" the imperative--rather than "make disciples" and "baptize"--and turned the Matthean version of the Great Commission into a slogan that comported readily with the spirit of imperialism. However, the context and mood of Jn 20:19-23 disallow such an association by forcing us to return to what is central to the gospel: the self-sacrificing love of God on which the salvation of the world is staked and linking discipleship to following Jesus Christ in his mission.

José Comblin (1979: vii) suggests that the Gospel of John is shaped by fifteen key words the writer uses: father (119 times), sent (41 times), man (35 times), world (77 times), to do (36 times), works (21 times) signs (16 times), testimony (46 times), glory (38 times), to know (88 times), disciples (77 times), to believe (43 times), truth (55 times), love (44 times), life (52 times). In the Gospel of John missionary action is based on the example of the Father, acting through the Son, in the power of the Holy Spirit to reach the world. Divine insertion in the human situation is in the form of utter vulnerability ("The Word became flesh and lived for a while among us" [Jn 1:14a]). The outcome is suffering and death--and the triumph of God over sin in the resurrection. It is on the basis of God's victory over death through suffering love that Jesus Christ entrusts his redemptive mission to his disciples with the clear instruction that they should imitate him: "As the Father has sent me, I am sending you" (Jn 20:21b). Just as the Incarnate Word challenges the imperial model of mission that was dominant throughout most of the period of the modern missionary movement, the Incarnate Word challenges the bent today toward "virtual reality" and "virtual relationships" by calling missioners to a discipleship modeled after our Lord.

C. Beyond Inculturation

One of the urgent themes in mission studies during the past thirty years has been inculturation or contextualization. Among the leading contributions to this discussion have been works such as *Christianity and Culture* by Charles H. Kraft (1979), *The Church and Cultures* by Louis J. Luzbetak, SVD (1988), *Constructing Local Theologies* by Robert J. Schreiter, CPPS (1985), and *Models of Contextual Theology* by Stephen B. Bevans, SVD (1992). It was clear that we had moved into a post-colonial phase and that the older concept of "indigenization" had to be superseded.

Yet the quest goes on. The effects of five hundred years of western domination are not easily and quickly set aside. Non-western theologians are grappling with more radical approaches and new conceptualizations. The starting point for considering witness is not culture but the gospel. The theological basis for the gospel to engage a culture is the incarnation. According to Andrew Walls (1996: 26-27), "God chose translation as his mode of action for the salvation of humanity. . . . Incarnation is translation." The power to transform people-in-culture does not reside in the context but in the gospel that so engages people-in-culture that all are renewed, i.e., made usable for God's purpose.

Second, it is being proposed to develop theology in dialogue with Christian theologians in the first three centuries rather than using western theology as the master grid. The issues faced by these early Christian thinkers, themselves new converts to the Christian faith, are typically similar to the issues that confront Christians in the non-western world today.

Third, what is at stake is the future identity of Christians in the non-western world. If they are to develop an identity that supports them in being both authentic Christians and authentic members of their cultures, then it must be based on the principle of translation. The Word must truly become flesh if men and women are to be "born anew."

D. *Summary*

The transforming power of the Word is discovered precisely as it encounters the World of human cultures and actions, not in some idealized extraterrestrial sphere. The missiological task is to seek to understand this interaction of humankind in the context of its cultures and in order to equip the missioner to be an effective agent of the Word.

3. *Church*

The third circle represents the church, the means by which the Word is proclaimed to the World. As Vatican II made clear, the mission is committed to the whole people of God, not a select few (AG 10). In order for the church to realize her full potential as witness to the gospel, both spiritual and structural renewal are needed.

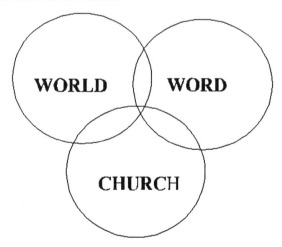

Nearly two decades ago I had an exchange of correspondence with W. A. Visser 't Hooft, founding general secretary of the World Council of Churches. Visser 't Hooft had published two articles in the *International Review of Mission* (1974 and 1977) concerning the evangelization of Europe's neo-pagans. I had written to ask Dr. Visser 't Hooft whether he had continued to work on this theme in the meanwhile. He replied promptly indicating that he regarded this to be "the main issue to which evangelists and missiologists should turn." He suggested that the challenge had to be approached through a re-reading of western literature and history in order accurately to define the issues and develop a strategy of response. Visser 't Hooft was convinced that pagan and anti-Christian elements had beguiled the church into compromises that weakened the Church in her witness. The only way forward was through renewal of the church in her missionary responsibility to the world. Although the example is drawn from the experience of the church in the West, I submit that it is the question the church has always faced and must continue to wrestle with.

Thus renewal has to do with the way the people of God understand what it means to be disciples of Jesus Christ. Authentic renewal results in an intensified commitment to the lordship of Christ in all areas of life. If the church of the future is to engage her culture in the name of the gospel, old habits of mind and action need to be thrown off. Although he was dealing specifically with the church in the West, Karl Rahner's comments in *The Shape of the Church to Come* readily apply to Christians of all traditions as he looked to the future: "Concretely and socially, the Church will no longer exist as formerly through the mere persistence of her office, of her socially firm structures, and through an awareness of being taken for granted by public opinion, recruiting new members simply because the children adopt and maintain the life-style of their parents and are baptized and indoctrinated by the Church" (Rahner 1983: 108). What Rahner is driving at is that a renewed church will be one that is motivated by a sense of mission rather than institutional loyalty.

The way Christians interpret their relationship to the cultural context can be visualized and described in terms of three metaphors: (a) *second generation immigrants*--who work assiduously to adapt to the new culture; (b) *colonizers*--who attempt to replicate the world they left behind; and (c) *resident aliens*--who establish their own haven in the new world. Each of these positions has problems and inadequacies. According to Miroslav Volf (1994: 18), "Christians are the insiders who have diverted from their culture by being born again. They are by definition those who are not what they used to be, those who do not live like they used to live. Christian difference is therefore not an insertion of something new into the old from outside, but a bursting out of the new precisely within the proper space of the old." It is essential that the church cultivate in the faithful a sense of identity that is secure in being "native born" but different.

4. *Mission*

These three overlapping circles--World, Word, and Church--identify the essential elements of Christian mission. As history makes clear, the church has not always had a clear sense of missionary purpose. It can co-exist with the world so that no missionary witness is made. We must hold all three elements together and see them as interacting continuously. I have indicated what I believe to be some of the important issues in relation to each of these three arenas as we think about mission in the twenty-first century. Now I will treat explicitly certain issues that have been left implicit in my discussion thus far.

A. *Location of Mission*

One of the unsettled debates centers on what constitutes a mission field. Many people react negatively when they hear Europe or North America described as *mission fields*. This betrays the fundamentally negative attitude modern people have toward mission. (It is scarcely tolerable when directed to exotic and primitive peoples but it is unacceptable in relation to sophisticated modern people.) Increasingly, however, Christians from Asia, Africa, and Latin America are preempting this discussion. They have little patience with the niceties of traditional definitions.

Three decades ago Alfred C. Krass returned to the United States following missionary service in Africa. He declared: "America is today very much a mission field. In any situation where people do not know to whom they belong, there is a mission field--the time is ripe for evangelism" (Krass 1973: 68; see Krass 1982). Krass is suggesting that we should test empirical reality and then respond accordingly. The church is to serve the *missio Dei* wherever she is and this includes evangelizing those who "do not know to whom they belong."

B. *The West as Mission Frontier*

I have advocated speaking about the West as a mission frontier for two reasons. First, the continued decline in active participation in the church in the historical heartland, especially Europe, cannot be ignored. To call this a pastoral problem appears to be unrealistic. A more radical response is required in view of the fact that growing numbers in Europe and North America are several generations removed from any formal relationship to the church. It is my considered conviction that nothing less than a fresh missionary engagement with people who "do not know to whom they belong" will prove effective. This is the first time in the history of the Christian Church that we are facing the task of evangelizing a large population that was, at some time in the past, considered Christian but that for a variety of reasons has abandoned or rejected that affiliation.

A second reason for using this terminology is that in the light of growing religious pluralism it is becoming ever more difficult for Christians to make credible geographical or territorial claims. Muslims comprise the second largest religious group in France today. Christians in other continents are no longer persuaded that the "Christian West" has the spiritual significance that it once claimed to have. They have experienced the use of "Christendom" versus "mission territories" as placing a stigma on them. As they increasingly have come into their own, they rightly resist all such labels that seem to assign them to a second-class status. It is incumbent on us to do all we can to remove this stigma.

C. *Mission Is Multi-directional*

One of the powerful characteristics of the modern missionary movement has been that it was *unidirectional*. It was a movement from Christendom to heathendom. Unfortunately, this happened to coincide with the fact that the European powers were using economic, military and political power to create a world system that served their interests at the expense of other peoples all over the world. Christian missions readily became identified as accomplices of western imperialism. Even today the legacy of western domination bedevils relations within the Christian movement. And yet, perhaps prophetically, churches from all continents are increasingly taking missionary initiatives directed to other continents. Undoubtedly, Roman Catholic missionary and religious orders have a great advantage in this regard as they develop multi-national memberships. We ought to do much more to make visible the fact that these missions are concrete testimony to the fact that the Body of Christ is not defined in terms of nationality, race, ethnicity, or language.

D. *Missio Dei*

World, Word, and Church overlap and interact; but if we are to develop a missional perspective, we must do so through the lens of the *missio Dei*. If we look at the World in a conventional way, we are not motivated to ask questions about its place in God's plan of salvation. Similarly, if we view

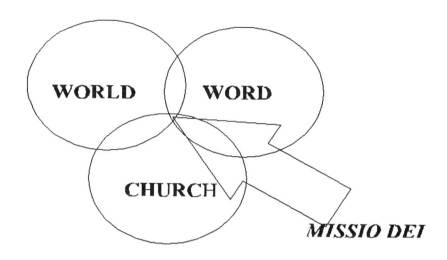

the Church as a religious institution providing certain services to its members, we are not challenged to think about the reason why Jesus Christ elected a people out of the World in order to be his continuing missionary presence in the World. The Word is central to God's missionary purpose and yet it has too often been treated as a religious message for the benefit of those who are already members of the household of faith. The *missio Dei* signifies the purpose of the Triune God--God the Father, God the Son, and God the Holy Spirit--that is being actualized through the church for the salvation of the World. Mission in the twenty-first century must be an expression of the dynamic of the *missio Dei* that holds in vital tension World, Word, and Church in such a way that the church is energized and renewed for the next phase of God's mission in which she is to play an indispensable role (see SVD 2000: 24-30, 47).

References Cited

Bevans, Stephen B., SVD
    1992   *Models of Contextual Theology*. Maryknoll, NY: Orbis Books.

Comblin, José
    1979   *Sent From the Father*. Maryknoll, NY: Orbis Books.

Ellul, Jacques
    1985   *The Humiliation of the Word*. Grand Rapids, MI: William B. Eerdmans Publishing Company.

Flannery, Austin P., ed.
    1988   "Ad Gentes," *Vatican Council II: The Conciliar and Post Conciliar Documents*. Northport, NY: Costello Publishing Company. Pp. 813-56.

Friedman, Thomas L.
    1999   *The Lexus and the Olive Tree*. New York: Anchor Books.

Giddens, Anthony
    1990   *The Consequences of Modernity*. Stanford, CA: Stanford University Press.

Jenson, Robert W.
    1993   "How the World Lost Its Story." *First Things* (October): 19-24.

Kraft, Charles H.
    1979   *Christianity and Culture*. Maryknoll, NY: Orbis Books.

Krass, Alfred C.
    1973   *Beyond the Either-or church*. Nashville, TN: Tidings.
    1982   *Evangelizing Neopagan North America*. Scottdale, PA.: Herald Press.

Luzbetak, Louis J., SVD
    1988   *The Church and Cultures*. Maryknoll, NY: Orbis Books.

Neill, Stephen
    1957   *The Unfinished Task*. London: Edinburgh House Press/Lutterworth.

Pope John Paul II
    1990   *On the Permanent Validity of the Church's Missionary Mandate: Redemptoris Missio*. Washington, D.C.: U.S. Catholic Conference.

Pope Paul VI
    1975   *On Evangelization in the Modern World*. Washington, DC: U.S. Catholic Conference.

Rahner, Karl
    1983   *The Shape of the Church to Come*. New York: Crossroad.

Ritzer, George
    1996   *The McDonaldization of Society*. Thousand Oaks, CA: Pine Forge Press. Rev. ed.

Schreiter, Robert J.
    1985   *Constructing Local Theologies*. Maryknoll, NY: Orbis Books.

Sennett, Richard
    1990   *The Conscience of the Eye*. New York: W. W. Norton.

SVD Publications
  2000   *Documents of the XII General Chapter SVD 2000. In Dialogue with the Word* 1 (September).

Visser 't Hooft, W. A.
  1974   "Evangelism in the Neo-Pagan Situation," *International Review of Mission* 63:249 (January): 81-86.
  1977   "Evangelism Among Europe's Neo-Pagans," *International Review of Mission* 66:264 (October): 349-60.

Volf, Miroslav
  1994   "Soft Difference: Theological Reflections on the Relation Between Church and Culture in 1 Peter." *Ex Auditu* 10:15-30.

Walls, Andrew F.
  1996   *The Missionary Movement in Christian History.* Maryknoll, NY: Orbis Books.

MISSION FOR THE TWENTY-FIRST CENTURY IN AFRICA

Gabriel Lionel Afagbegee, SVD[*]

Introduction

Mission in Africa has a long history, though one could say it has been an interrupted history with three distinct phases. The first phase covered the period of the first seven centuries of the Christian era. During this period there was a flourishing Christian presence in North Africa, Egypt, Ethiopia and parts of present day Sudan. Unfortunately however, except for traces of this Christian presence left in Egypt and Ethiopia, the Arab-Muslim invasion of the seventh century wiped out all the gains.

The fifteenth century marked the beginning of a second phase of Christian evangelization in Africa with Portuguese explorers and traders establishing Christian settlements along the western and southern coasts Africa. And during the first half of the sixteenth century there were also missionary activities carried out on the east coast of Africa particularly in Mozambique. These efforts however, failed to produce any lasting results.

The third phase of evangelization began towards the middle of the nineteenth century and the flourishing local churches one finds all over the continent are fruits of the missionary endeavors of this phase.[1]

The theme for this workshop, "Mission for the Twenty-First Century in Africa," presupposes that there is a reason and/or need for the church to engage in missionary activity in Africa in the twenty-first century. But the question is: Is there really any reason or need for mission in Africa today? Does Africa need mission? Can Africa not do without mission? Even if there is a reason and/or need for mission, is such a need urgent?

Based on the above questions our discussion would focus on the meaning, necessity, and how to approach mission for Africa in the twenty-first century.

---

[*]*Gabriel Afagbegee, SVD, from Ghana, is director of the Lumko Institute in Johannesburg, South Africa.*

Meaning of Mission for Africa

Africa has often been referred to as "mission territory"--i.e. a continent at the receiving end of missionary activity in terms of personnel, finances, etc. This "territorial" designation has influenced the understanding of 'mission' and 'being missionary' in Africa. For many people "mission" and/or "being missionary" is something/someone foreign--i.e. the message and the messenger come from outside.

Such an understanding of mission is of course partial as it fails to capture the complexity and dynamism of mission.

Based on the definition of Pope Paul VI that "evangelizing means bringing the Good News into the strata of humanity, and through its influence transforming humanity from within and making it new" (EN 18), we would define mission for Africa as that complex and dynamic process by which the gospel message proclaimed by the church permeates and transforms the core and fabric of the culture (life) of the people of Africa. In the transformation process the culture of the people remain authentically African but purified. The process takes place on two levels: 1) at the level of peoples, groups, and socio-cultural contexts in which the gospel message is not known and/or which lack Christian communities sufficiently mature to be able to incarnate the Christian faith in their own environment and proclaim it to other people or groups. This will be primary evangelization or mission 'ad gentes', and 2) at the level of those already baptized or communities with adequate and solid ecclesial structures.

Necessity of Mission for Africa

The splendid growth and achievements of the church in Africa (that are the results of the selfless dedication of generations of missionaries) have led some people to argue that there is no need for missionary activity in Africa today. The church in Africa, it is argued, has come of age and should be able to take care of itself. In essence the point being raised here is that there is no need for mission among the already evangelized. The second argument against mission in Africa today concerns those not yet evangelized. It is argued that, it is now an accepted fact that, long before the first missionaries set foot on African soil, Africans had their religious beliefs, worshiped their Creator and had a high sense of morality. In support of this argument it is pointed out that the church itself acknowledges that the "Kingdom and . . . salvation, . . . are available to every human being as grace and mercy. . ." (EN 10), and that "Christ died for everyone, and since the ultimate calling of each of us comes from God and is therefore a universal one, we are obliged to hold that the Holy Spirit offers everyone the possibility of sharing in the Paschal Mystery in a manner known to God" (GS 22).

If the church really believes and teaches the above and if mission is what it is said to be (as explained above) then, is there a necessity for mission in Africa today? Is there a need for evangelization to continue among the already evangelized? And do those who have not yet heard the Good News necessarily need to hear it to be saved? So why mission today, be it among the evangelized or the un-evangelized?

To the argument against mission among the already evangelized it must be pointed out that the flourishing local churches (the result of the successes of the missionary endeavors of the past two centuries) are an indication of the establishment of the church on the African continent. This very fact is reason for continuing mission today because the Church is missionary by nature (AG 2). And because it is missionary by nature, the tasks of evangelizing all people--be they people already evangelized or not, constitutes its essential mission.[2] As Pope John Paul II puts it, mission or missionary activity "is the primary service which the Church can render to every individual and to all humanity in the modern world, a world which has experienced marvelous achievements but which seems to have lost its sense of ultimate realities and of existence itself" (RM 2). Thus the fact that it is already established among a group of people in a given context is no reason for the cessation of her missionary activity. She exists for no other purpose than to "to point *beyond* itself, to be a community that preaches, serves and witnesses to the Reign of God." Hence it is not an institutions that exist for its own sake or to "provide refuge from a sinful world, nor to provide a warm and supportive community for lonely souls, nor even less to be a plank of salvation on a tempestuous sea that threatens damnation."[3] Mission is therefore not a matter of choice for the church in Africa. It is an obligation (see EN 5). It is that which gives the meaning and purpose of the very existence of the church even among the already evangelized.

As to the necessity of mission in Africa among those not yet evangelized, it must be stated that, though the church teaches that God saves all people regardless whether they are Christians or not, it also makes it clear that its "fundamental function in every age, ... is to direct man's gaze, to point the awareness and experience of the whole of humanity toward the mystery of Christ" (EN 4). It further teaches that it is the redemptive event of Christ that brought salvation to all humanity, Christian or not. We are here in the realm of faith. That is why Pope John Paul II explains: "It is only in faith that the Church's mission can be understood and only in faith that it finds its basis" (EAf 47). This is not a denial or a show of lack of respect for non-Christian religions in Africa. But "neither respect and esteem for these religions or the complexity of the questions raised is an invitation of the Church to withhold from these non-Christians the proclamation of Jesus Christ. On the contrary the Church hold that these multitudes have the right to know the riches of the mystery of Christ (cf. Eph 3:8)--riches in which we believe that the whole of humanity can find, in unsuspected fullness, everything that it is gropingly searching for concerning God, man and his destiny, life and death, and truth" (Ibid.).

If as Christians we really believe that Christ is the absolute and unique mediator, then we can not but urgently proclaim this Good News "to the millions of people in Africa who are not yet evangelized" (Ibid.), notwithstanding the fact that explicit awareness and/or belief of the very special role of Christ and the Church are not indispensable for salvation.[4]

Challenges for Mission in Africa

If the Church in Africa has an obligation to be missionary, how should it carry out that mission in such a manner as to remain faithful to its mandate and at the same time be relevant for Africa?

We are of the opinion that the approach to mission in Africa today-- be it renewed evangelization or primary evangelization must--be premised on the understanding and appreciation of the fact that 1) the church (through its missionaries, whether expatriate or African) did not in the past nor does it today bring God to Africa, and 2) mission in Africa today is not merely a matter of passage of people from a non-Christian religion to Christianity through certain types of conversion. Mission in the twenty-first century in Africa has to do with helping Christians and non-Christians alike to discover abiding "hidden" presence of the loving, gentle and compassionate God whom Jesus calls Abba, and with making this presence relevant and credible in the present concrete situation or realities of Africa.

The teeming millions of unevangelized people in Africa need to hear the saving message of Jesus Christ. This need is not derived from the fact that they are "unbelievers" (in the sense that they have no knowledge or belief of God) but "believers" who are either unaware and/or unconvinced of the riches of the mystery of Christ (see Eph 3:8) who has reconciled humanity with the Father and is the only means of salvation. So it is not as if to evangelize them is to bring them the knowledge and experience of God the Creator for the first time. Evangelization/mission among them would or should entail sharing the experience of the personal and/or communal encounter of Christ, and helping them to have what Pope John Paul II calls "this overwhelming and exhilarating experience of Jesus Christ who calls each one to follow him in an adventure of faith" (EAf 57). This is the challenge of primary evangelization.

Among those already baptized, the challenge of renewed evangelization is how to help them continue to deepen their faith and become really convinced and committed Christians--i.e. people for whom Christianity is a "way of life" and not merely something one has learned. Such a need is underscored by the statement of Pope John Paul II that in Africa "formation in the faith--as many adults, and especially the intellectuals, admit--remains too often at an elementary stage, and the sects easily take advantage of this ignorance."[5] In support of this renewed evangelization, Paul VI stresses that "the Church does not feel dispensed from paying unflagging attention . . . to those who have received the faith and who have been in contact with the Gospel . . . . . Thus she seeks to deepen, consolidate, nourish and make ever more mature the faith of those who are already called the faithful or believers, in order that they may be so still more" (EN 54).

These challenges facing the church are accentuated by the fact that Africa is menaced on all sides by all sorts of problems such as: the HIV/AIDS pandemic which is causing catastrophic havoc in terms of human and economic resources; ethnic and tribal conflicts that breed hatred and a cycle of violence leading to increase in the number of refugees and internally displaced people; problems associated with urbanization and globalization resulting in rising unemployment, breakdown of traditional social systems and values; and the corruption and the naked rape of the continents natural resources by unscrupulous people and forces.

In the face of such seemingly hopeless and precarious situations, how can the church (God's People, Christians) live and engage in its mission in such a manner as to be a sign and instrument of change or transformation and hope--hope that is rooted in the Paschal Mystery?

These challenges call for a comprehensive, integrated and systematic on-going formation programs or catechesis that in the words of Pope Paul VI are "full of Gospel vitality and in a language suited to people and circumstance" (Ibid.). Such programs or catechesis should be designed in such a manner as to cater for the different stages and situations of life-- programs which, touching on the real issues of life, that do not merely impart knowledge but also (more especially) mold people's character. They should be programs inclusive of relevant rituals performed or celebrated at major turning points in people's life, from cradle to grave. The emphasis of such catechesis must not be on learning about the faith but on living it; a catechesis that facilitates a living personal and communal encounter with the Risen Lord, so that Christianity would not be merely a matter of belief but principally a matter of behavior, ensuring a life in which there is no dichotomy between the sacred and the profane.

Mission and Inculturation in Africa

In light of the above, it is clear that any consideration of mission in Africa that is not linked to inculturation is incomplete. We read in Jn 1:1: "In the beginning was the Word, and the Word was with God and the Word was God." This Word became incarnate from the Virgin Mary and was made flesh--became human and dwelt among us (Jn 1:14). This "sublime mystery of the Incarnation of the Word, . . . took place *in history*: in clearly defined circumstances of time and space, amidst a people with its own culture . . . ." (EN 60).

This Word, the Second Person of the Blessed Trinity is Jesus, the Good News that the church proclaims. This Word if it is universal must be at home in every culture; a message that takes root in the concrete life situation of its hearers. This must be the reason behind Pope Paul VI's teaching that the church should "in practice incarnate in the individual Churches made up of such or such an actual part of mankind, speaking such and such a language, heirs of a cultural patrimony, of a vision of the world, of an historical past, of a particular human substratum." The Pope further explains, "In the mind of the Lord the Church is universal by vocation and mission, but when she puts down her roots in a variety of cultural, social and human terrain, she takes on different external expressions and appearances in each part of the world" (EN 62).

The incarnation of the Word --the *Good News*, in the cultural milieu in which it is proclaimed, is what inculturation is all about. The gospel message takes root in the actual life situation of its hearers, becoming meaningful and relevant and serves as the anchor and motivating force in their life.

Traditionally, religion for the African is part and parcel of life. There is no dichotomy between the sacred and profane. "Religion pervades the life of the African."[6] Hence Mbiti observes "wherever the African is, there is his religion; he carries it to the field where he is sowing seeds or harvesting a new crop; he takes it with him to the beer party or to attend a funeral ceremony."[7]

Therefore, as discussed earlier, if mission is the complex and dynamic process by which the gospel message (proclaimed by the church) permeates and transforms the core and fabric of people's life and culture, then mission for Africa invariably involve the process of inculturation. This might be the reason why Pope Paul VI stated that mission (or in his own word "evangelization") "loses much of its force and effectiveness if it does not take into consideration the actual people to whom it addresses, if it does not use their language, their signs and symbols, if it does not answer the questions they ask, and if it does not have an impact on their concrete life" (EN 63). Thus if mission is urgent for Africa in the twenty-first century, so also is inculturation. For without inculturation the *Good News* will remain foreign to the people. It would be something learned, but not lived; a fashion taken after but without (much) conviction, a matter of belief but not of behavior, a belief that is professed but which does not serve as the anchor and motivating force of life. Because inculturation is indispensable for mission in Africa in the twenty-first century, the Synod Fathers could confidently assert that it is "an urgent priority in the life of the particular Churches, for a firm rooting of the Gospel in Africa . . . a requirement for evangelization, a path towards full evangelization" (EAf 59).

Conclusion

Through the heroic, dedicated and selfless service of generations of missionaries from other continents, the church has taken root in the African soil. Some of the fruits of those endeavors are the flourishing local churches, the increase in the number of native clergy and members of Consecrated Institutes, the building and managing of health and educational institutions and social development projects and programs aimed at uplifting and improving the quality of life of the people.

The challenge for mission in Africa in the twenty-first century is not so much how to sustain the achievements of the past centuries, but how to continue with mission in such a manner as to ensure that the seed of faith in Jesus Christ will continue to take deeper root in the African soil--in the hearts and minds of the African, permeating the core and fabric of his/her being and transforming him/her into a true (Christian) witness of the Kingdom. A true witness will not be one with a two-fold faithfulness, operating with two thought systems and having two parallel behaviors. He or she will not be like the Christian the Congolese musician has lamented: "Miserable Christian, at Mass in the morning, to the fortune teller in the evening, amulet in the pocket, the scapular round the neck." Rather the true witness will be one whose faithfulness to Christ is solid and can carry him/her through times of crisis, and whose thought system and behavior are anchored in Kingdom values.

***

Cry of an African Christian

I hear a cry, a silent cry
A cry so fervent and yet so faint.
I sense a plea, an honest plea
A plea so powerful and yet so patient.
I feel a groan, a painful groan
A groan so crushing and yet so calm.

This cry that I hear,
The plea that I sense
And the groan that I feel
Are those of the African Christian.

It is a cry for respect for his culture and values,
A plea for understanding and sensitivity towards his symbols.
A groan for patient-love for his mode of expressing himself.

It is a crying out to the missionary,
A pleading with the evangelizer,
A groaning out to the messenger,
Who seeks to help him discover the Good News
In the profound riches of his culture and values
And in the priceless value of his symbols.

So that in the expression of his faith
He will remain authentically African
And a convinced and committed Christian.

Gabriel Afagbegee, SVD

Notes

1. "The African Synod: Lineamenta and Questions," *Africal Ecclesial Review* (AFER), 33 (1991): 11.

2. "Declaration of the Synod Fathers, " #4, *L'Osservatore Romano* (27 October 1974): 6

3. Stephen Bevans, SVD and Roger Schroeder, SVD, "Missionary by Its Very Nature: A Reading of the Acts of the Apostles, " *Verbum SVD*, 41, 2, (2000): 200.

4. Anthony Bellagamba, *The Mission of the Church* (Nairobi: St. Paul's Publication, 1993), p. 24.

5. John Paul II, "Address to the Episcopal Conference of Cameroon" (13 August 1985) as quoted in AFER , 33 (1991): 21.

6. Andrew Moemeka, "Communication and African Culture," *Communication and Culture--African Perspective* (WACC--African Religion, 1989), p. 8.

7. John S. Mbiti, *African Religions and Philosophy* (London: Heineman).

MISSION FOR THE TWENTY-FIRST CENTURY IN ASIA:
Two Sketches, Three Flash-Backs and an Enigma

John Mansford Prior, SVD*

Introduction

In this workshop we are invited to reflect upon three ecclesial documents from the particular perspective of Asia,[1] focusing on questions of theology and mission for the future. These three documents are quite different in genesis, weight and impact. The key text is *Ad Gentes* (AG--1965); it is a document of an ecumenical council and therefore of the highest ecclesial authority. Historically AG helped trigger fundamental new directions for mission in Asia. Next in weight comes *Evangelii Nuntiandi* (EN--1975), a synodical--or more accurately quasi-synodical--document, drawn up by a papal commission after the bishops failed to reach a consensus.[2] And thirdly, *Redemptoris Missio* (RM--1990), a papal text, which, twenty-five years after the event, gives John Paul II's interpretation of the council, in particular of AG. The pope sees Asia as the major challenge for mission while voicing concern about developments in theology (primarily in Asia?). Fissures already apparent in the compromises of AG came to the surface in the synod that birthed EN and were unambiguously answered in RM. Thus, this workshop is asked to reflect upon theology and mission in Asia over the coming years in the light of a council, a synod and a pope.[3]

In the first place we wish to understand whether, and to what extent, the Council has renewed the life of the Asian Catholic churches and how these churches have assimilated the conciliar enterprise. In the second place we wish to see how the Asian Churches have positioned themselves to face the future. The real and effective power of AG and, subsequently of EN and RM, depends upon the intrinsic validity or otherwise of the ideas and issues behind the text. How have AG, EN and RM led the churches to respond

---

John Mansford Prior is Professor of Missiology at Divine Word Seminary, Ledalero, Flores, Indonesia and Coordinator of the SVD Asia/Pacific Zone (ASPAC). He worked in the secretariat for the 1999 Asian Synod of Bishops in Rome.

authentically in faith to God's mission in Asia? We must look both behind as well as in front of the texts, for in many ways the most vital energies mobilized in the Asian Churches by the conciliar dynamic were largely unforeseen in the wording of the texts themselves and unexpected by many who subsequently implemented the conciliar vision.

An Interpretive Key

The "new Pentecost" of John XXIII swept through the Asian Churches within a generation of most countries reclaiming their political independence. As Asian nations re-appropriated their political and cultural identities and faced the challenge of development, so the scattered pockets of Christians rediscovered themselves as fellow Asians and threw in their lot with the common struggle for a more just and humane society. This double dynamic decides how we are to interpret the impact of individual ecclesial texts on the churches.[4] The same dynamic also informs us as to how prepared the churches are for mission in the coming years.

Many Asian churches have recognized the deep dynamism at work in the conciliar event. These churches have creatively appropriated the conciliar vision through a renewal both fruitful and demanding. The liberating power of the council has taken concrete form in ways that are surely enduring. This post-conciliar discourse in Asia is multi-vocal and multi-directional. However systematically the Roman Curia has attempted to regulate reform from the center, post-conciliar history has proved how irrepressible is the power of the Spirit.

That is why, at this distance from the Council I shall be listening to the ongoing evocative power of the Johannine Council rather than monitor implementation of specific decisions. I shall speak from three decades of immersing myself in the self-confident local Churches of Asia as they leave behind their pre-conciliar ghettos from pre-independence days. I am convinced that we can learn from the way that the Asian churches are reinventing themselves as laboratories of hope amidst stark political tensions, intransigent inter-ethnic violence, increasing religious extremism and crass economic exploitation of the continent and indeed of the entire globalizing world.

Establishing Boundaries

The scope of this workshop paper is at once too wide and too narrow. Too wide, for Asia contains around 60 per cent of the world's population and a greater cultural and religious plurality than any other continent. However, the numerous widely dispersed churches, each with its own issues, can be coped with by limiting ourselves to key ideas and events, to major paradigmatic shifts and to the alternate paths that have opened up. At the same time the scope is too narrow. An overtly confessional approach is more or less demanded by our focusing upon three Roman Catholic documents. However, this should not make us unmindful of the strongly ecumenical character of the recent history of the Asian churches. The Johannine Council has had an enormous impact upon the Reformation Churches, for instance on their rediscovery of conciliarity. In a similar way Protestant global and regional events have impacted Catholic developments, for instance on our acceptance of the integrity of creation as an integral part of justice and peace.[5] The Catholic Federation of Asian Bishops' Conferences (FABC) and the Protestant Christian Conference of Asia (CCA) have close working relationships on theological, ethical and pastoral issues.[6]

I present two straightforward sketches, three flash-backs and conclude with the present enigma that we are facing. Through the words of a Filipino bishop and the work of FABC I observe that the greatest renewal of the Asian churches is their rebirth as base communities, as contrast cultures, both Christian and inter-faith. I accept the provisional nature of the AG text; it is not and was not intended to be definitive. Yet the comprehensive vision of its opening and its rediscovery of patristic horizons, have hugely influenced the reform of the churches and are still germane today. Rather than treat the many themes of EN, I look at the two alternative theologies and world views voiced during the 1974 synod, each represented by one of the special secretaries. This allows me to relate the work of updating mission in India in the immediate post-conciliar period with the new frame for mission. While the curia successfully scuttled that vision in 1974, it is at the heart of divergent views that separate Rome and Asia today. My treatment of RM is also individual. I contrast the theological basis in chapters 1-3 with that of AG chapter 1. Finally, I look at the challenges that we shall have to face if the churches of Asia are to live out their mission as dynamic diasporas of hope.

Sketch 1:
Towards a more Participatory Church working for a Participatory Society

When a tree falls it makes a great noise, but when a forest is growing nobody hears anything (Chinese proverb)

Participation

Twenty years after the Johannine Council (1962-1965) Bishop Francisco P. Claver summed up the Council's impact on the Catholic Churches in Asia in a single, short phrase: the Council has led to the building up of *a more participatory church*.[7] Claver sees participation as the single key conciliar idea that has brought about the most radical renewal of the church and its work. For Claver participation is the pivotal idea upon which all other reforms depend. In this one word he sums up the entire work of the Council and its impact upon the Asian Catholic Churches who have set out once again as pilgrims of the gospel. Participation is behind both the reform of church life, and political, economic and cultural renewal. Through the work of the FABC, the vision and practice of bishops such as Claver have had a marked impact on the Asian Churches.[8]   The gradual building up of a more participatory church led to a change of focus away from hierarchical leadership towards lay follower-ship. This Claver describes as a true "paradigm shift." Ecclesial horizons have been extended so that old ecclesiastical boundaries have been replaced by a lay-led, multi-centric evangelizing mission. Participation envelops the whole of life--individuals, communities and societies. This shift demands much rethinking and consultation. The Asian churches have had to become listeners, probers, questioners. For this to happen we have had to discover *a new way of being church*:

> The church becomes local, practically inevitably . . . (for) when people begin participating in its life, they bring into its ambit of concern their own life concerns. This has the effect of both broadening and narrowing the Church's concerns: broadening them . . . beyond its explicitly spiritual concerns, narrowing them to the specificities of the people's life . . . a truly participatory and discerning Church, given the change of focus and the acceptance of social transformation and inculturation as legitimate tasks in the general mission of the Church . . . .[9]

Since 1981 the Federation of Asian Bishops' Conferences (FABC) has formulated an ecclesiology of communion, the churches as, "a communion of communities."[10] With the collapse of western imperialism and in line with the autonomy and independence of Asian nations, the Council saw the establishment of authentic and autonomous local churches as a key aim of missionary activity (LG 17, AG 6).[11]

Participation is the rediscovery that the church is conciliar/synodical and that society is democratic. This rediscovery has led to seven major shifts that have redefined the mission task in Asia. These were presented to the Seventh General Assembly of the FABC in January 2000 by Archbishop Orlando Quevedo.[12] Archbishop Quevedo summed up the thirty-five year renewal of the Asian churches as a seven-fold movement. As a result of the Johannine Council we are moving from largely passive and somewhat anxious minority churches (closed, foreign enclaves cut off from the vast mass of Asian peoples) and are becoming active, evangelizing church communities increasingly confident in complex, inter-religious situations. We are moving from an abstract and non-involved universalism to becoming truly local churches, rooted in the people, a church at once indigenous and inculturated. We are moving from large, powerful social institutions to a deep interiority where prayer engenders clear options and transparent witness. We are moving from an inherited western individualism towards participatory, co-responsible communities of faith, open to other local churches and other faith-communities. We have been trying to move from clericalism towards an authentic lay empowerment where a vast majority of the laity live among and minister to followers of other religious traditions. We have been trying to ease away from a comfortable and uncritical relationship with the rich and powerful--a temptation inherent in small, minority middle-class churches--and reposition ourselves as a church of the poor and a church of the young. We are moving from a passive acceptance of militarized and brutalizing cultures of death towards active involvement in generating cultures of peace, human rights and life.

To these seven movements, the FABC Assembly participants added an eighth: from churches busy with themselves we are moving towards becoming churches in dialogue with the marginalized, with living cultures and with other faith-traditions.[13] This three-fold dialogue has been a hallmark of FABC activities since the very first meeting of Asian Bishops with Pope Paul in Manila in 1970.[14]

Base Communities

The participatory church is returning to its roots, its base among the poor and the marginalized. Claver himself says that the spearhead of this new way of being church is the replacement of the conventional, large parish with networks of base communities, both Christian and inter-faith. The old institutional church has not been able to engage with the great religious and cultural traditions of Asia whether Buddhist, Islamic or Hindu. Participatory base communities--in particular inter-faith communities at the grass roots of society--are opening up a new way of being "church-in-mission."[15]

Most Asian churches have adopted this "new way of being church." For instance, the national Catholic Jubilee 2000 Congress in Bogor, Indonesia, shared experiences of base communities in the light of contemporary political and social turmoil as the country is inching towards a more participatory, civil society.[16] The development of networks of base communities is supported by the Asian Integral Pastoral Approach (AsIpa) promoted by the Office for the Laity of the FABC.[17]

Integral Liberation

Concomitant with this, the church has been breaking out of its ritualistic cocoon and pietistic mode as it works with majority communities in developing a more humane, participatory civil society founded upon basic human rights and duties. Unsurprisingly, the Office for Human Development of the FABC that began with great verve and imagination, has its headquarters in Manila. As the single largest Catholic nation in Asia,[18] the Philippines is showing the other Asian churches how a Christian nation is developing a practical social teaching.[19] While all this can certainly be traced back to the conciliar event, the particular emphasis upon liberation and base communities does not from AG. Conversely, this two-pronged strategy, with equal input from other continental churches, helped shape the content of the post-synodical exhortation EN[20]

Flash-Back 1:
AD GENTES:
A Commanding Vision and an Impending Earthquake

Read today, AG is not that impressive a document; and yet thirty-five years ago, together with other conciliar texts, it set a revolution in progress. In Chapter One we find key elements of a rediscovered, patristic theology of mission. At this distance we would do well to concentrate on this majestic, opening vision drawn up on the insistence of hundreds of "missionary" bishops looking for encouragement and inspiration.

Undergirding Vision

The Johannine Council wished to do away with the idea that mission is a peripheral phenomenon of the church, constituting a sphere of activity reserved to specialists.[21] Anchored in the ecclesiology of LG, AG sees the church as the missionary, pilgrim people of God, as God's envoy, destined to extend to all regions of the earth (LG 9-17). As universal sacrament of salvation, the church must be present to all people in order to bring them into contact with the saving message of Christ and incorporate them into his body. The aim is not a naive Christianization of the world but a renewal of the world in the spirit of the gospel. This comprehensive mission vision, coming as it did at a time of national, cultural, religious and economic renewal throughout Asia, was decisive in the drive of the Asian Churches to move out of their minority enclaves and enter the mainstream of society as prophetic diasporas.

AG 2-9 elaborates the theological justification for mission. The basis of mission lies in the missions of the Son and the Holy Spirit motivated by the love of God. But mission also means a fulfilment of the striving of human nature. Thus traditional elements of missiological thinking are taken up, but influences from more recent Protestant missiology are also evident, especially with reference to the eschatological perspective (paragraph 9). As such the church is "on the way" and remains oriented to service in the world.

> The church on earth is by its very nature missionary since, according to the plan of the Father, it has its origin in the mission of the Son and the Holy Spirit. "Fountain-like," this plan flows from the love of the Father. He is the origin without origin. From him comes the Son and through the Son the Spirit. God wishes to call humans not only one by one but also in relation to each other to partake in his life. The Father wishes to gather all people to *become* one people, in order that his children, scattered around the world, become one (AG 2).

Mission is the *missio Dei*. Mission is cosmic in scope. Mission arises wherever there are local Christian communities. In the words of Yves Congar, according to AG, "No local church is not missionary and no mission is not ecclesial; there is no Church which is not mindful of the whole Church and which does not provide universality within itself."[22] This commanding vision is returned to in article 9:

> Missionary activity is nothing else, and nothing less, than
> the manifestation of God's plan, its epiphany and realisation
> in the world and in history; that by which God, through
> mission, clearly brings to its conclusion the history of
> salvation.

This is an holistic vision bringing together personal and cosmic salvation, a mission to transform the world, to change all its structures, economic, political, cultural and religious so that it expresses and heralds a new humanity of love and fellowship, justice and peace, freedom and wholeness, solidarity and sharing, together with all people of good will.

Replete with patristic references[23], the first chapter incorporates the Christo-centric concept of mission from the Münster school of Josef Schmidlin with its emphasis upon the proclamation of the gospel with the curial-canonist (territorial) concept of Pierre Charles and André Seumois from the Louvain school which focuses upon church plantation. However, both conceptions still view the church chiefly as an institution, and the missionary is still pictured as a foreigner who travels to distant lands.[24] The consequences of LG Chapter Two have not been absorbed.

Salvation and Other Religions

AG both reaffirmed the necessity of mission activity while holding out the possibility of salvation for adherents of other religions (e.g. LG 16, AG 7). AG refrained from putting forward a theory about the consistency of the two principles. The main concern of *Nostra Aetate* (NA) was to see religions in a positive light and thus as open avenues for dialogue and co-operation without playing down the missionary consciousness of the church in any way (NA 2). There was no decision on the value of other religions for salvation. Christ and Christianity appear as "fulfilment, goal and accomplishment, as crisis and judgement" of other religions. There is no word as to why Asian adherents to other religions do not see Christianity as the fulfilment of their religious experience. In spite of a new esteem for other religions and the recognition of the possibility of salvation for all people of good will, the Council wanted to emphasize the meaning and necessity of missionary activity. Thirty-five years on, these apparently conflicting statements of the Council have produced divergent stances that distinguish the approaches of Asia and Rome.

Issues left Open

Today, and from an Asian perspective, we might note what AG did not say about issues already evident on this continent in the 1960s. Important in Asia would have been a greater self-criticism with regard to mission history, in particular regarding the Euro-centrism of mission and its uncritical link with colonialism (cf. the strident conciliar intervention of Arrupe). The socio-political dimension is included but could have been more strongly stressed as the Asian Churches embarked on an active engagement in the "decade of development." Also, AG had virtually nothing to say about ideological atheism (China, North Korea, Viet Nam, Laos) or pragmatic agnosticism (the secularist commercial sub-culture, for instance).

At the turn of the century, another comment is worth making. The Johannine Council attempted to allow the church to come to terms with the modern world. Unfortunately, the modern world was about to give way to a post-modern world. The church was coming to terms with the *disappearing world* of modernity. Thus, the council was unaware of the collapse of metaphysics, the pursuit of hermeneutics, the emergence of critical methods, and the whole world of deconstructionism--present in Asia above all in its literature and poetry.[25] The Council concluded just before the revolt of young people who were already forming a semi-autonomous world of their own, resulting in a radical break in continuity with the past. Such generational breaks have been intensified by mass economic migration and even more so in the instant, click culture that has subsequently enveloped the globe. The Council had little to say about women, secularization or urbanization, or indeed anything about the crisis of the magisterium itself. The Council attempted to answer the problems of the modern world, not the post-modern world that was already on the horizon.

The broad vision of the opening chapter was not followed through. There was no time to integrate the thought and direction of *Gaudium et Spes* (GS) into the conciliar understanding of mission. There was not enough time to re-work the draft into a coherent whole. The different origins of individual parts are still evident, and unnecessary repetitions can be found. Results from other documents were slotted in, although the influence of AG on the rest of the conciliar texts is virtually non-existent.

AG not an innovative draft, but it is a valuable transition document taking account of previous theories and results without committing itself to one side or the other. In some important passages it gives pointers to the future without blocking possible developments. The broad horizon of AG could have radically altered the subsequent chapters--and the subsequent policy of the Congregation for the Evangelization of Peoples--if the bishops had had the energy to work at the issues.[26] While crucial theological and pastoral problems were recognized, their solutions were left in abeyance. Asia has pursued these open paths; Rome has systematically tried to block them.

Seismic Shifts, Personal Rapport

Four conciliar insights have radically influenced Asian Churches over the past thirty-five years. This process of reform was trigged by the clear statement of the priority of the local church (LG 23), the necessity of incarnating local churches (AG 22), the equality of each and every rite within the Catholic communion of churches (OE 2), and the imperative of ecumenism (UR). Meanwhile the classical paradigm of mission was gradually subverted by four other major conciliar shifts: God's saving plan encompasses the entire cosmos, leading it towards ultimate unification (AG 1); the universal salvific will of God offers everybody the possibility of salvation (LG 16, GS 22); all peoples are part of a single human community with God as origin and goal (NA 1) and, because human beings are social by nature, the quest for God is not limited to the individual conscience but finds outward, social expression (DH 3).[27]

There was also a more intimate effect of great significance. In the Council for the first time Asian bishops met each other; began to recognize each other as colleagues and began to recognize issues in common. They had yet to find a common voice or a sense of unity. However the conciliar experience paved the way for the Asian meeting of bishops in Manila five years later and made possible the establishment of the Federation of Asian Bishops' Conferences (FABC) in 1974. At the very least, it can be said that due to the conciliar experience, Asian bishops were no longer isolated from each other or locked up in the old traditions of their western, founding churches. In this sense, the Council was a point of departure for pastoral, theological and mission renewal. One excellent example of that is India.[28]

Sketch 2:
Birthing the Council in South Asia

All-India Seminar

Within a year of the Council's conclusion, the bishops of India already saw the need for establishing research centers to assist in the development of new models for mission in line with AG 22:

> In imitation of the plan of the Incarnation, the young Churches rooted in Christ and built upon the foundation of the apostles take to themselves in a wonderful exchange all the riches of the nations which were given to Christ as an inheritance . . . . If this goal is to be achieved, theological investigation must necessarily be stirred up in each major socio-cultural area.. As a result avenues will be opened for a more profound adaptation in the whole area of Christian life.[29]

The bishops set a process in motion which culminated in the All-India Seminar.[30] A remarkable post-conciliar spirit of open and courageous dialogue ensured that every possible viewpoint in both the Eastern and Western Rite Churches be listened to in the context of contemporary society. This was in line with India as a whole which was trying to synthesise its traditional ethos (culture, religion, values) with modern society (economics, politics, plurality). Seven orientation papers were written, circulated and discussed nation-wide.[31] No fewer than nine national consultations, fourteen Regional and Diocesan seminars, fifteen seminary seminars and thirteen studies by special groups involving over 10,000 participants from every part of the country and every sphere of the apostolate were held. From these regional and diocesan seminars 485 delegates were chosen for the All-India Seminar.[32] Material submitted by the preparatory seminars were published in a 583 page volume. The seminar was in session for ten days opening on Ascension Thursday and concluding on Pentecost Sunday, 1969. The first ten sessions were in sixteen workshops followed by ten more sessions in four clusters of the original sixteen workshops.[33] Only then came the twelve plenary sessions that approved the resolutions.

During a short eighteen month period, the Latin and Syrian Catholic Churches of India faced the question of mission as a single communion of churches. A tremendous impetus was given to the inculturation of the whole of Christian life--language and culture, ashrams and religious life, theology and catechetics, lifestyle and the liturgy. Very soon this move towards "deep inculturation" combined with work for liberation as the Dalits rediscovered their voice and their dignity. Initiated and led by D. S. Amalorpavadass for its first fifteen years, the NBCLC ("National Centre") in Bangalore kept the conciliar flame alight. Amalor was secretary to the Biblical, Catechetical and Liturgical Commissions which formed the heart of the "National Centre." This remarkable person was one of two special secretaries for the Roman Synod on Evangelization five years later (1974). With the All-Indian Seminar behind him, and countless other workshops at regional and national levels, he was thoroughly prepared for Rome. If the Indian experience was articulated during the 1974 synod which produced EN, then further developments in India were behind much of the concern expressed in RM.

The All-India Seminar released a vitality and courage that has marked important elements in the Indian Church ever since. This pioneering theological and practical investigation is being carried out in a sub-continent with a population of one thousand million people. It would not be historically correct to say that all latter developments were triggered by the All-India Seminar. Perhaps it is more correct to say that the energies released by the council combined with the dynamism of the Indian people. This is one of the more remarkable cases of a "statistically insignificant" church (a mere 2 per cent of the total population) yet with a substantial number of members (over 20 million) birthing itself as Asian rather than remaining confined in a quasi-Western womb. The importance of Medellín, 1968 and Latin American liberation theology cannot be overestimated; and yet the majority of the peoples of the Americas are racially and cultural western. In the Indian sub-continent we have churches re-rooting themselves in their own cultural soil. Little wonder that a cardinal in Rome has called India the "epicenter of heresy."

"Without dreams the people perish" (Prov 29:18). Many of the dreams of the All-India Seminar have not been realized. The multiplicity of rites and jurisdictions have not been replaced by a common rite based on Indian tradition; quite the contrary, the three rites now each have their own separate episcopal conferences. The episcopal conferences themselves have not been re-constituted to include clergy, religious and laity. And so forth. Yet, ashrams are thriving, solidarity with the struggle of the Dalits continues in the midst of increasingly violent communalism, and some of the most creative are articulate theologizing anywhere continues to fill countless books and journals. The All-India Seminar is both sign and instrument of what

Asian churches can do when they have the freedom to uncover the paths of mission for themselves.[34]

Inter-Faith Dialogue

The Catholic churches of the Indian sub-continent, with twenty million members running across more languages and cultures than the whole of Europe combined, are scattered as small communities throughout the nation with a solid base in Kerala and a growing presence in the North East. They have learned over the past four decades to live with, and learn from, other faith traditions. This ongoing, reflective experience with members of other faith traditions, in contemplative *sadhana*, in Dalit struggles, a vibrant dialogue of life and action has perhaps done more to radicalize and Asianize the church and any one other single issue. If participation is the key to the reform of many of the Asian Churches beginning with the majority church of the Philippines, then the inter-faith dialogue of life and action is surely the key experience in India and much of Southeast Asia--Myanmar, Thailand, Cambodia, Laos, Viet Nam, Malaysia, Singapore, Brunei and Indonesia.

Asian Catholics now know that their neighbors are people of faith and that their faith inspires them to live out the will of God and come to divine-realization and self-realization. We know that our neighbors live the truth in love through their faith tradition.[35] Dialogue is the key term and the key experience. Dialogue is not an alternative activity let alone a competitor to the announcing of the Good News. Dialogue is a way of living and thinking; it is the mode of mission in Asia today. However hard elements in Rome try to separate "the announcement of the gospel" from "dialogue with people of other faith traditions," in Asia we witness by life and action and when possible by word, but always as an ongoing, living dialogue.[36] This three-fold dialogue in faith brings about cultural transformation, integral liberation and pluralistic expressions of the Truth as experienced and lived. Proclamation *is* dialogue where the dialogue of life-witness and committed action with all people of good will is carried out with the values, perspectives and the power of the incarnate, crucified and risen Word of God. And precisely here, the key term "participation" and the key experience "dialogue" come together in an open, listening, pilgrim people of God.

Flash-Back 2:
EVANGELII NUNTIANDI
A Broadening of Horizons and a Warning of Things to Come

After the success of the 1971 Roman Synod on Justice in the World, there was every reason to look forward to the 1974 Synod on evangelization. AG was not quite the inspirational document sought by the conciliar bishops. Subsequent paradigmatic shifts in both the theology and practice of mission led to confusion as well as pioneering breakthroughs. Asian and African contributions to the 1971 synod were already significant. The Third World bishops might well have been decisive in the Synod of 1974 if the curia had not allied with a minority of bishops and manipulated the proceedings.

There were two special secretaries. From the Gregorian University, Rome, came Domenico Grasso, a member of the commission that had drafted AG 10 years previously.[37] From India there came D. S. Amalorpavadass. Amalor combined both an original, brilliant mind with managerial abilities. As the month-long synod progressed it became apparent that these two secretaries interpreted the voice of the world's bishops very differently. Grasso was the voice of Rome, re-interpreting AG in a minimalist way, avoiding any reformulation made necessary by a decade of experience with inter-faith dialogue and living with the marginalized. Grasso's synthesis of the theological discussion made "either-or" statements out of every issue. It was crystal clear from his version of the final statement which of the alternatives he backed: the cautious minority fearful of the dangers of the new, creative approaches to mission. Amalor, on the other hand, penned a coherent, comprehensive, contextual theology of mission, drawing in both the bold new ventures of the majority and the questions of the cautionary minority into a "dialectical tension, one calling for the others." Amalor's kaleidoscopic summation admits to both approaches, bring them into a creative tension. It could (and should) have become the basis of a remarkable synodical document.

When Amalor learned that his work had been ignored in the drafting of the final text to be voted on, he had his more comprehensive version duplicated and distributed among the bishops. There was no time for debate between the reading of the final draft and the vote. However, the official draft was decisively rejected by the bishops for they had been able to compare it to the alternative version drawn up by Amalorpavadass during a marathon, all-night labor of love. The official version simply did not reflect the bishops' contributions. With only four days left to the end of the synod, it was decided not to attempt another draft but simply to draw up a list of topics discussed in the course of the synod as a framework for a future document to be arranged by Paul VI. The result, as we well know, is *Evangelii Nuntiandi* (1975).[38]

This snippet of ecclesiastical politics is worth recalling. Firstly, it shows quite clearly that episcopal synods are not free to discover their own voice where this is not in tune with curial thinking.[39] Secondly, the impasse caused by the manoeuvrings of the synodical secretariat by marginalizing Amalor, and with him much of Asia, Oceania, Africa and Latin America, resulted in the synods becoming mere talking shops. Since then, no synod--except the extraordinary synod of 1985--has produced its own report. The proceedings are reduced to a number of secret propositions which are presented to the pope who is asked to write up the report, usually in the form of an apostolic exhortation. And thirdly, just ten years after the conciliar promulgation of AG, two quite different interpretations of the text have emerged. One is associated with the Congregation for the Evangelization of Peoples, the other with the self-confident, evangelizing churches of the Third World.

What then was so dangerous about the mission voice of Asia and the rest of the Third World?[40] According to Amalor, the two main contributions of the synodical discussions were on the local church and liberation. These were unacceptable to a centralizing bureaucracy in alliance with conservative worldly powers. Mission takes off when local churches become authentically Christian (back to the radicalism of the gospel including the option to be with the marginalized of society) and authentically local (in lifestyle, theology, spirituality, ethics, cultural ethos and worship). This demands a radical decentralization of the Latin communion of Catholic churches in solidarity with society's victims. This was stated clearly during the 1974 synod. This is what many local churches have been attempting since the Council. This is the theological thrust of the FABC–in its Office for Human Development (integral liberation), Office for the Laity (base communities and lay leadership), and the Office of Theological Concerns (propositions on a theology of the local church and on inter-religious dialogue). Above all, in the central thrust of the FABC Statements published by their regular General Assemblies: mission through the three-fold dialogue with the marginalized, with Asian cultures and with other faith traditions.

Amalor himself observes that the two tendencies in the 1974 synod come from two clearly discernible theological approaches due to two different world-views:

The one starts from above, outside the world, deducing conclusions from principles and applying them to various situations and cultures. This approach is inclined to overemphasize uniformity, transcendence, the divine and the supernatural. The other approach starts from below, from the dynamic realities of the world and history, and identifies with humans and is involved in human life situations where through the spirit of Christ God is at work and reveals God's designs in a ongoing process. The duty of the church is to discover God and interpret God's designs for today through the signs of the times in the light of the gospel. This approach from below will obviously join people as they are and where they are; it will emphasize pluriformity, immanence, the historical, anthropological, communitarian and cultural dimensions, political action, call for social change and care for relevance, credibility, experience, inner unity and communion. At the basis of these two approaches there are also two different ways of understanding divine revelation and the church.[41]

A year after the synod, EN was promulgated. EN is much broader than the final draft rejected by the bishops in 1974. Many of the issues discussed and captured in the unofficial draft by Amalorpavadass get a hearing. One issue, though, disappears entirely, namely that of inter-faith dialogue. Becoming a listening, pilgrim church dialoguing with majority faith traditions has brought about a paradigmatic shift in the self understanding of the Asian Catholic churches. While participation is the key hermeneutic that unlocks the dynamic alive in the Asian churches, dialogue is the key experience that has brought about a seismic change in the way we express our faith in life witness (partners not competitors), in action (for common human-divine values such as justice, basic rights and duties, democracy, above all human dignity), in spirituality (not just Christian use of Buddhist, Muslim, Hindu or tribal "*sadhana*", but a creative unfolding of our unique experience of the divine in experientially Asian terms), and in theology (Asian theologies are the only major alternative to western Theologizing to date).

Having stated "the Asian case", allow me to add that much in EN reflects what had been happening in the Asian Churches; much mission work such as integral liberation and base communities are given official recognition. EN is a positive document. Concern is more with what was left out (inter-faith dialogue, radical decentralization of the communion of Catholic churche, etc.) rather than what is stated. One of the conditions of genuine evangelization is dialogue in a attitude of mutual openness and acceptance, in respect and love, willingness to listen and to share, and readiness to be inspired, edified and converted by the other, and thus to journey together. However, Rome was not content to leave well alone.

Flash-Back 3:
REDEMPTORIS MISSIO
A Vigorous Return to a Pre-Conciliar Frame

Read meditatively, RM is a call to renew our discipleship for, "in the church's history, the missionary drive has always been a sign of vitality, just as its lessening is a sign of a crisis of faith" (RM 2). Mission springs from personal faith (RM 87). As Thomas D'Sa puts it, "The Samaritan woman was putting up barriers of race, sex, religion and tradition, Jesus did not argue with her on these. He simply offers his very person."[42] Looking beyond the frozen letter of the encyclical we can seek out key, creative metaphors and let them come to life in our lives. Such a spiritual reading of RM is possible for many who wish to share with their neighbors their God-experience of peace, reconciliation, self-surrender and prayer. However, as professional cross-cultural missioners we do not approach RM primarily as spiritual reading, but as an authoritative guide post for mission. Read as such in Asia, RM is a truly disturbing document.[43]

Allow me to begin by making my own a few comments by confrere Augustine Kanjamala:

> The encyclical, from beginning to end, projects a sense of anxiety... The tone... tends to be aggressive... To many in Asia RM appears to be primarily a response to the missionary crisis in Europe and America. It does not take seriously the Asian and Indian theological reflections... In essence, however, this encyclical, despite its many good and valid points, only indirectly and then inadequately addresses the problems and life experience of Asia, home of all the major world religions.[44]

Every paragraph of AG breathes with the hope engendered by John XXIII's call for a new Pentecost. EN is imbued with a genuine pastoral concern and, as such, was widely welcomed by the Asian churches. RM is a one-directional message from headquarters, framed without a shadow of doubt. While AG broke through the defensive, often frightened, attitudes of the fortress-church of pre-conciliar days, RM returns the petrine office to battle mode. AG left certain key issues open for further reflection, RM shuts the door on further development and returns to a traditional, petrine missionary framework.

Briefly put, RM mirrors the compromises arrived at in AG and then goes on to turn them into stone. AG was a transition document written at the beginning of a new era in both church and world. As such it is broad in its horizon and gentle in its recommendations. To avoid controversy during the final days of the Council, it sets pre-conciliar notions and mission administration side by side with the new understanding of the church (LG) and the opening towards a rapidly changing world (GS). Since its promulgation, the churches in Asia have taken up the challenge of converting western, institutional churches into a network of authentically Asian evangelical communities within cultural, social and religiously pluralistic societies. Asian theologians have accompanied this task as articulate pilgrims. They have set out to comprehend the plan of God in multi-cultural and multi-religious environments where glaring wealth and stark impoverishment live side by side. Biblical symbols and narratives, together with patristic practical wisdom, have combined with an Asian approach to social and cultural analysis to plumb the depths of the mystery of existence. RM dismisses this articulated experience, indeed blames it for helping to create a failure of nerve in mission (RM 3, 4, 6, 8, 17, 18, 35, 36, 65). RM aims to make the preliminary conciliar contours permanent, without feeling any need to listen to what the Spirit has been saying to the churches in the meantime. In both its vision (Chapters 1-3) and its elaboration of the mission task, it is a Roman-centric, reactionary document, looking back to the pre-AG era, caricaturing and then denigrating most developments in the meantime. Because most objects of its attack are Asian and, to some extent African, RM is of particular interest to ongoing mission renewal in these continents.

In looking at the future of mission in Asia[45] I shall concentrate on two issues, namely the undergirding theological paradigm and the question of inter-faith dialogue. Both issues are crucial to the future of mission in Asia.

Theological Paradigm

Historicity: It can be claimed, validly I think, that Christian mission has had an impressive impact on many Asian societies: on independence leaders educated in Christian schools, on national constitutions, on renewal movements in Islam and Hinduism, on modern education and the development of a secular, civic society, in revivifying the most profoundly human values in culture and religion.[46] In terms of church growth, Christian mission has barely convinced 2 per cent of the continent to become members of one of the competing churches, and most of these are tribals and other ethnic minority groups. While Jesus is rejected by some, he is accepted by many others such as in the Bhakti movement in Hinduism and among Sufis in Islam. However, generally speaking the churches are dismissed. That is where Asia and RM part company.

RM ignores the experience of dialogue and inculturation, and disregards the concrete historicity of the churches. RM is thus incomplete in a disturbing way. It passes over the history of mission and western colonialism as though it were no longer an issue. And yet this painful story still plays an important part in the collective memory of Muslims, Buddhists and Hindus.[47] Without a painful healing of historical memories, there will be no long-term renewal in mission. While RM re-iterates over and over again that Christ is the fulfilment of other religions, it does not feel the need to listen to why others do not regard themselves as a preparation for the Christian gospel. Listening and systematic analysis are absent. In dialogue we listen and learn; RM proclaims and teaches the answer already in its possession. RM does not feel the need to learn from the experience of dialogue in Asian countries since 1965. The failure of the Christian churches to expand in the presence of strong Buddhist, Muslim and Hindu religions and cultures cannot be answered by simply repeating models of mission that have "failed" since the sixteenth century, however great the increase of conviction, however warm the fervor.[48] RM reduces the dialogue with cultures to pre-conciliar accommodation. Such a "primitive" approach does little to alter the western shape of the churches, and does much to engender suspicion (inculturation as pre-conversion tactic).[49] RM regards sects as problems, whereas they are alternate answers. When we listen we can hear how real needs are being met by the sects. At the same time we become aware of how our response is different due to the inclusion of justice as an integral and indispensable dimension of mission. Lack of listening is also apparent in that RM does not come to terms with religious fundamentalism and the communal conflicts that have irrupted throughout Asia from India to

Indonesia to the southern Philippines. By confining mission by the laity to a subsidiary role to that of the hierarchy, countless contemporary forms of mission are ignored. RM is reactionary and pre-conciliar above all in its fear of religious pluralism and its rejection of the tentative attempts of Asian theologians to understand the positive role that God has for other faith traditions. And, finally, by tying Christ and the Reign of God so exclusively to the Roman Catholic Church, the key issue of mission and ecumenism reaches an impasse.

In the whole of RM mission is from the church to others; there is little about the conversion of the missioner, the conversion of the church as it shares its experience of Christ across boundaries of faith. Precisely the conversion of the church through rereading the sources of faith in the light of inter-faith dialogue and solidarity with the marginalized has been placed at the heart of mission activity in Asia. Thus, we do not find in RM any assistance in the ongoing renewal of the church-in-mission in Asia.

Horizon: In a decisive way, RM returns to the mission frame of pre-conciliar times. RM begins with Jesus Christ as the only Savior, as does *Ecclesia in Asia* nine years later. By way of contrast, AG begins with the comprehensiveness of God's saving love and only then goes on to its realization in Christ and the Spirit. Neither the "will of God (Trinitarian) nor the "Christo-centric" frame need be absolutized. However, the comprehensive vision of AG makes room for a positive role to other religions, while also leading some, perhaps, to relativize the role of Jesus and the church. Placing Jesus as the first word attempts to retain the integrity of the Christian gospel, but may well lead Christians into becoming blind to the truth of other religions and cultures, and lead us to a false sense of superiority, indeed of arrogance. This is what happened in the days of western imperialism.[50] This is the attitude most repugnant to Asian peoples.

Inter-faith Dialogue

Apparently RM has not succeeded in reducing inter-faith dialogue into a strategy for conversion to Christianity. The dialogue of life and action continues apace among those who feel it is important. In 1999 the pope promulgated *Eccelesia in Asia* as his response to the deliberations of the Asian bishops in the continent-wide synod held the previous year.[51] Much of the mission concern of the Asian bishops comes through in this document, yet the theological frame is unrepentant: it begins with Jesus as the one savior and sees church growth as the aim of mission.

In 2000, Jozef Ratzinger's Congregation for the Doctrine of the Faith published *Dominus Iesus* (DI). Here all semblance of listening to experience is eschewed from the start. Ahistorical, exclusivist statements claim to uphold orthodoxy without a breathe of love or a mention of the poor. Remove love and the poor from the gospel, and hardly any verses remain! The *symbolon* (creed) is reduced to a source for doctrinal statements which then lead on to tendentious conclusions. The Roman Catholic Church has the full means of salvation, all others, including other Christian churches, are severely deficient. We have faith, the others mere belief; we have revelation, others purely human wisdom. *Dominus Iesus'* God is a tribal god, a small-minded, puny deity content with looking after its own. On hearing these arrogant, abstract propositions devoid of any historicity, I say: the louder and longer Rome bangs its empty tin drum, the more hollow the sound. This is a monologue of the deaf. It is time to pause and listen. As inter-communal strife overtakes the Asian continent, the times call for a sharing of truth in love, for living out the truth in solidarity with the victims of society. Authentic cross-cultural missioners have always been those who have empathized and suffered with the communities they nurture.

If mission has a future in Asia, if the western, pious, Christian enclaves, islets of comparative wealth in an ocean of poverty, are to be reborn as dynamic communities of hope, truly Christian, authentically Asian, as partners with all of good will in the struggle for a more humane society with God as its source and goal, then we must ignore the theological frame of RM and return to the majestic opening of AG. Yes, we need to be attentive to the concerns of Rome but only while courageously listening to the victims of society.[52] We are evangelized when we learn how Buddhist, Muslim and Hindu faith traditions, together with tribal and regional cultural traditions, maintain human dignity in the face of uncountable odds and sustain a peoples' identity in the face of rapid social change. We are moving in similar directions; we need to be partners not competitors. The alternative is bleak: exclusivist language is welcomed only by warring extremists, absolute truth is the preserve of sects not of a universal *communio*. "Truth that is outside of charity is not God, it is only an image and idol that no one should love or adore."[53]

With an increase in communal violence, expressed in ethnic and religious conflict, we need an openly ecumenical discourse, an inclusivist language that can be heard and understood in other faith communities. Ethnic and religious conflict will not be overcome with confessional claims impervious to the rightful claims of others. If we wish to move beyond AG, then we must listen to how the Asian Churches have been doing this over the past 35 years.

A Sustaining Spirituality for the Long Haul
and The Enigma of the SVD

I shall now look at the future of mission, keeping in mind the key insights, major thrusts and crucial challenges that have emerged since the conciliar dynamic transformed mission in Asia.

Asia is facing two crucial challenges. Firstly, the dangerously expanding gap between rich and poor with the concomitant devastation of the environment as Asian economies are locked into a globalizing capitalism. Secondly, the resurgence of cultural and religious identities as mass migration has re-awakened our sense of plurality in both culture and religion. Faced with these challenges, the Asian Churches are somewhat defenseless. Our privileged place, hewed out through prolonged collusion with western colonial states, has disappeared. Most Asian countries are reasserting one or other Asian religion to as they struggle for social cohesion and self-respect. God is revealing Self through these issues; context is not just context, it is *logos*.

Towards a New Way of Being Church-in-Mission

The pre-conciliar, hierarchical church produced isolated Christian enclaves scattered across the face of Asia. Experience since the Council has shown that only by a radical transformation of these churches into a participatory, communion of communities, have the Asian churches been able to face the key challenges above. The road ahead is to become prophetic diasporas of hope.

Religious and Economic Split

Many Asian Churches consist of two economic classes, somewhat equally balanced numerically. Roughly half the church is extremely rich, the other very poor.[54] It is all too easy for the conventional, pyramidal church to accommodate itself to the spiritual needs of well-to-do entrepreneurs. Thus, in the cities, it is quite common to observe the clergy busy as "private chaplains" to elite groups, many charismatic in nature. Interestingly enough, charismatic groups are often "half-way" houses to joining Pentecostal churches or sects eventually, at first with "dual membership" (Catholic for sacraments, Pentecostal for revivals), and then more permanently. There has been a marked increase in the unusual in the religious sphere: miracles, visions, apparitions, countless apocalyptic messages from "the other side." This is "religion as entertainment." This sector continues to finance the hierarchical church.

Pentecostalism is the only Christian movement experiencing statistical growth world-wide as we move into a new century. Pentecostalism has long been the largest Protestant denomination (if it can be called "Protestant"!).[55] Main stream Christianity is declining, dramatically in the North Atlantic, more gradually in much of Asia.[56] Dialogue with Pentecostal Christianity is crucial. And since many Catholics now hold "dual allegiance" (Pentecostal and Catholic), as bi-cultural missioners, we can and should be bridge-builders, without in any way compromising the evangelical option to be with and for the poor and oppressed.

Meanwhile, around 50 per cent of the church consists of those at the edge of society, from whom the rich obtain their wealth through exploiting their labor. These Catholics survive with their popular religiosity and routine sacramental life. Popular religiosity is becoming increasingly separated from conventional Catholic life, while routine sacramental worship is no longer sustaining the poor. We can no longer take for granted that the poor will be with us always (pace Mk 14:7, Jn 12:8). They are simply "voting with their feet."[57] As social cohesion fragments, so does religious adherence.

The choice ahead for Christianity is as clear as it is stark: either Pentecostal-like religion--generally without a social conscience--or a network of ecumenical, mainstream base communities who consciously opt for and with the marginalized. For the former mission is for salvation in the next world; for the latter, salvation is integral: Jesus came that we have life in all its fulness now (Jn 10:10).

Mission Networking

This move away from the conventional institutions into which confreres and provinces are embedded is parallel to a wider shift in society. The dynamism of state institutions is transferring to regional and global networks. The nation-state, product of modernity, is on the wane. Smaller communities are uncovering their local identities while linking up with other communities world-wide. This could be globalization at its best, yet it finds humans at their most vulnerable. However, the model is there to be emulated: smaller groupings in a host of interacting networks. This obtains both for the way we organize as a cross-cultural mission society, and also for the way we participate in mission.

The transformation in progress is clear: from a top-down managerial style to a communitarian, relational style; from working within a closed monopolistic frame to feeling at home in more openly pluralistic frameworks, from being "right-brained" chauvinists to becoming holistic, fellow-pilgrims (*syn-odus*); from being dependent with little initiative to creative questioning. This paradigmatic shift involves our picture of ourselves, of who God is to us, and of our relation to others and the earth. This fundamental change of perspective influences the way we relate to cultures, faith traditions, people at the periphery, women, and the laity. This change of paradigm expresses our *koinonia*, our *shalom*, the heart of our mission.

This relational paradigm is trinitarian and encourages us to move from thinking and acting in mono-cultural ways to multi-cultural ways, from a single center to many centers, from pyramidal arrangements to egalitarian relationships, from a clerical church to a community of disciples, from mission as conquest to mission as pilgrimage, from benefactor to mediator and advocate, from a position of superiority to becoming a brother, from an instruction mode to a facilitating one, from power to defenseless, from being owners to becoming servants.

Mission Studies

Both the urban poor and the rural marginalized breathe a dominantly oral culture. Here we have to re-invent our SVD Anthropos tradition. Contact over the past 125 years between the academic researcher and the oral culture of the people among whom we live has not been particularly successful. And yet only this will prevent our professionalism from turning us into an elite club, far from the grind of marginality. A renewed contact will also prevent our scientific findings from domesticating, freezing, stifling, in a word commandeering, tribal wisdom, a wisdom that holds the seeds of global redemption.[58] The marginalized express truth in energizing stories rather than bland statements, in vivid descriptions rather than dry definitions, in vibrant song rather than verbal systems. Oral culture is embedded in a more or less cohesive life-way, the academic sub-culture is specialist, analytic, elitist. Mission studies are bridge-studies between the oral majority and the literate minority, the practitioner and the professional. We bridge the Christian and, say, the Muslim worlds as we seek a place to breathe in this fast-moving world.

Obstacle

The greatest obstacle on our part that opposes this ongoing transformation is neo-clericalism. Seminaries are still a ticket to a middle-class way of life. High social status combined with more than adequate financial remuneration has produced in many Asian countries a clerical leisure caste.[59] Neo-clericalism is in line with both the re-clericalized ideological training received by many younger staff members and with the authoritarian ideology of most Asian regimes. "Asian values" is a phrase on the lips of some of the least democratic national leaders and political movements. A neo-clericalized church is a church that, in practice, has opted to be with the rich and the powerful. Such a church is partner to the elite in the globalizing world.

Challenge

The challenge for the SVD is straightforward: to ease out of conventional institutional work like the conventional parish and the elite school which still absorb the majority of our confreres, and opt for a more creative, vulnerable mission of animation and empowerment in collaboration with the myriad inter-faith base communities that have emerged everywhere. The past four decades have shown that the cutting edge of mission is no longer with the conventional parish whatever the rhetoric.[60] We should be wherever people are organizing themselves for justice, human rights and the restoration of dignity, among scavengers, industrial workers, minority groups, legal aid NGOs and gender-empowerment networks. From these movements we learn professionalism while we readily offer our lives in the struggle for a more participatory and humane society. Martyrs of hope, as in Timor Lorosae and the Moluccas in Indonesia, inspire us. The victims of society evangelize us by opening us up to the power and defencelessness of the God of Jesus the Christ. Our presence states as clearly as possible, what needs to be said about our convictions concerning human dignity. Our willingness to suffer with, to live in personal solidarity, shows others who Jesus of Nazareth is for us.

As church we are moving from conventional parish to a flexible network of inter-faith communities. As missioners we need to ease out of our more traditional institutional roles and work as pioneers, "free lancers," networkers.

An Enigma

I am not sure that we are training *formandi* for this type of mission task. Quite realistically, we have to admit that most confreres feel more at home working within conventional frameworks. However, that is not where the cutting edge of mission is.

Towards a Church in Dialogue in Societies in Conflict

The City

Enormous social upheavals are causing mass displacement of the peoples of Asia. Villages are emptying as megacities expand phenomenally. Each day the urban population of Asia increases by more than 100,000 people, that is, approaching 40 million a year. This issue is intimately related to the globalization of capitalism. The more the Asian economies get locked into the globalized, transnational machine, the faster the urbanization. This is arguably one of the more urgent mission fields. Have we ever really been at home in the city? That is, with the underbelly of the urban sprawl?

Unplanned growth of cities is bringing about rapid cultural change. Formerly "quiet" Christian villagers are now neighbors with people of other religious groups with different linguistic and cultural roots. Formerly quietly pious villagers have found themselves in multi-cultural and multi-religious urban environments. Politically voiceless, socially marginalized, economically failures, educationally challenged, they are easy prey to escapism (religion as comfort) and extremism (intolerance, conflict and violence). Conventional, large-scale parishes are simply not responding.

Here two dialogical issues intertwine. Firstly, cultural and religious dialogue. We challenge increasing extremism with an increasingly open church with an ecumenical and inter-faith spirituality. We network with everyone of good will in honest and transparent ways. Secondly, social dialogue, namely, societal reconciliation. As social conflicts spread, there is a whole new meaning to mission as peace making.

Cultural Issues

We all need to be acknowledged, our dignity needs to be valued. Thus, the whole question of inculturation needs revisiting. Perhaps a majority of our people--Catholic and otherwise--are culturally and socially uprooted. What is the meaning of inculturation--being rooted in one's culture--when socially one no longer has firm roots? This problem is compounded by the globalization of communications. We live in an instant culture, a "click culture." Those who have the personal and communal resources can move from inherited traditions to personal options. This minority is certainly benefitting from rapid social change, including, I presume, we participants in this consultation! In mission we are concerned with the majority who see even their traditional options being taken away from them. Neither dialogue nor inculturation make sense outside of a people's generating a secure identity.

Cultural Memory

Our central Eucharistic liturgy is a narrative of remembrance, *anamesis*. How do we relate a religion that "remembers" to an instant culture that lives for the here and now, forgetful of the past and oblivious of anything except the immediate future? Given that the dominant model of globalization is capitalist, this instant culture becomes consumerist, its values materialist. Sustaining cultural values are displaced by the shallow value of the market place. Everyone and everything is reduced to a priced commodity.

Cultural Images

We need to re-image our cross-cultural mission for the future. We need to place at the heart of our formation communities--and in the heart of each confrere--to image other religions as fellow-pilgrims, as partners seeking out to do the will of God; to image cultures as enriching, completing, making more whole; to image the poor and discriminated against in terms of empowerment and advocacy; to image the earth as a fellow creature; to image the church as an open communion of communities in a prophetic network of disciples; to image the SSpS and SVD as equal and complementary; to image God as Immanuel, the one who walks with us (Ex 30), as fellow pilgrim and co-sufferer.

Transforming the Cultural Frame

The "last frontier" is that of gender. If mission is to be credible, then we shall have to transform our chauvinistic sub-culture and learn from women's movements for empowerment of the victims of society. In becoming partners with women, we can break through any cynicism eating away at our ideals, and break out of celibate obsessions such as the abuse of nicotine, alcohol and television, and reemerge as more transparently human. In Indonesia, and perhaps in many other Asian countries, the breakthroughs in conflict situations such as in Jakarta and the Moluccas are invariably led by women. The most sustaining movements in a sectarian society are run by Muslims, Protestants and Catholics together.[61] The way to combat sectarianism is to think, write and act in non-sectarian ways.

Issues concerning the Missioner

Mission challenges us to become living examples of dialogue with people undergoing cultural turmoil while being threatened by a loss of religious identity. This entails a vision and a spirituality which sustains mission strategies and clear priorities. I do not see how this can be undertaken except by letting go of our primary role as religious functionaries and re-birthing ourselves as people of the Spirit. A prophetic religiosity rather than an institutional religion. But then we would have to revamp our novitiates[62] and dismantle our mass-transit seminaries. But if we do not encourage--and give the necessary support--to more and more confreres to work in situations of conflict - religious and cultural and social - then I do not see much of a future for the SVD as a cross-cultural mission society in Asia. We will be just one more transnational foundation-- running schools in Japan and Philippines, and conventional parishes in Indonesia.

Mission is not about building up a power-base, busily marking out and defending our patch, whether for the church as a whole or our mission society in particular. Mission is a matter of cross-cultural listening and questioning, it is an ongoing self-critical process which probes to the heart of life. Mission is learning the meaning of life in the light of the gospel in another's language, another's culture, another's religious symbols and convictions. The crucial conversion is that of the missioner. All this is absolutely essential for the survival of our broken, violent world. More positively, it is needed for the "eruption" of justice and peace, solidarity and reconciliation between peoples.

The Enigma

This is a world away from the language of RM and DI. So be it. If we do not put ourselves at the cutting edge of cross-cultural mission then I think the SVD might well survive as a religious foundation for another generation, but not as a frontier-blazing, cross-cultural movement. It is only by uncovering our fundamental charism and by putting on the stubbornness of an Arnold Janssen, that we have be gifted with the necessary sustaining spirituality to live in uprooted, conflict-ridden cultures, to witness amidst political brutality and economic crassness, to live in solidarity with the poor with all their violence and inhumanity, that our Society in Asia will uncover its charism and be born again. Paraphrasing T.S. Eliot--the end will be the beginning and we shall glimpse the beginning for the first time.

APPENDIX 1
Ad Gentes Reconsidered
On Interpreting a Conciliar Document in Asia 35 years after the Event

If the language, concerns and the immediate commentaries on AG seem somewhat distant from the seven-fold movement towards a participatory church in a participatory society, this only goes to show how great a distance the communion of Catholic churches in Asia has journeyed in mission over the past 35 years.[63] It will not be amiss to recall the history of the text of *AG* in order to recognize its strengths and limitations, and how it came to bring a participatory church to birth in Asia.

The two preliminary drafts of *De missionibus*, written with great difficulty by the Preparatory Commission for the Missions under the direction of Cardinal G. P. Agagianian of Propaganda Fidei, were rejected prior to any debate in the conciliar assembly. Devoid of any explicit theology of mission, the two drafts were little more than a list of practical reforms in the training of cross-cultural missioners and ways of promoting mission work. Excessively theoretical and juridical in tone, the drafts took up the concerns of Propaganda Fidei while largely ignoring the numerous concrete proposals of bishops from Africa and Asia.[64] But even this meager fare was twice reduced before any debate in St. Peter's.[65] Five of the seven sections were removed by the Central Commission and then re-worked as integral parts of other documents, more importantly in *Sacrosanctum Concilium* (1963) and *Lumen Gentium* (1964). This is by no means to be regretted: mission moved from being the business of overseas *afficionados* and was placed at the heart of the mystery of the whole church.[66] And then, in an attempt (unsuccessful as it turned out) to draw the Council to a conclusion by December, 1964, the Central Commission demanded that the remnants of the by now truncated draft be compressed even further into a few proposals and guiding principles. Despite these latter being formally supported by the unprecedented appearance of Paul VI in the conciliar assembly on 6 November, 1964, the resultant "dry bones" were decisively rejected by the bishops.[67]

The rejection of the first three drafts necessitated the drafting of a completely new text by a new commission.[68] This is worth recalling for two reasons. Firstly, although AG is the third longest document approved by the Council, it was the result of one of the shortest debates. The third longest conciliar text, AG was the last schema to come before the council.

Secondly, AG was written as a response to the concern of many bishops in council that the positive attitude towards other religions expressed in other conciliar decrees such as *Lumen Gentium* (16), *Nostra Aetate* (2), *Dignitatis Humane* and *Gaudium et Spes* (22, 26, 38, 41 & 57) would dampen missionary zeal. They called for a reaffirmation of the traditional stand regarding the necessity of the church. "The plurality of religions remains a fact, but to suppose that it is intended by God would be a great mistake" (Cardinal Jornet). On the other side stood Cardinal Koenig, supporting AG's recognition of the religious values found in the great religions and that dialogue should commence the work of evangelization. "Give witness to a truly Christian life. They should look upon (other) religions as ways of seeking God. Even if these religions are not *the* way to salvation, they nevertheless lead people toward it. The grace of God is the way to salvation . . . ." Thus, the purpose of dialogue with others is not merely the discovery of common ground for philosophic contemplation or social action, but the recognition and evaluation of truths that would help us better to live out our Christian calling. However, the tension between "direct proclamation of the Good News" and "inter-faith dialogue" was not resolved at the Council. This concern is more frequently expressed by those unaffected by actual dialogue. The tension, at times destructive, still awaits an urgent transformation into a creative polarity.

Unsurprisingly, the final decree is neither highly polished as a text nor over consistent theologically.[69] Key issues that have marred the relationship between Asia and Rome ever since, were not ironed out in the conciliar assembly. This has allowed at least two seemingly contrary interpretations of AG to surface ever more sharply during the intervening years.[70] The broad, contextual interpretation is exemplified in the mission praxis and theological reflection of a large number of Asian local churches, for instance in the final statements of the plenary assemblies of the Federation of Asian Bishops' Conferences (FABC). The narrow, minimalist interpretation has been taken up by the Congregation for the Evangelization of Peoples.[71]

Thus, AG is a compromise document. There was no time --nor energy--for a thorough reappraisal of the missionary role of the church in all its aspects. Anyhow, such a reassessment was blocked by an important curial office whose effectiveness and relevancy would undoubtedly have been reduced by too drastic a revision.[72] The struggle here was between ecclesiastical bureaucrats anxious to maintain control over a highly centralized bureaucracy and a reasonably successful enterprise, and those in the field who felt that all concerned should have a greater share in the direction of the church's mission work. This would be in keeping with the doctrine of collegiality and the renewed emphasis on the church's awareness of itself as being, by definition, missionary.

Also, Chapters 2 to 6 are still too hierarchical in outlook. The vision of Chapter 1--the church is missionary by its very nature, and therefore mission work actually belongs to the whole People of God--is replaced by the traditional curial scheme whereby only the hierarchy were really involved, the laity are reduced to their assistants.[73] LG Chapter Two had not been appropriated.

None of this takes away from the importance of AG. The comprehensive vision is there. Unable to resolve the tension between "proclamation" and "dialogue" the two were left side by side. Rome has chosen to subsume dialogue under the overarching paradigm of traditional proclamation. Asia has chosen to take on dialogue as the way of mission. The Council's "breakthrough was to validate a kind of irenic ambivalence toward others, not weaken the church's christocentric view of salvation."[74] Anyhow, by December, 1964 the bishops were suffering from "conciliar fatigue." The sub-commission under John Schütte's direction was instructed to recommend nothing that would cause prolonged debate or be too upsetting to the existing missionary structure. Conscientiously, the sub-commission endeavoured to insert some phrase that would satisfy each major intervention or submission; the result, naturally enough, is "something of a mish-mash." They were tasked to satisfy each major intervention, that is, all but proposals that would flesh out the broad theological sweep of Chapter 1.

Looking back we can say that while the Asian Churches have renewed their mission in line with the "dialogical imperative" of the Council, the central bureaucracy has remained essentially unreformed. A centralized and centralizing machinery holds power in the Latin Rite, while the Asian Churches are evolving into a communion of communities. A "Copernican" revolution is underway, unforeseen in the texts of the Council yet made inevitable by its by its openness to the world and its call to dialogue with all people of good will.

Appendix 2:
Resources on FABC

Occasional Papers:

Regular documentation found in FABC PAPERS. Documents preparatory to General Assemblies, Final Statements of General Assemblies and the various offices. In January, 2000 FABC Paper No.92 was published. Often a single number consists of a series of separate papers, eg. FABC Paper No. 92 has 20 separate papers running from No.92a to No.92s. Address: FABC, 16 Caine Road, Hong Kong, SAR. Email: <hkdavc@hk.super.net>

Collections of Documents

1992   Rosales, Gaudencio & Arevalo, C.G. (eds.), *For All the Peoples of Asia: Federation of Asian Bishops' Conferences Documents from 1970-91*. I. Manila/New York: Claretian/Orbis, xxx-356pp.

1997   Eilers, Franz-Josef (ed.), *For All the Peoples of Asia: Federation of Asian Bishops' Conferences Documents from 1992-96*. II. Manila: Claretian Publications, xi-319pp.

Collected proceedings of Colloquia:

Rarely published in book form. The exceptions are:

1977   Achutegui, Pedro S. de, ed., *Asian Colloquium on Ministries in the Church*. Hong Kong: FABC, xxiv-496pp.

1993   *Colloquium on the Social Doctrine of the Church in the Context of Asia*. Manila: Office for Human Development FABC, xvi-214pp.

1997   *Colloquium on Church in Asia in the 21ˢᵗ Century*. Manila: Office for Human Development FABC, 502pp.

Collected Documents of Bishops' Offices

1994   Gnanapiragasam, John & Wilfred, Felix, eds., *Being Church in Asia: Theological Advisory Commission Documents, 1986-92*. I. Manila: Claretian Publications, xi-140pp.

no date Rogers, Anthony, ed., *Your Kingdom Come in the Context of Asia: Teachings of the Federation of Asian Bishops' Conferences.* Manila: Office for Human Development FABC, xvi-89pp.

Books and Theses on the FABC

1985   Putranta, Carolus Borromeus, "The Idea of the Church in the Documents of the Federation of Asian Bishops' Conferences (FABC) 1970-1982." Rome: Gregorian University, 179pp.

1993   Handoko, Petrus Maria, "Lay Ministries in the Mission and Ministry of the Church in Asia: A Critical Study of the Documents of the FABC 1970-1991." Rome: Gregorian University, viii-340pp.

1994   Nemet, Ladislav, "Inculturation in the Philippines: A Theological Study of the Question of Inculturation in the Documents of CBCP and Selected Filipino Theologians in the Light of Vatican II and the Documents of FABC." Rome: Pontifical Gregorian University.

1995   Ezhanikatt, Vincent, "Evangelization in India in the light of Federation of Asian Bishops' Conferences Documents from 1970 to 1991." Rome: Pontifical Urban University.

1997   Bula, Agustinus, "A Study of the Evangelizing Mission of the Church in Contemporary Asia in the Light of the Documents of the Federation of Asian Bishops' Conferences: 1970-1995." Rome: Pontifical Urban University.

1999   Alangaram, A., *Christ of the Asian Peoples: Towards an Asian Contextual Christology Based on the Documents of the FABC.* Bangalore: Asian Trading Corporation, xviii-223 + 8p index.

2000   Quatra, Miguel Marcelo, *At the Side of the Multitudes: The Kingdom of God and the Mission of the Church in the FABC Documents (1970-95).* Manila: Claretian Publications, x-234. Shortened and simplified version of, *Regno di Dio e Missione della Chiesa nel Contesto Asiatico: Uno Studio sui Documenti della FABC (1970-1995).* Rome: Pontifical Gregorian University, 1998.

Notes

1. I shall refer in this paper primarily to South and Southeast Asia.

2. The 1974 Synod was split between two very different ways of theologizing about mission, the one associated with the cutting edge of Asia (D. S. Amalorpavadass

was one special secretary), the other with the concerns of Rome (the other special secretary was Domenico Grasso, one of the drafters of AG).

3. Perhaps it should be noted that not many theologians in Asia do their theology as commentaries on conciliar, synodical or papal texts. Most Asian theologians use a practical methodology which begins with experience and leads to praxis. However, given the growing gap between Rome and Asia, perhaps it is not amiss to look for both the source of disagreement and also for possible rapprochement in three recent conciliar, synodical and papal documents.

4. This hermeneutical key is obviously different from that used by the bishops in the Extraordinary Roman Synod of 1985. See Xavier Rynne, *John Paul's Extraordinary Synod* (Wilmington, DE: Michael Glazier, 1986). The Synod's "Message to the People of God" and "Final Report" together with a number of interventions are published in *Origins* 15, 27, (December, 1985). See also Avery Dulles, "The Reception of Vatican II at the Extraordinary Synod of 1985," Giuseppe Alberigo, et al., *The Reception of Vatican II* (Washington, D.C.: CUA Press, 1987).

5. Ongoing mutual enrichment between the Ecumenical and Roman Catholic traditions of social teaching are exemplified in the 1999 Asia Conference on Church and Society organized by the Christian Conference of Asia with FABC participation. See Feliciano V. Carino & Marina True, eds., *Faith and Life in Contemporary Asian Realities* (Hong Kong: CCA, 2000).

6. The paradigmatic shift in the Asian ecumenical movement came during the Situation Conference of the East Asia Christian Conference in 1963. See John Fleming, ed., *One People--One Mission* (Singapore: EACC, 1963). The conference discussed eight key questions on mission. Papers previously published in *South East Asia Journal of Theology* (October, 1963).

7. Francisco Claver, "The Church in Asia: Twenty Years after Vatican II. Personal Reflections," *East Asian Pastoral Review*, XXII, 4 (1985): 316-323.

8. Since 1974 the FABC has brought bishops together to share experiences and develop their perspectives on a host of practical theological issues. Important meetings, papers and conclusions are published from Hong Kong in the occasional series "FABC Papers." See "Appendix 2" of this paper. For the 1974 Statement of the First Plenary Assembly see, *Teaching All Nations* XI, 2 (1974): 120-128.

9. Ibid., 319.

10. The Asian Churches as a "communion of communities" was first formulated at the FABC General Assembly of 1981; subsequent General Assemblies have reaffirmed this open, participatory ecclesiology.

11. See Jacques Dupuis, "FABC Focus on the Church's Evangelising Mission in Asia Today," *Vidyajyoti*, LVI, 9 (1992): 449-468.

12. Archbishop of Cotabato in Mindanao. In 1999 he was elected President of the Episcopal Conference of the Philippines, and in 2000 he finished his term as General Secretary of FABC.

13. In Archbishop Quevedo's address the seven movements "from . . . to . . ." are explicitly stated. In the Assembly's Final Statement the sense is expressed positively by including only the "to . . ." referent.

14. Latin American bishops met in Bogota in 1968, African Bishops in Kampala in 1969 and the Asian bishops in Manila in 1970. The purpose of each continental-wide assembly was to determine how the churches, each in its specific political and cultural zone, should make, "the struggle for justice and the transformation of the world . . . a constitutive dimension of the preaching of the gospel" (as the Roman Synod of 1971 phrased it a year later). For the message of Paul VI as well as the Message and Resolutions of the Asian Bishops' Meeting see, *Teaching All Nations*, VIII, 1 (1971): 5-31.

15. The Philippines has had regular communication with the Americas ever since the Spaniards first landed in Cebu in the sixteenth century. Thus, Latin American experience of base communities came to Asia largely through the Philippines. Meanwhile more multi-faith societies such as India, Indonesia and Sri Lanka developed new "bases" that have been termed, "Basic Human Communities" and "Basic Inter-Faith Communities."

16. Congress held from 1 - 5 November, 2000. Proceedings to be published by the Documentation Office of the Indonesian Bishops' Conference. For an appropriation of Base Communities in India, see Gilbert de Lima, *Evangelisation in India through Basic Communities* (Mumbai: St. Paul's, 1996).

17. The FABC-OL holds workshops with both bishops and laity working with a participatory church and small Christian communities. It is publishing a large collection of training material based on similar material from the Lumko Pastoral Institute of Southern Africa.

18. Timor Leste (or Timor Lorosae) is the other Catholic nation in Asia. South Korea is 35% Christian, Indonesia 9%; other Asian nations have statistically small, though vibrant, Christian communities.

19. For publications of the FABC including those of the Ofice of Human Development (OHD), see Appendix 2.

20. More recent developments in the Philippines can be followed in the National Pastoral Plan approved by the Second Plenary Council of the Philippines. See *In the State of Misison: Towards a Renewed Integral Evangelisation* (Manila: Catholic Bishops' Conference, 1993). Most recently in the preparation and proceedings of the National Jubilee Mission Congress, October 2000.

21. AG 6 distinguishes between "mission" and "*activitas misionalis*" endeavoured to break out of an outdated geographical understanding of mission. This description of "*activitas misionalis*" obviously comes from, and is intended for the use of, the Congregation for the Propagation of the Faith: " *'Missions' is the term usually given to those particular undertakings by which the heralds of the gospel are sent out by the Church . . . .*" Not unambiguous, the chapter combines three tendencies: the narrowly geographic frame of Propaganda fidei, the personal approach of Yves Congar, while taking into account the concern of South America and the North Atlantic with de-christianization. The aim is not to produce a missiological text but an inspirational essay to preface more practical reforms in order that all bishops (local Churches) be conscious of their responsibility for mission. Twenty-five years later RM distinguishes between "mission as such" and the need for re-evangelization in the North Atlantic and South America, but then goes to see them both as mission in the sense of AG 6.

22. Yves Congar, "A Last Look at the Council," in Alberic Stacpoole, ed. *Vatican II by Those Who Were There* (London: Goeffrey Chapman, 1986), 344.

23. The preface was written by Yves Congar while the theological foundation of the First Chapter was written by Congar with Jozef Ratzinger. The remaining chapters return to the Vatican custom of referring almost exclusively to previous councils and papal statements.

24. The scathing denunciation of the inadequacies of the whole western approach to mission made by Arrupe in the Council assembly are now largely outdated; Asia receives few western cross-cultural missioners and itself is a major source of missioners *ad gentes, ad extra, ad vitam.*

25. For my own comments on the Indonesian literary scene see "Portraying the Face of the Nazarene in Contemporary Indonesia: Literature as Frontier-Expanding Mission." To be published in 2001 in *Pacifica.*

26. For similar reasons voices suggesting that the Constitution on the Liturgy be rewritten in the light of the renewed ecclesiology of LG were not accepted. We are having to live with the consequences today.

27. See John M. Prior, "New Missionary Thrust," *Verbum SVD*, 38, 1-2 (1997): 101-127.

28. Cletus Colaco analyses mission in India in the context of AG and developments in FABC. See *25 Years of "Ad gentes" in India* (Bangalore: Asian Trading Corporation, 1991).

29. Although called "young Churches" many Asian Churches are of course older than the oldest in Europe. Churches in both West Asia (Middle East) and South Asia (Kerala) are apostolic in origin while Christian communities have existed in China and Southeast Asia long before the conversion, for example, of Poland and Russia at the turn of the first millennium.

30. The seminar secretary, Aloysius Fernandes, wrote up a short report, "All-India Seminar: Church in India Today," *Teaching all Nations*, VII, 1 (1970): 31-42. The proceedings of the seminar were published by the Bishops' Conference.

31. The seven papers dealt with four fields, namely 1) Theological Perspectives (The Church and her Mission); 2) Realistic Perspective (Socio-Economic forces, political forces, cultural forces, religious forces shaping India today), 3) Theological and Realistic Perspectives Combined (Responsibility of the Church in India, and 4) Plan Perspective (Personnel and Resources).

32. Together with the observers and secretariat the total number at the All-India Seminar came to 531. Over 25% were below 35 years of age. Lay participation was 33.4%.

33. The four clusters were 1) Spirituality, Liturgy/Catechetics, Pastoral Life, Leadership; 2) Ecumenism, Dialogue with Other Religions, Evangelisation, Personnel/Resources; 3) Educational Activities, the Family, Indian Culture, Social Communications; 4) Socio-economic Activities, Civic and Political Life, Labor, Health and Social Services.

34. Further developments can be traced through ongoing national consultations. For instance, *Paths of Mission in India Today*, Statement of the National Consultation on Mission, 4-9 January 1994 (Pune: Ishvani Kendra, 1994).

35. See for instance, Edmun Chia, fcs, "Of Fork and Spoon or Fingers and Chopsticks: Interreligious Dialogue in *Ecclesia in Asia*," *East Asian Pastoral Review*, 37, 3 (2000) 242-255. Also published in *Jeevadhara*, 5 (2000). Edmund is the secretary of the Office for Ecumenical and Interreligious Affairs of the FABC.

36. Not only Rome makes this false dichotomy, also Sedos and the SVD. See Mary Motte & Joseph Long, eds., *Mission in Dialogue* (Maryknoll, NY: Orbis, 1982), p.634. Also, "Final Document" of the Fifteenth General Chapter of the SVD, 2000.

37. Domenico Grasso's own interpretation of AG is laid out in articles such as, "The Church's Missionary Activity," *Teaching All Nations* III, 2-3 (1966): 38-45. "The Reasons for Missionary Activity," *Teaching All Nations* III, 4 (1966): 258-274. A similar interpretation informs RM (1990) and DI (2000). At the very least we have to admit that Rome is consistent--but at the price of not learning from, let alone interacting with, ongoing experience in love.

38. Amalor himself has been extremely circumspect in his written record of events. He states the bare essentials calmly in his book leaving out the "dramatic" distribution of his own version. See, *Evangelization of the Modern World* (Synod of Bishops, Rome, 1974), (Bangalore: NBCLC, 1975), esp. 18-21. He told the fuller story to only one or other close friend.

39. Amalor evaluates the 1974 synod and makes a number of concrete suggestions for improving the procedure. Ibid., 70-76. Unfortunately, over twenty years later at the Synod for Asia, Amalor's suggestions had not yet been taken up, and the same weaknesses obvious in 1974 were plain for any thinking bishop or observer to note in 1998.

40. India had prepared for the synod by holding an All-India consultation on evangelization in October 1973. See, D. S. Amalorpavadass, *Approach, Meaning and Horizon of Evangelization* (Bangalore: NBCLC, 1973).

41. Amalorpavadass, *Evangelization of the Modern World*, 31-32.

42. Thomas D'Sa, "The How of Redemptoris Missio," *Vidyajyoti*, LVI, 10 (1992): 543-547. The author also quotes John Paul II at Haiti on 8th March 1983, "We are not to pass on a doctrine, but a touch of the person of Christ." (Ibid., 546-547).

43. A wide selection of positive reactions to RM from Asia can be found in *Indian Missiological Review*, 14, 3-4 (1992).

44. See Augustine Kanjamala, "Redemptoris Missio and Mission in India," in William R. Burrows, ed., *Redemption and Dialogue* (Maryknoll, NY: Orbis Books, 1993), 198; 202.

45. According to RM 37 the greatest challenge for present day mission is Asia.

46. Even anti-Christian figures such as K.M. Panikkar acknowledge this. See *Foundations of New India* (New Delhi: 1963).

47. In Indonesia this "selective memory" on the part of groups or nations is called, "memory-cide".

48. It is humiliating to recall that five major crusades to "convert" China over the past 2000 years, the last taking place in the nineteenth and twentieth centuries, produced very meager results. The Chinese mission consumed the greatest number of cross-cultural personnel and logistics, and yet church growth is almost certainly greater since the expulsion of the expatriate missioners in the early 1950s than at any point previously. This needs a calm and thorough analysis.

49. Indonesia is only the latest case of where skin-deep inculturation is being rejected as piracy by both Muslims and Hindus (the latter in Bali).

50. In his careful and quiet way, J. Neuner contrasts the two approaches. See, "Mission in *Ad gentes* and in *Redemptoris missio*," *Vidyajyoti* LVI, 5 (1992): 228-241.

51. For my comments on the 1998 Synod for Asia see "A Tale of Two Synods," *Sedos Bulletin*, 30, 8-9 (1998): 219-224. Also published in *Vidyajyoti*, 62, 09 (1998): 654-665. Urdu translation from Multan, Pakistan. Also, "Apostles and Martyrs: Consecrated Life at the Special Assembly of the Bishops' Synod for Asia," *Review for Religious*, 58, 1 (1999): 6-27. For my comments on *Ecclesia in Asia* see "Unfinished Encounter: A Note on the Voice and Tone of *Ecclesia in Asia*," *East Asian Pastoral Review*, 37, 3 (2000): 256ff., and in *Verbum SVD*, 3 (2000). Shorter version published as "Proclaiming Christ in Asia Today: A Brief Note on the Sources and Nature of *Ecclesia in Asia*," *Mission Today*, II, 2 (2000): 180-91.

52. We await the next pontificate and the calling of a new General Council of the Roman Catholic Church. The reform of the Roman Curia is a top priority. Ideas were already expressed at the last council and have been repeated quite consistently at Roman Synods ever since. A "consensus" has been put together in Gary MacEoin, ed., *The Papacy and the People of God* (Maryknoll, NY: Orbis Books, 1998).

53. Blaise Pascal, quoted by Leonardo Boff, "Ratzinger's Iesus omits Love, the Poor" *National Catholic Reporter*, 24 November 2000. Fuller Portuguese text found online at www.uca.edu.ni/koinonia/relat/233e.htm.

54. I do not have post 1997 monetary crisis figures. To take the Indonesian example. Prior to the crisis, 49% of Indonesian Catholics lived below the poverty

line while 51% were super rich. The rich are largely ethnic minorities in the cities (Chinese traders, financiers etc.) while the poor are tribals either in the outer islands or urban workers in Java.

55. Many studies of Asian and Pacific Pentecostalism have been carried out from India to PNG. How many of us SVDs are "Pentecostal literate"? Interesting papers were read at the Nanzan Asian-Pacific Missiological Symposium of 1996. (Papers yet to be published).

56. Also of note: numerically Muslims have just about caught up with Christianity for the first time in history and are posed to become the largest global religion of the coming decade.

57. Forty percent of "secular" British Catholics go to regular Sunday Worship; less than 10% of "religious" Flores in Eastern Indonesia do the same.

58. For my views on tribal and globalized cultural values see John M. Prior, "Human Values and the Pursuit of a Full Humanity in Asia," *FABC Papers No.92p* (Hongkong: FABC, 2000), esp. 13-18.

59. See John M. Prior, "Towards a Pastoral Approach to Culture: Reflections from Eastern Indonesia," *Cultures et Foi/Cultures and Faith/Culturas Y Fe*, III-4 (1995): 289-291. Republished in *Verbum SVD*, 36, 4 (1995): 401-404. This trend is clear, for instance, in countries as diverse as South Korea, Thailand and Indonesia.

60. The promotion of base communities in conventional parishes has led to their being subsumed into a centrally-run and clerically led enterprise. A similar comment can be made about promoting the four "essential characteristics" of the SVD in conventional parishes and apostolic institutions.

61. This is the case in the "Fact-Finding Commission" after the mass rape in Jakarta (May 1998) and also in the ethnic-religious conflict in Ambon where a Muslim lady, a Protestant pastor and Sister Brigita run a "Concerned Women's" NGO tending to the victims and their families (sustaining, nurturing, empowering).

62. The SVD novitiate at Nenuk, West Timor, accepted over a 100,000 displaced persons forced from their homes in East Timor. The novitiate program was maintained "as usual" throughout the chaos. How different if the presence of the 100,000 traumatized people, continually intimidated and terrorized by Indonesian army-trained militias, were accepted not as an *interference* but as a *calling*. In this case, Bible sharing, "conferences" and daily worship would grow out of the

novices' listening to the individual stories. The regular timetable would be put aside, and the novices would eat with the expelled Timorese. NGOs assist displaced persons professionally; we are called to empathize, to be with the victims and see in them the face of Christ.

63. Quotes from conciliar documents are from Austin Flannery, ed. *Vatican Council II: The Conciliar and Post Conciliar Documents.* Study Edition (New York: Costello, 1987).

64. Asian bishops showed keen interest at all stages of the process that produced AG. For instance, of the 67 suggested emendations to the draft of December 1964, 21 of the bishops came from Asia while 16 came from Africa, 17 from Europe and 13 from the Americas.

65. On the origin and history of AG, see Suso Brechter, "Decree on the Church's Missionary Activity," in Herbert Vorgrimler, et al., eds., *Commentary on the Documents of Vatican II* , Vol. IV (London: Burns & Oates, 1969), 87-111.

66. During the opening session in 1962 few bishops outside Africa, Asia and South America were interested in "the missions." A paradigmatic shift in awareness subsequently took place as is evidenced by the debate and acceptance of LG 16-17, which later formed the theological frame for AG.

67. The six pages contained a preface (later used in AG), and thirteen topics. Donal Lamont, the Carmelite bishop of Umtali, Rhodesia (Zimbabwe), gave the death-knell with his Celtic-eloquent "dry-bones" intervention of 7 November, 1963. For Donal Lamont's recollection see, "Ad Gentes: A Missionary Bishop Remembers," in Stacpoole, ed., 270-282. For the complete text, see F. Anderson, ed., *Council Daybook. Vatican II, Session 3* (Washington, D. C.: National Catholic Welfare Conference, 1965), 238-239. With comparable oratory, Lamont approved of the final draft in October 1965, *inter alia,* "No land is so primitive as to be unfit for the Gospel nor is any so civilised as not to need it." For the original Latin text see, *Acta et Synodalia Sacrosancti Concilii Vaticani II* (Vatican City: Typis Polyglottis Vaticanis, 1970-1980), Series IV, 4, 223-224.

68. The present decree was written during a marathon session of a new five-member sub-commission at Nemi from 12 to 28 January, 1965 under the able guidance of J. Schütte. This new draft was revised by a plenary session of the Commission in March and circulated to the bishops in June. The conciliar debate took place during only four days between 7 and 13 October, even then having to time-share with the ongoing debate on GS.

69. For example, the opening theological chapter makes mission the duty of the local church as People of God; subsequent chapters often revert to an hierarchical

view--with other members of the church as "assistants." Also, having abandoned the geographical model of mission in Chapter One it is presupposed in some subsequent passages.

70. See for instance the recent declaration of the Congregation for the Doctrine of the Faith, *Dominus Iesus.* Vatican City, 5 September, 2000.

71. See, for instance, Marcello Zago, former Secretary of the Congregation for the Evangelization of Peoples, "Implementing the Council Guidelines on the *Mission ad gentes*," *Omnis Terra*, 34, 304 (2000): 49-56. He begins, "The Second Vatican Council Decree *Ad gentes* is the arrival point and the synthesis of the pontifical teaching of this century . . . ." Conciliar teaching has been absorbed by and become a support of papal teaching.

72. See Xavier Rynne, *The Fourth Session: Debates and Decrees of Vatican Council II September 14 to December 8, 1965* (London: Faber & Faber 1966), 135-147.

73. A new paragraph (21) was inserted and minor changes were made in Chapter V, paragraph 41; however, the hierarchical slant was retained.

74. Such is the conclusion of William R. Burrows. See "Concluding Reflection," *Redemption and Dialogue*, 239-244. Quote from p. 240.

MISSION FOR THE TWENTY-FIRST CENTURY IN EUROPE

Heribert Bettscheider, SVD*

The New Concept of Mission in Ad Gentes, Evangelii Nuntiandi and Redemptoris Missio

I will address the question how the new concept of mission in the three Roman documents has been determining the view of mission and the concrete realization of mission in Europe. In a first part I will present the basic impulses of the three documents. The second part will then elucidate how these impulses have changed the understanding of mission and how this informs concrete practice.

Vatican II: **Ad Gentes**

Ad Gentes (AG) represents a milestone in the formulation of the modern concept of mission, continuing earlier beginnings such as the encyclical *Maximum Illud* of Benedict XV. In AG the insight that the church is a "World Church" takes shape. In theological terms the essentially missionary nature of the church is emphasized. Mission is not *one* of the Church's activities alongside others but part of the essence of the church. And so it is the mission of the church, in the singular, that is discussed, not missions, in the plural.

The basic argument is as follows: the church is determined by its mission for the world. This mission is the essence of the church. Therefore mission has to do with the whole church. It is not something added onto the church, no special task of the church. "Whoever says 'Church' says 'mission'--there is no room for an 'and' here. One cannot say 'Church and mission,' it has to be 'the mission of the Church.'"[1]

Heribert Bettscheider is director of the SVD Missiological Institute (Missionswissenschaftliches Institut), Sankt Augustin, Germany, where he is Professor of Fundamental and Dogmatic Theology. He is author and editor of many books and articles.

The original version of the decree[2] had drawn conclusions from the Constitution on the Church and declared in paragraph 2: "The pilgrim Church is missionary by its very nature." It used mission in the singular and described it as having its origin in the *missio Dei*, the mission of the Son and the Holy Spirit. It spoke of mission as a fundamental duty of the people of God (MD 35); each member of the church has the duty to "cooperate in the Gospel, according to opportunity, ability, gift and position" (MD 28). This view extends to the missionary societies which are seen as delegates or respresentatives of the parishes from which they come. Through them the community as a whole carries out its activity among the peoples (MD 37). They do not pursue particular aims of their institute, they have no monopoly on mission, and no special privileges. All they do is "assume as their specific task . . . the obligation of preaching the Gospel, which is the responsibility of the whole Church" (MD 23).

Another point relates to the goal of mission, which is no longer described as "implanting the Church," but as "gathering the people of God," in order to underscore that missionary activity does not come to an end with the establishment of the local church, since the local church in its turn is to become missionary. God gathers a new people for himself in order to target the world again out of it. The church does not exist for its own sake, but for the salvation of the world. The establishment of the church as the goal of missionary activity is too ecclesiocentric a view; it obscures salvation as the real intent of mission. Mission is centrifugal, it is directed beyond itself, to the world.

In the fourth and last session of the Council, however, corrections were made in the text as it then stood, which watered it down considerably. Cardinal Gregorio Pietro Agagianian, President of the Commission on the Missions, insisted on including a statement on the mission *territories*, Bishop Stanislaus Lokuang of Tainan/Taiwan on using the plural, *missions*, in the definition of mission in the strict sense. And so the document as adopted did present a correction of the previous concept of mission, but was not a Magna Charta on mission, as J. Glazik put it.[3]

The compromise attempted shows most clearly in the first chapter on the theological foundation of missionary activity. Up until paragraph 6/2 the text always speaks of the "mission of the church," in the singular. Then, abruptly, "missions," in the plural, is introduced. These are "special undertakings," in which preachers of the gospel, "sent by the Church," . . . make known the Good News among people who do "not yet" believe in Christ and "implant the Church" there. In these formulations the original insights were rescinded:

"1. The text no longer speaks of the essentially missionary nature of the Church, but of 'special undertakings.'
2. The Church appears as 'sending' body again, not as 'sent' itself.
3. The message of salvation is not directed to the whole world, but only to those 'who do not yet believe in Christ.'
4. It is not preached in the whole world, but only 'in defined territories.'
5. The goal is the 'implantation of the Church'--mission is not the task given to the Church, the Church is the objective and aim of mission!"[4]

Because of this compromise in AG, further efforts to define the nature of mission had to be made.

Evangelii Nuntiandi

The Apostolic Exhortation *Evangelii Nuntiandi* (EN) takes the Magisterium's reflection on the mission of the church some steps further. It clarifies a number of points and states them more precisely than AG did. The definition of "mission" in AG is rejected as "defective and incomplete" because it does not do justice to the "complex, rich and dynamic reality which is called evangelization" (EN 17).

Evangelization in EN is universal and global, addressed to the whole world in all spheres of life. This continues a line of thought which has begun in the twentieth century and, on the Catholic side, reached its-- temporary-- culmination in Vatican II.

This change in the concept of mission was expressed at the World Missionary Conference of Bangkok (1972/73) by the phrase "from western mission to world mission." This meant, in the first place, that the so-called young churches, too, have a duty to be missionary. The experience in the so-called Christian countries which, as a result of the process of secularization, find themselves also in a missionary situation, points in the same direction. Therefore, since the Plenary Assembly of New Delhi (1961) and the World Missionary Conference of Mexico City (1963), the expression "mission in six continents" has been in use.

Vatican II does speak of the Church as missionary by its very nature (AG 2), but this was often understood in a reductionist sense, as meaning that the whole church had to engage in "the missions." It is the insight that the so-called Christian countries need re-evangelizing which allows EN to develop a global and universal understanding of mission. This shows also in what EN says about the goal of evangelization, which is not to make proselytes or increase the numerical membership of the church, but to renew the world and the human race. All sectors of the world are to be influenced by the spirit of the gospel and so be transformed.

Evangelization, therefore, must not be reduced to the purely spiritual sphere--EN speaks of development and liberation--but includes structures, too. The goal, however, is not a mere change of structures, but the New Humanity. "It is the aim of evangelization . . . to effect this interior transformation" as well as the transformation of all sectors of human life, "the criteria of judgment, the standard of values, the incentives and life standards of the human race which are inconsistent with the Word of God and the plan of salvation" (EN 18; 19).

The statement that cultures must be evangelized shows the same basic attitude: evangelization is directed to the world. In addition, EN states not merely the universality of evangelization, but goes into concrete detail in enumerating the people to whom it is addressed. First proclamation is addressed to people who do not know the good news of Jesus, and is considered "a prototype of this work" (EN 51). (This has to be kept in mind when other groups are mentioned later. First proclamation has a very special place and importance.) According to EN the followers of non-Christian religions belong to this group.

Another specific group is that of non-believers. In this context EN distinguishes between the legitimate autonomy of the secular world as creation and a secularized world which "is entirely self-explanatory without any reference to God, who thus becomes unnecessary and is, as it were, an embarrassment" (EN 55). Both groups mentioned can be described as non-Christians. But Evangelii Nuntiandi also mentions groups with a Christian background, who are in need of a new evangelization. Paragraph 52 lists more particularly: 1. "Many people who have been baptized [but who] live lives entirely divorced from Christianity"; 2. "simple people who have a certain measure of faith but know little even of its fundamental principles"; 3. "intellectuals who feel that they need to approach Jesus Christ from a different standpoint from that which was taught them in their childhood days." In the same category fall those who do not practice their religion, "who have been baptized and, while they have not formally renounced their membership of the church, are, as it were, on the fringe of it and do not live according to her teaching" (EN 56).

This does away with the earlier distinction between home mission and foreign mission, even if Evangelii Nuntiandi does not explicitly draw this conclusion. But it is obvious from paragraph 54, where even those are counted among the addressees of evangelization whose faith needs consolidating and fostering.

One question which Evangelii Nuntiandi leaves open is the relationship of evangelization and mission. One remarkable point is the frequent use of the term "evangelization," which on the Catholic side has not been much employed until post-conciliar times, whereas the word "mission" does not occur very often. The question is, why? D. Grasso's explanation is that the term "evangelization" is less burdened with historical associations than the word "mission," for instance, in its connection with colonialism. Furthermore, "evangelization" can also be used for the formerly Christian countries.[5]

Does this mean that "evangelization" has replaced "mission"? Is it the new term for mission? Has the idea of mission changed? One important point is that the term evangelization is not restricted to preaching, but includes the whole world, the whole human being, the entire task of humanization. And how is the word mission used in EN? An analysis of the text shows that *missio* is only and exclusively used for the state of "being sent," not for the concrete activities that implement it. *Missio* in this sense is used of Christ (EN 6; 75; 77), of the Holy Spirit (EN 12), of the Apostles (EN 6) and finally of the church. In connection with concrete missionary activity, only the adjective *missionalis* appears, otherwise the term *munus* (task) is used. The conclusion from this, it seems to me, can only be that evangelization means the concrete realization of what the church is sent to do, in a comprehensive sense.

Another point of importance for the concept of mission is what EN says about the relationship between church and mission. An intense missiological discussion has been going on about this, with terms ranging from ecclesio-centric mission to church-less mission, or even a completely ex-centric Church. EN does not propose an ecclesio-centric view of mission. It does use the term *plantatio ecclesiae*, but rather in passing; this view is certainly not predominant. Paragraph 7 speaks of Jesus, not the church, as the source and origin of evangelization.

Furthermore, the church does not find its identity in concentrating on itself but in the proclamation of its message: "Evangelization is the special grace and vocation of the church. It is her essential function" (EN 14). In paragraph 15 the relationship between evangelization and church is defined: 1. The Church itself has come into being through and is the result of the proclamation of Jesus and the Apostles. 2. Therefore the church in its turn is sent by Jesus, "it is above all his mission and his work" which the church "perpetuates." 3. The church has to begin by evangelizing itself, if it "is to preserve the freshness, the ardour and the strength of [this] work of preaching the gospel." 4. The good news has been entrusted to the church, not primarily to guard it, but to proclaim and spread it. 5. The church, "having been herself sent forth and evangelized, sends out evangelizers in her turn."

Paragraph 16 emphasizes the close connection between Christ, the church and evangelization: "During this 'era of the church' the task of evangelization is entrusted to her. This task cannot be carried out without her, and much less in opposition to her." Paragraph 60 points out that it is the whole Church which evangelizes. Evangelization is, therefore, never the work of an individual, but an essentially ecclesial act, which is why heralds of the gospel must be sent out. This also means that the church has the responsibility of spreading the gospel "for the whole world and for every part of it." Here again we see the global understanding of mission.

Redemptoris Missio

The encyclical *Redemptoris Missio (RM)* continues the Magisterium's reflection on mission in line with AG and EN in the context of a new situation. The more recent missiological debate discusses the tension between the saving action of God in and through the church on the one hand and his action in the world, even outside the church, on the other.[6] In the recent documents we discern a tension between the mission of the church and "holistic liberation." Neither can replace the other, but they are, as EN states, inseparable. Inculturation and interreligious dialogue have also been intensely discussed lately. All this has to be kept in mind in reading RM.

The encyclical intends to present a precise definition of mission. It emphasizes the one mission of the church. AG 9 is cited: "Missionary activity is nothing else, and nothing less, than the manifestation of God's plan, its epiphany and realization in the world and in history; that by which God, through mission, clearly brings to its conclusion the history of salvation" (RM 41). Mission has its origin in the mission of the Son, its beginning and fundamental function is to proclaim Jesus Christ, who is "the one Savior of all." The "definitive self-revelation of God is the fundamental reason why the Church is missionary by her very nature." In every age mission has the one objective: "to direct man's gaze, to point the awareness and experience of the whole of humanity towards the mystery of Christ." (RM 5; 4). Mission is seen as "a single but complex reality" (RM 41). It is "one and undivided, having one origin and one final purpose; but within it, there are different tasks and kinds of activity" (RM 31) which arise "from the variety of circumstances in which . . . mission is carried out" (RM 33). The whole Church is missionary. Therefore no distinction is made between "sending" and "receiving" churches, because "the universal Church and each individual Church is sent forth to the nations" (RM 62).

Another characteristic of RM is its holistic concept of mission. There is "a close connection between the proclamation of the Gospel and human promotion" (RM 59). "A commitment to peace, justice, human rights and human promotion is also a witness to the Gospel when it is a sign of concern for persons and is directed towards integral human development" (RM 42). The encyclical mentions the modern forms of the Areopagus, and here the same view of mission is evident: "for example, commitment to peace, development and the liberation of peoples; the rights of individuals and peoples, especially those of minorities; the advancement of women and children; safeguarding the created world. These too are areas which need to be illuminated with the light of the Gospel" (RM 37).

Special emphasis is laid on the mission *ad gentes*, which is seen as best realizing the essence of mission. The main aim of RM is to emphasize the unchanging legitimacy and validity of the mission *ad gentes*, which it defines as the church proclaiming the gospel to "peoples, groups and socio-cultural contexts in which Christ and his Gospel are not known, or which lack Christian communities sufficiently mature to be able to incarnate the faith in their own environment and proclaim it to other groups. This is mission *ad gentes* in the proper sense of the term" (RM 33).

RM delineates three situations for mission *ad gentes*. There are first of all specific areas in which mission is carried out. Here a geographical understanding of mission prevails: "The growth in the number of new Churches in recent times should not deceive us. Within the territories entrusted to these Churches-- particularly in Asia, but also in Africa, Latin America and Oceania--there remain vast regions still to be evangelized" (RM 37). Secondly, the encyclical mentions new "worlds" and social phenomena: "Today the image of mission ad gentes is . . . changing: efforts should be concentrated on the big cities, where new customs and styles of living arise together with new forms of culture and communication, which then influence the wider population" (Ibid.). Thirdly, RM speaks of cultural sectors, the modern Areopagus. This is the world of commnications, scientific research and international relations (Ibid.).

So, within the one mission of the Church the pope distinguishes three situations which each require different activities: 1. the mission *ad gentes* proper; 2. the pastoral care of the faithful; and 3. the new evangelization or re-evangelization. The document states that "the boundaries between" these "are not clearly definable" (RM 34). Here the encyclical is somewhat ambiguous. On the one hand it proposes a strictly theological definition of mission, on the other it also uses a geographical understanding of the term.

Finally, RM addresses two subjects of importance in connection with mission: inculturation and dialogue. In its encounter with different peoples and cultures the Church necessarily "becomes involved in the process of inculturation" (RM 52). Without an appropriate inculturation the message of the gospel cannot be presented "in a credible and fruitful way" (RM 53). Inculturation has two aspects: "Through inculturation the Church makes the Gospel incarnate in different cultures and at the same time introduces peoples, together with their cultures, into her own community. She transmits to them her own values, at the same time taking the good elements that already exist in them and renewing them from within. Through inculturation the Church, for her part, becomes a more intelligible sign of what she is, and a more effective instrument of mission" (RM 52). In the process of inculturation the distinctiveness and integrity of the faith must not be compromised (Ibid.). The two basic guidelines are "compatibility with the Gospel and communion with the universal Church" (RM 54).

Inculturation is not the work of a few experts but must involve the whole people of God. "It must be an expression of the community's life, one which must mature within the community itself, and not be exclusively the result of erudite research. The safeguarding of traditional values is the work of a mature faith" (Ibid.) And finally RM emphasizes the necessity and distinctiveness of interreligious dialogue which is "part of the Church's evangelizing mission" (RM 55). It is not a question of tactics but "is demanded by deep respect for everything that has been brought about in human beings by the Spirit who blows where he wills" (RM 56). And the Spirit can act not only in individuals, but also in religious traditions. Therefore, the "other religions constitute a positive challenge for the Church" (Ibid.). RM insists, however, that dialogue is not opposed to the mission *ad gentes*. A Christian taking part in dialogue does so in the certainty that salvation comes from Christ and that the church is the way to salvation.

Another point addressed is the relationship between dialogue and proclamation. Both are inseparably linked, but distinct, and must not be confused or interchanged. Dialogue "does not dispense from evangelization" (RM 55). The relationship described is one of tension and, on occasion, contrast. In any case, for the church there is no dialogue outside the missionary context.

Vatican II and the subsequent pontifical documents have developed a new foundation for the concept of mission. Mission is now understood theologically as the church sent into the world to carry on the *missio Dei*. The different social conditions and cultural and religious traditions form its starting point. In this way the various contexts of "world" determine a broad spectrum of forms of missionary work. Mission is to shape the world, an idea expressed in the term "holistic liberation." Such a concept of mission does away with the distinction between evangelization, respectively new evangelization, of the baptized and "foreign missions" among the unbaptized. There is no need any more for a one-sided fixation on "missions abroad." Important aspects of mission in this sense are inculturation and dialogue in a comprehensive sense, especially interreligious dialogue.

The document of the fifteenth General Chapter of the Society of the Divine Word (SVD) is also based on this concept of mission. It speaks of the *missio Dei* in which the church and the SVD participate. The SVD realizes this mission in the form of a fourfold prophetic dialogue, carried out in four perspectives or dimensions. Against this background, we now ask the question: What is the mission of the church and the SVD in present-day Europe?

Mission and Europe

The changes described in the understanding of mission and the development of this concept in contact with the realities of the modern world have begun to influence the concrete shape of the church and its proclamation. Today we apply the term mission territory to Europe as well; we speak of missionary situations, of re-evangelization or new evangelization. An intense discussion of the missionary dimension of the church is carried on in the German churches, for instance. The German Bishops' Conference is preparing a substantial document entitled: "A Church in Mission." In 1999 "mission" was the theme of the year in the Protestant churches of Germany and at their synod. The term mission, so long reviled, is being rehabilitated.

The SVD, too, has been discussing the consequences of this new concept of mission for its work in Europe. The process began with the meeting of the provincials of the European Zone at Roscommon/Ireland. What should the contribution of the SVD be in the process of new evangelization and, in some places, first proclamation in Europe? What should its presence look like within the missionary church of Europe under present-day circumstances? Another question is the specific contribution of the SVD for the European church that results from its special charism.

The Context of Mission in Europe[7]

Secular and Postmodern Culture

The first context for mission in Europe is secularization in the form in which it has developed in modernity and post-modernity. Secularization means a process begun in the Enlightenment which has resulted in the increasing emancipation of the human being from Christianity, the church, and religion in general. It is a process which the sociologist of religion F. X. Kaufmann describes as "a loss of the significance of religious meaning in ever more areas of life."[8] Church-related religiosity and Christian tenets of faith are not fought, they simply evaporate.[9]

Modernity and post-modernity present us with other phenomena which go beyond secularization. One vital experience today is the "changeability of all things,"[10] which is seen as a law of reality. Social scientists call it the legitimation of continual change.[11] Something is seen as good simply because it is new. Not the past is important, but the present, and especially the future. And the future is totally open. History does not have a discernible goal. Not even the category of progress is accepted today. Continual change is its own legitimation. The buzzwords are: openness, flexibility, mobility, adaptability, innovation. Modern industrial society is rapidly changing. From the radicalization of the elements of modernity results something new called post-modernity. It is characterized by an increasing differentiation in all areas of life. The integrated milieux of a past age are dissolving, both in the social and the religious spheres. Catholics no longer speak with one voice, not in politics, not in the economy, in culture or society, not even in the religious field.

This differentiation of life leads to another fundamental phenomenon of post-modernity: social and religious pluralism. It is no longer the group that forms the individual's attitudes; everyone has direct access to culture, primarily through the media, especially television. This produces a sort of mass culture which, however, presents various opinions, among which the individual has to choose. The result is an experience of liberation from pre-determined social patterns and a greater possibility of shaping one's life individually.

But this development has its dangers as well. The necessity to continually choose and decide is too great a burden for most people, especially since they are left without any orientation. In earlier times the Christian faith offered this, but this function is accepted less and less today. On the contrary, any social or religious claim to absolute truth is suspect and rejected out of hand as ideology or fundamentalism. Christianity is only one among a whole range of competing worldviews on offer. As a result of this development individuals feel less and less bound by the views and values of their families, their group, their religion, whose interpretation of life and the world are no longer simply acceoted as naturally valid. People shape their lives according to their own individual ideas.

The European churches have to a large extent lost contact with this post-modern world, which has next to no impact on proclamation, liturgy, community life or religious and pastoral practice. Traditional Christian life does not correspond to the needs, ways of thinking and understanding of people in this post-modern society. Christianity in modern Europe can be described as de-culturated or ex-culturated (see EN 20).

But the Church has to concern itself with this post-modern culture. Merely rejecting it will not get us anywhere; it has to be seen as a chance to proclaim the faith in a new way. In order to do this the church has to take a good look at it first of all, and then discuss its limitations.

Religious Pluralism

The emphasis on individual choice in post-modernity is linked up with another important phenomenon, namely religious pluralism. As a result of social and cultural change, migration movements and the modern media, this is a constitutive part of life in present-day Western Europe.

One important element in modern society is the increasing recognition of the limits of a purely rational explanation of the world. The rationality of the Enlightenment is seen as "weak rationality" (H. J. Verweyen) and therefore relative, "the religious dimension is again given a legitimate place in general culture."[12] Since both reason and knowledge are limited, an answer to the basic questions is sought in the irrational. Religion therefore is again in demand among post-modern people, who look to it as a "shield" against the manifold threats to which everyone is exposed.[13]

But this new interest in religion is not at all related to or interested in institutions, so that the churches do not profit from it. In addition, it is realized within our pluralistic and individualistic society where everyone is confronted with a wide variety of lifestyles, worldviews and religions. On the basis of these, the individual is expected to build up a religious identity by free choice, no longer restricted by social group or milieu. But this freedom of choice means also an obligation to choose, from among the new possibilities, some view of the world on which to base an existence. Today, however, people no longer take over complete sets of interpretations, rather, everyone tinkers with elements of the given patterns to build up an individual view of the world. "Religious patchwork" is what sociologists of religion call the result. An interest in other religions and cultures or experiences from the world church is motivated by purely egocentric concerns. And it is too easily forgotten that everyone is strongly influenced by their social conditioning, the attitudes of their milieu, by education and fashions, whether they realize it or not.

Inculturation of the Faith in Europe

We have mentioned the de-culturation of the faith in Europe. In my opinion this is the basic problem of the European church. What de-culturation means in this context is that the Church does not take modern culture sufficiently into account, knows too little about it and lives and proclaims its faith in such a way that post-modern people cannot understand what it's supposed to mean.

The inculturation of the faith in the post-modern context is not primarily the task of academic theology, but has to occur in the way believers live the faith. Their lives have to show that God can be experienced here. Inculturation becomes possible if the reality of God--or God's withdrawal--can be experienced in the interpretation of everyday life.

There are several reasons for this failed inculturation in Europe. The Christian communities are not sufficiently able to open up spaces for a Christian experience or interpretation of everyday life. They lack a language--as, for that matter, do theologians and pastoral workers--to express their life experiences as "talk about God." People cannot interpret and express their experience in the light of tradition. Theology has to find a new language as its specific contribution to inculturation. In addition, one must admit that Church authorities are often sceptical of such attempts, where they do occur, and try to restrict them.

A second reason is that pastoral workers do not have enough courage and creativity. Everything is still too much oriented towards the bourgeois individual. There is a lack of clear options. The social and political significance of the faith is not sufficiently obvious.

Theological studies do not foster the inculturation of the faith, either. Academic theology still sees itself mainly as a hermeneutic of the faith as found in Scripture and Tradition in debate with German philosophical idealism. There is no relation to practice so that the validity and importance of the faith as it finds shape in everyday experience is not realized. There are not enough "frontier people" who do theology from the basis of a shared everyday life.[14]

Now what should inculturation of the faith in Europe look like? I proceed from the assumption that there must be a critical relationship between culture and the gospel, between everyday life and Church proclamation. Otherwise the Good News will not be understood. *Gaudium et Spes* (GS) has a well-grounded theological understanding of inculturation and emphasizes the connection between the gospel and culture: "The joy and hope, the grief and anguish of the men of our time, especially of those who are poor or afflicted in any way, are the joy and hope, the grief and anguish of the followers of Chist as well. Nothing that is genuinely human fails to find an echo in their hearts" (GS 1).

Just like the Church in Africa should the Africanized, Europe has the right to Europeanize its own Christian self-realization, in the sense of a unique authenticity.[15] This is not the same as a right of the European churches to Europeanize other churches, quite the contrary! As far as inculturation is concerned we notice a peculiar development: While the European churches in the nineteenth century began fantastic operations of missionizing abroad, they did not manage to realize the faith in their own context. I give only one or two suggestive examples: Instead of siding with the victims of industrialization, the church chose to fight leftist ideologies-- and so lost the world of industry and the workers. Popular religiosity was despised and not taken seriously, instead of taking note of the vital concerns of the faithful that it expresses.

It is true that in social welfare the churches are still present through their big organizations, but there is a distinct split between this type of presence and the symbolic world of the church. Culture and the media are seen and treated as a problem. And in areas where the church has responded to people's felt needs, for instance in ecological questions, the initiative usually came from the outside. "One might almost say in an adaptation of Matt 27, 42: They saved others; they cannot save themselves."[16]

During the past two centuries the church has failed to respond in a positive way to the social changes that occurred. On the contrary, it went into opposition to the developments of the time, and so lost the future. Change was not seen as a "sign of the times" (Vatican II), but considered unacceptable, any dialogue refused. As a result the European church needs a "root treatment."[17] Fuchs uses another simile: The Church has to return to the wellsprings, the ground-water level of our cultures, our history and our contradictions in order to find new strength in those depths.[18]

The basis for an inculturation of the Gospel is this: "Cultures are not vacuums devoid of authentic values, and the evangelizing work of the church is not a process of destruction; rather, it is a process of consolidating and fortifying those values, a contribution to the growth of the 'seeds of the Word' present in cultures (GS 57)."[19] The important thing, then, is the realization that God and God's Word are already present in the cultures. Theologically speaking, we have to look for the Spirit of God, the Risen Lord, the Reign of God, the Trinity, the Creator, or whatever other terms are used to identify the presence of the good God among humankind, and, secondly, for the acceptance of the Word by the grace of God. There are many more signs of God at work than we dare consider. And if the gospel is not inculturated into them, it will not be able to develop its full power.

This principle of inculturation is also valid for the ambivalent aspects of a culture. Here the point is the closeness to sinners. Gregory of Nazianzus said in this context: "What has not been taken in is not saved."[20]

One Example of an Inculturation of the Gospel:
The Project "A Church in Mission" of the German Bishops' Conference

The German Bishops Conference is preparing a document about the mission of the German Church.[21] Even though it has not yet been promulgated, I want to present its basic points here. It proceeds from the assumption that the church is missionary by its very nature, so mission does not occur only in Asia, Africa or Latin America, but in Berlin, Hamburg and Munich, too. The worst shortcoming of the church today is the lack of conviction that it can win new Christians. The Church continues the mission of Jesus who saw himself as a messenger of God, sent to bring good news to the people of his time. He asked his disciples and he asks us to be messengers of God for our generation. "Make disciples of all nations!" This is the essential task of the church, which does not exist for its own sake, but in order to establish contact between Jesus Christ and humankind. This movement of Christians towards people is called mission. I am supposed to pass on to others what has enriched me spiritually in my own life. Evangelizing means pointing to the source from which these riches flow: the gospel, Jesus Christ and the communion of life I have with him.

The first step in the mission of the church is the "witness of life" (p. 12). Even people with no interest in the church will listen and react when I speak of my own personal experience, my life, including those bits where things do not run smoothly. My own, personal faith in God, complete with questions and doubts, is telling. Telling other people how my faith helps me cope with my life can help them see their life in the light of faith. The witness of life can open doors, encourage others to "try out" the faith, too.

The second challenge for us Christians is the "witness of the word" (p. 13). I have to tell others about my faith. It is true that today advertising is regarded with scepticism, especially aggressive advertising. This goes for religion, too. People do not want to be recruited into some big organization-- and that is what the church is in the eyes of many people. It is a different matter if people see " human faces," concrete individuals who speak about their faith and invite them in the name of Christ. However, in the religious sphere especially a certain reticence is necessary, a special sensitivity, since the faith is a very personal and intimate thing. A space and a form are needed which are not intrusive. Many faithful feel rather shy about expressing their faith. It is almost a taboo. One of the reasons may be that the terms "mission" and "evangelizing" had and still have negative connotations, because they often come coupled with the experience of intolerance and aggressive conversion attempts. But the New Testament encourages us to have an answer ready for people who ask us. The question is how to do this, what language to use to pass on what gives a firm foundation to our own life. What I say will only reach people if it is convincing, plausible. The language of academic theology and official Church documents is all too often completely divorced from people's life experience. Ordinary Christians, too, have to learn a new language that is related to their everyday world in its terms, images and signs. The document goes on to mention specific *loci* of proclamation, in the first place the liturgy, which is to be celebrated in a way that allows people to find a place in it. In addition, though, other offers of religious instruction are necessary. The text mentions vigils, prayer services and pilgrimages which relate to people's experiences. Dialogue groups are important too, for instance "Bible sharing." Here people can share their experiences, their questions and doubts. Finally the document speaks about the different forms of catechesis and the indispensable role of the media for religious instruction. The internet is mentioned particularly.

A third challenge for missionary proclamation which the bishops mention is the Christian community. It is here that people actually experience "church." In our modern, very mixed society, from which the old milieux have disappeared, it makes "missionary sense" to look for new "faith milieux." The term "biotope" is used: "These 'biotopes of Christian life' can be spaces for acquiring, trying out and testing faith in practice" (p. 20). Therefore the development of such groups should be fostered, especially the type that is oriented towards solidarity, self help, participation, exchange and networking. Parishes, Christian communities and new spiritual movements can offer such spaces for Christian life that help to practice and experience the faith. These groups are not, however, ghettoes or closed refuges, but open to the world.

This document of the German Bishops' Conference wants to go beyond a mere recognition of the religious situation in post-modernity and therefore develops a "missionary ministry." Concrete possibilities are proposed for getting in touch with the people of this modern world and talking with them about the faith.

The Missionary Task of the SVD in Present-day Europe

The church in Europe is a missionary Church. The SVD in this modern Europe does not simply have the task of the Church as such, but has to make its proper contribution on the basis of its special charism. My statements are based on the document of the last General Chapter in June / July, 2000, which defines the SVD charism as a fourfold prophetic dialogue: with people who are searching, with the poor and marginalized, with people of different cultures and adherents of different faith traditions and secular ideologies.

The post-modern world is characterized by secularization and pluralism. People are thrown back on themselves, on their own individual resources in their search for orientation, identity, security, meaning. We have to find contact with these people, we have to address them, accept them, find out where and how they live and show them that they are welcome among us. Our Northern Province in Germany has three parishes where we live and work in small teams: in Hamburg, Berlin and Dresden, which are all special social foci. Here we have to use our special charism to come into touch with people, many of whom have never been evangelized. In the former German Democratic Republic great numbers of people are in need of first proclamation. I can only mention some relevant terms here: a renewed adult catechumenate, urban ministry, adult education, student ministry.

In the modern world people learn to believe in the context of their very individual biographies. It is experience and choice which makes people Christians today. This presupposes spaces where religious experiences can be made and talked about. This also presupposes freedom, including the freedom to revise decisions. Our communities should offer such space for God-experience. Small contemplative communities and centres for spiritual life also belong to this context.

Today the faith has to live in the context of modernity and post-modernity. We can learn a lot here: individual freedom and liberation from heteronomy, more direct participation of every member of society, worldwide exchange and contact.[22] The collaboration of the laity is indispensable here. And laypeople are able and willing to participate, as the German churches' consultation process on the economic situation or the 1995 "Petition of Catholics to Their Church" have shown.[23]

Another ongoing subject is violence, particularly violence against foreigners. Since this is linked to cross-cultural contacts it is a special challenge to a missionary church and a pivotal concern in a multicultural and multireligious society. In Germany immigration is a much-discussed subject in the political arena and in society in general. A learning process is required to get to know, to respect and accept those who are different. This is part of the dimension Justice, Peace and Integrity of Creation.

Globalization is increasingly influencing our society. This is a special challenge to the SVD as an international congregation. Catholicity means linking the local with the global, which results in dialogue and exchange. It is a question of intercultural communication which approaches the truth from different perspectives and experiences, and of exchange in different directions, including from Africa, Asia and Latin America to Europe. The goal is a sharing of resources in all spheres. Another goal could be an intercultural theology which does not simply take over elements from other cultures, but in contact and exchange with them finds new paths.

An enormous challenge for the European Church is the inculturation of the faith in Europe. We must really get to know the modern European culture, learn to understand it. This, it seems to me, is also one of the biggest challenges for the SVD in Europe. In practice this concerns especially our parishes, our educational institutions and, above all, our academic institutes. Here we have barely scratched the surface.

Finally, another task of the SVD in Europe, and certainly not the least, is the missio *ad gentes* in the strict sense. We are called to go to the ends of the earth. Our time demands solidarity, exchange among the churches in all spheres, religious, cultural, social and economic. The mission of the SVD in Europe is and remains rooted in the missio *ad gentes*.

Notes

1. J. Glazik, "Vor 25 Jahren Missionsdekret 'Ad Gentes'," *Zeitschrift für Missionswissenschaft und Religionswissenschaft* 74 (1990): 261.

2. This was the version of the missions decree (MD) as elaborated during the third session under the chairmanship of Fr. John Schütte, SVD.

3. See J. Glazik, "Eine Korrektur, keine Magna Charta," in J. Ch. Hampe, ed., *Die Autorität der Freiheit*, Vol. III, Ch. IV: "Das Evangelium für die anderen. Konzil und Missionen" (Munich, 1967), 543-553.

4. Cf. J. Glazik, "Vor 25 Jahren Missionsdekret 'Ad Gentes'": 270.

5. D. Grasso: "L'evangelizzazione. Senso di un termine," in M. Dhavamony, ed., *Evangelisation* (Documenta missionalia 9) (Rome: Gregorian University Press, 1975), 43.

6. See David J. Bosch, *Transforming Mission. Paradigm Shifts in Theology of Mission*)Maryknoll, NY: Orbis Books, 1991), esp. 474-489.

7. I am limiting myself here to speaking of the German-speaking areas of Central Europe, since these are the areas with which I am most familiar.

8. F. X. Kaufmann, *Religion und Modernität. Sozialwissenschaftliche Perspektiven* (Tübingen, 1989), 213.

9. See H.-J. Höhn, " 'A Test of Rupture.' Will It Hold? European Christianity in the Tension of the Social Process of Modernisation," in *Yearbook of Contextual Theologies* 97 (Frankfurt, 1998), 63-72.

10. Kaufmann, 19.

11. Ibid., 35.

12. See F. X. Kaufmann, "Auf der Suche nach den Erben der Christenheit," in M. Haller et. al., eds., *Kultur und Gesellschaft* (Frankfurt, 1989), 277-288.

13. See P. M. Zulehner, *Helft den Menschen leben. Für ein neues Klima in der Pastoral* (Freiburg, 1979).

14. For the whole subject see M.Bücker, "Europa-ohne Grenzen und ohne Mission. Zur Notwendigkeit und Chance inkulturierter Mission im deutschsprachigen Raum," *Neue Zeitschrift für Missionswissenschaft* 56 (2000): 233-234.

15. O. Fuchs, "Gott hat einen Zug ins Detail. 'Inkulturation' des Evangeliums hierzulande," in O. Fuchs et. al., *Das Neue wächst. Veränderungen in der Kirche* (Munich, 1995), 59.

16. Ibid., 61.

17. See H. Halbfas, *Wurzelwerk. Geschichtliche Dimensionen der Religionsdikaktik* (Düsseldorf, 1989).

18. Fuchs, 66.

19. "Evangelization in Latin America's Present and Future." Final document of the Third General Conference of the Latin American Episcopate, Puebla, Mexico, 1979. In John Eagleson and Philip Scharper, eds., *Puebla and beyond : Documentation and Commentary* (Maryknoll, NY: Orbis Books, 1979), No. 401.

20. See Gregory of Nazianzen, Epistola 101. PG XXXVII, 175-193.

21. German Bishops' Conference, *"Zeit zur Aussaat." Missionarisch Kirche sein* (die deutsche Bischöfe 68) (Bonn: 2000).

22. See Bücker, 241.

23. Secretariats of the German Bishops' Conference and the Protestant Churches in Germany, ed., *Zur wirtschaftlichen und sozialen Lage in Deutschland. Diskussionsgrundlage für den Konsultationsprozeß über ein gemeinsames Wort der Kirchen* (Gemeinsame Texte, 3) (Bonn, 1994).

MISSION FOR THE TWENTY-FIRST CENTURY IN LATIN AMERICA:
A View from the Perspective of the Missionary Religious Life

Edênio Valle, SVD[*]

Introduction

An outstanding Spanish missiologist says that the church is at an historic crossroads of mission.[1] This is a metaphor which, as well as being colorful, points to something very real. In particular for people of my generation who have lived through the creative effervescence of the 1960s and 1970s, it is amazing to think that after so many years of speaking about evangelization and renewal of the church and mission, we didn't get enough clarity about some quite important aspects of very fundamental issues of missiology.

In this context, the metaphor of "crossroad" is very useful under two conditions. First, it should be used with a certain caution so as .not to loose sight of the positive pathway already traveled. Second, the image should not be used so as to obscure the basic problem, which for me, as I will try to show, is that of the *self-definition of a new historic figure or form* of the missionary activity of the universal and local church and of missionary religious life (MRL), constantly called in question by transformations that are occurring in a world which, it seems, is going through a process of fundamental change.[2]

Edênio Valle is a Brazilian SVD missionary. After studies in theology and psychology in Europe, he returned to Brazil and served as president of the Brazilian Conference of Religious (CRB) and Confederation of Latin American Religious (CLAR). He also served for many years as the vice-president of the Catholic Pontifical University of São Paulo, where he is presently Professor of Psychology and Religion in the graduate department of religious studies. He has published several books and articles on the Psychology of Religion, Education, Religious Life, and Pastoral Theology.

It is not only or not so much the *theological* concept of mission and of missionary religious life which shows insufficiencies; it is its sociological concrete shape and its historic self-definition that are not well-defined. The greatest difficulty is in determining what concrete objectives, relations, organizational and behavioral styles should be given to the missionary charism of the church as a sacrament of salvation for all humankind.

Generally speaking, we all accept the importance of the missionary charism as such, but we are understanding it from differing and sometimes contrary perspectives. In this sense our efforts to affirm a really new model of mission in the concrete pluralistic contexts of today's culture cannot succeed without a previous consideration of those starting points. In this very moment there is a temptation in the church and in some sectors of MRL to turn in upon itself, unable to let itself be questioned by interpellations coming from "outside." Here I will attempt to describe more this cultural and sociological side of this dilemma. Toward the end of my text I will touch a little on the theological dimension of it.

I am not a missiologist; I'm only an SVD missionary coming from Latin America. What I know comes from my own experience in the field, more specifically, in the area of missionary religious life, during many years in leadership of religious life (RL) in Latin America and in Brazil. I'll leave to the competent missiologists here present the theological issues which are hidden behind our efforts toward a new manner of doing mission. I would like to say, from the very beginning, that it is clear for the Latin American missiologists that the new emerging non-European missionary forces have a fundamental contribution to give for the world mission of the church. They are not simply going to repeat what was done before. Coming from other cultural and religious backgrounds the "Third Church" (W. Bühlmann[3]) will give an unprecedented qualitative input in the whole question of the creation of a new figure of mission and MRL. We SVDs are already living this process, as our last General Chapter shows.[4] So my contribution to this Symposium is very modest. I will speak preferentially about the affirmation of this "new historic form" of MRL which is taking shape in Latin America. I don't feel competent to enter in the other questions which will be discussed in this Symposium and to cover the opinions coming form Asia and Africa.

Let me begin stating a personal conviction. At a time of crossroads, we need an attitude of humble and patient searching, in order to discern and re-contextualize the options and practices that were adopted at other ancient or recent times. This is a basic condition for living that *"creative fidelity"* about which the document *Vita Consecrata* (VC) speaks[5] (VC 37). There is no possibility of refounding MRL without this attitude.

But, on the other hand, in this process of highs and lows what is at stake is more than this or that element, taken in isolation. The present form of MRL[6] --as a whole--seems incapable of explaining to the world, the church and to men and women religious themselves, all of the charismatic creativity that should belong to it.

I fear that the hierarchical church, and even some leaders of MRL, despite their open discourses, are focusing more on questions of *means*, forgetting that the situation is asking from us to give first priority to the *purpose* of MRL to be a sign of the Kingdom of God in this very concrete continent, inside this equally concrete pluralistic post-Christian era with its context of crude injustice and selfishness.

We all know that there is not, and never has been *one* Latin America. In reality it is neither *Latin* nor *one*. It is multi-ethnic and multi-cultural, the fruit of an uneven historic process which I cannot attempt to outline here.[7] It is clear that there do exist some links of convergence between different stories in a pathway that has many common points. Puebla and Santo Domingo speak, maybe too optimistically, of a "cultural Catholic substrate" and insinuate the existence of a "Catholic identity"[8] common to all of Latin America.

When one looks at Latin America as a whole, one may even say that, especially for the last decades of the twentieth century--with the polarization of all our countries around the North American colossus--social, political, economic, and cultural elements, as well as popular religiosity, have taken on somewhat of a unidirectional aspect. A basically similar North Americanized cultural climate has arisen all over the continent.

From the viewpoint of MRL the most fundamental aspect in this process of convergencies and divergencies has been the rediscovery of the *originality* of the historic formation of the Latin American MRL, both relating to the cultures and to the contextual transformations brought by the world-changing trends we detect in the present globalization process.

Our missionary self-image is no longer seen from the viewpoint of the "center"; we see ourselves rather from our own "peripheral" place in the global context of the world and church today. In cutting the link with the centers of power which traditionally limited the Latin American church and MRL in its vitality and self awareness, we have managed to better our insertion among our people and to rethink our role on this continent. We are also developing at the same time a really new consciousness of our responsibilities regarding the challenges of the universal mission of the church.

In no way am I saying that there already exists in the Latin American church and MRL a full consciousness of its role in the world church. What I want to say is that especially the new Latin American MRL can no longer imagine itself apart from solidarity of destiny with the poor and the excluded of the whole world. For me, from a more strictly missiological viewpoint, what is important at this moment of transition is to include the "missio *ad gentes*" in the prophetic option made by the Latin American MRL in Medellin[9] and other major events of our church, within a history that does not cease to march on.

Of course, this attempt has to consider the newly emerging challenges in the light of our own history and way of being Christians and Catholics. We cannot ignore our pre-colonial and colonial experience. Our roots are still there. In fact, they are in pre-Colombian times and in Africa,[10] since two thirds of our population comes from there. I see in this origin a prophetic sign of our most profound but still dormant missionary vocation.

A History of 500 Years of Missionary Activity

I am unable to describe here the whole path traced by the missionary church and MRL in the five hundred years of its presence in Latin America. I'll focus mainly on the reality of Brazil, the country I know best, but I will seek to follow an approach that may apply to the majority of other Latin American countries, including the Caribbean.

The Colonial Inheritance

It will be useful to recall for those who don't know Latin America that our church has always played an outstanding role in social and political life of all our countries. For many years we have had an active and generous missionary life all over the South American continent.[11] Brazilian historians,[12] for instance, describe four very vigorous missionary movements which took place between the seventeenth and nineteenth centuries. One high point was the famous "mission of the seven Guarani peoples,"[13] in the territory bordering Paraguay, Uruguay, Argentina and Brazil--one of the most impressive missionary works in history.

There were also serious limitations in the action of those missionaries because of their relations with the constituted power. In fact the Portuguese and Spanish colonial system bound the church tightly to the state. The church and MRL were partly an instrument of the state's control over the newly discovered territories and peoples. Catholicism remained the only official religion for more than three centuries.

In the seventeenth century and later, with the entrance of Enlightenment ideology (around 1750), during the wars of independence (around 1800-1822), and with the introduction of the Freemason ideas among the elite (around 1820-1900), there came misunderstandings and persecutions; but in general, the influence of the Catholic Church continued to be strong, especially among those people and families who were deeply religious. During the persecution years the older orders were expelled or repressed.[14] They almost disappeared. But towards the end of the nineteenth century they started coming back. Dozens of new congregations--also female[15] orders [a novelty!]--arrived and began to act as the main agents of the restoration of the Catholic Church in Latin America.

Three Periods of the Last 150 Years of MRL

Let me make just a few observations about what happened during the approximately last 130 years of MRL in Latin America. I would discern three phases in this period:

Phase One

This is the time of the transplantation of a new model of religious life, called by our historians the "Romanized" form of MRL.[16] It was very different from the Iberic[17] model built during the colonial times. Thanks to the efforts of Pius IX and Leo XIII thousands of missionaries were sent to South America. We SVDs and the SSpS were among them.[18] It is important to underline that in this period religious women[19] played, for the first time in history, an important cultural and social role. RL was soon reinvigorated and moved in to fill a supplementary role in responding to the social needs of the white urban populations and of the European immigrants. So there developed a huge network of social works (especially of schools, hospitals, parishes and seminaries) which contributed to greatly strengthen the prestige of the Catholic Church in the first half of the twentieth century.

Sociologically speaking, therefore, the new RL became an integral part of the urban middle classes, for whom it furnished most of its services, and from whom came the majority of its vocations. Clearly, this picture differed from country to country, but I maintain that throughout the whole continent the new model of RL made an effective preferential option for the emerging middle classes. Because of this development, in the middle of the twentieth century, it found itself separated from the majority of the population. The huge system built by the very active religious army which disembarked on our shores kept its European lifestyles and thought pattern, avoiding a real dialogue with the mentality of our Latin American cultures. The existence of a great number of vocations in Europe reinforced the conventional attitudes of distance and superiority of the foreign congregations--especially the male orders--with respect to the lower sectors of the population, specially to peoples of African and indigenous descent.

Phase Two

Vatican II introduced a *second phase*, weakening the Europeanized RL model that had seemed so stable and durable. Medellin brought back the missionary sense of RL. The hierarchical church called on RL to make a profound revision in its presence in Latin America. The "elegant" modifications proposed by *Perfectae Caritatis* were soon swept aside by the process of renewal[20] unleashed by religious in most of the countries. In contrast to what happened in the United States, the dialogue of RL with the modern world did not lead to what Gerald Arbuckle[21] calls the "liberal model." In Latin America the process moved RL much more closer to the people, leading finally to a kind of social exodus from the place that RL had occupied in the first half of the twentieth century.

The preferential option for the poor persuaded most of religious-- especially religious women--to change their point of reference. From the world of the middle classes, thousands of them passed over (also in geographic sense) to the poor areas of the population. Their way of relating to black and indigenous people changed drastically. These were the foundation years for the theology and practice of liberation. Along with the bishops, and often urged by their devoted pastoral care, RL began to engage in a revision of its missionary presence and role in the continent. The so-called inserted and inculturated RL began to take form. RL rediscovered its essential missionary character.

The Synods of Bishops that followed the Council, still under Paul VI--one on justice in the world, the other on evangelization--strengthened the process begun by Vatican II and Medellin (1968). *Evangelii Nuntiandi,*[22] the church document of the greatest influence in Latin America after Vatican II, reinforced the evangelization process indicated by Medellin. The theology of liberation was the theoretical expression of this practical solidarity with the poor, in view of their liberation.

This period was characterized in some sectors and countries by social activism of an urgent kind. Three words summarize the experience of the Latin American MRL between 1960 and 1985: *liberation, inculturation and insertion*. There is another term, however, which I consider just as fundamental: *biblical spirituality*. Biblical spirituality provoked a profound change in our way of conceiving and living the following of Jesus on a continent of poverty and injustice. As we used to say in those days: the poor became our evangelizers. They became the living fountain of the missionary dimension of our vocation.

Phase Three

A third phase followed in the 1980s, which was a decade of great energy and vitality. As I have just said, evangelization was understood by MRL mainly from the viewpoint of the "insertion among the poor." From this viewpoint it was impossible for MRL not to take a political position regarding the military governments who entered in partnership with interests of the USA, imposing silence on the claims of the people. In some countries, especially those of Central America, there was an active political, ideological and even armed resistance to the military dictatorship. Religious moved into the front line of political involvement. This involvement was not a kind of theorizing by scholars and pastors with broad views and generous hearts. It was a pervading movement of change. Those were days of repression and persecution of MRL. For the first time, after centuries, religious men and women were killed because of their commitment to justice. This was seen by MRL as a sign of the times; we were indeed disciples of Jesus Christ.

In this complex controversy, John Paul II, in my view, took a line favorable to the conservative side. But MRL kept tending more toward the line of social transformation, in alliance with the lower social classes. Despite the conservative attitude on the part of the Catholic hierarchy,[23] MRL reinforced the tendency to move towards the poorest classes and to enter into their conditions of life; to get in touch with the base Christian communities; to move towards a direct pastoral work in the local churches, living in small communities, in a life-style much more similar to that of the poor. For the first time in this century MRL became significant for the popular movements outside the church, collaborating with the trade unions and taking oppositional stand in relation to the regime. It was not accidental that in those years Latin America became a mission-sending church. Inside each country there developed the same missionary movement. The SVD and

SSpS of Brazil, for instance, left the better established churches and the schools built in the southern part of the country and went to the poor dioceses of the northeast and the Amazon area, assuming a clear missionary position regarding the pastoral urgencies of the Brazilian church.

The Present Transitional Phase

In the 1990s MRL was apparently going through a *transition phase*. The changes occurred after the decline of socialism and the affirmation of the neo- liberal model[24] in economy, culture and politics put MRL at a "historical crossroad," marked by the typical problems of postmodernity[25] and was closed linked to what is happening inside each of our countries[26]

Inside the Catholic Church, this final part of the pontificate of John Paul II is highlighting an instability[27]. Many religious are receding to a more individualistic and passive attitude regarding the possibility of resolving the problems of the Latin American church. This feeling is still stronger among those who are active in the social areas. Apparently there are no viable alternatives except those of conformism and retreating to the defence of small and immediate interests. In this situation, it is not easy for MRL to maintain, on the one hand, the principle of the option for the poor and the spirituality of liberation, and on the other, to exercise a prophetic and critical role in the new situation, distinguishing in it what is destructive for the people and what offers them opportunities which call for action. In other words: MRL finds itself in a crossroad.

Many people are asking what should be the profile of the MRL in the immediate future? This question depends on various as yet unresolved questions.[28] It depends also on what direction will be taken among the different possible scenarios or tendencies[29] present today in the church in Latin America. It is hard to say to which of these RL will most adapt itself.

A final observation. From what has already been said, the reader might well have the impression that in Latin America everything revolves around a religious life mission-oriented and inculturated among the poor. In fact it is not so. On the contrary, it seems that there is a tendency to come back to a more closed model. This is part of the present crossroad situation. Even so, I would say that today there pulses in the vast majority of MRL an Abrahamic[30] and prophetic spirit which, like Abraham and the prophets in former times, is involved in a faith-ful search of a new earth and a new heaven.

The Religious Conference of Brazil (CRB) says it with courage in its main objective for 1998-2001, which is the following: "to refound religious Life . . . inserting it in our social, cultural, political, economic and religious reality; through the identification with the values, patterns and ways of being and thinking of our people and with a definite commitment to the struggles for the dignity and justice for all and in very special way for those excluded by the neoliberal economic process."[31]

Life as the Completion of Liberation

There are a few significant new words which are typical of this transitional phase. Here is a short list of terms currently in use: "mercy," "gratuity," "fruitfulness," "attention," "tenderness," "prayerful reading," "reconciliation," "Mother God," "solidarity," "sensibility," "hope," "symbiosis," "ecofeminism."[32] In my view, these words should not be seen as a denial of the strong political words which were used at the time when a well-known hymn spoke of God as "Our Revolutionary Father,"[33] underlining the need for more radical changes in the economic, social and political systems. At least partially, I regard these new terms as different modes of expressing the same concerns we used to express in the radical terms used in the 1970s and 1980s. I resume the new and the old vocabulary: *compassion and liberation.* In these two words I find a synthesis of our main present theological and missionary insight: to fight for justice and to be merciful meet and complement each other.

That means that MRL remains committed to the defense of the dignity, freedom and quality of life; to the valuing of the fundamental rights of persons and minorities; to the effective solidarity between peoples and religions; to the cry against any and all forms of injustice; to the sensitivity to situations of misery, hunger and war; to the interest for ecology; to the critique of economic injustices. All those objectives are seen as central in the action of MRL in the beginning of the next century. In other words, Latin American MRL is trying presently to create a new mode of presence centered in insertion, liberation and inculturation and animated by the missionary biblical spirituality which we relearned in the last thirty or forty years.

Problems of the Crossroad Context
It would take too long to enumerate all the characteristics that mark, both positively and negatively, the pathway traced by Latin American MRL in the last decade. At the risk of over-simplifying, let me sketch briefly a few aspects which I find significant for the present moment and for immediate future.

The *diversity of cultures* is already a fact within Latin American MRL. Vocations are coming mainly from the poorer sectors of society. Understanding Afro- and Indian-American cultures are becoming a must for all congregations. These new missionaries will bring a breath of fresh air to our way of conceiving and doing mission.

In MRL traditionally directed by men, the *interplay of the genders* represents a challenge that cannot be resolved merely by rhetoric, because it puts deeply into question the androcentric ideas and structures that we still keep within the missionary activity of the church.

The same can be said regarding the *laity*. In Latin America the involvement of the laity is proclaimed as a fundamental right and as a need for evangelization. In practice, however, little has been done. On the contrary, one hears of a revival of clericalism. Even MRL does not offer very promising conditions to establishing a more adequate way of relating and sharing the religious missionary charism with the laity. Canon Law, our ingrained habits and structures, plus an inadequate theology of the laity are still blocks to our creativity in this field. We are not able to imagine our missionary congregations as a family open to *all ecclesial vocations* and ministries.

Another important area in which we are poorly prepared is that of *ecumenism and interreligious dialogue* or "macroecumenism," as we say in Latin America.

Another problem, often poorly resolved within RL, of *the human and affective maturity* of our members. In a time of massive individualism, only the personalization of this dimension and a new kind of missionary community life can offer a solid affective and social basis for a more fruitful entry in the *different areopagi* pointed by John Paul II in his missionary encyclical (RM 37) .

Finally I would mention as a problem for MRL the *lack of missionary consciousness of our local churches* in regard to the universal mission of the church. Most of our dioceses are poor. The bishops are primarily preoccupied with the pastoral urgencies within their own churches. It is difficult for them to think of the responsibility of the Latin American church in the future of the mission *ad gentes*. I have the impression that "*ad gentes*" and "*Redemptoris Missio*" did not have a really effective influence on the Latin American way of seeing the whole question of mission.[34] This lack of consciousness is often present also inside the RL, some missionary institutes not excluded.

Changes

The changes that will be mentioned here should not be seen as an "either/or" but as a "both/and." They are simultaneously novelty and provocation, passage and matrix. They have an essentially spiritual dimension which comes from the living spring of our religious past, but that offer a response to the quest and desires of the new generations of missionary men and women.

I wish to draw your attention to some changes of viewpoint and practices[35] that are already becoming visible among people committed to the refoundation of MRL. Here we see emphases and trends to be further discerned in light of our evangelical vocation to holiness, prophecy and mission:

> From a situation of exodus, joy, courage and clarity about our target, we have passed to one of *bewilderment and hesitations.* We are camped by the banks of the rivers of Babylon, in need of a deep purification of those motivations that sustain our faith and our willingness to convert ourselves and invest our life in the missionary following of Christ;

> From the dream of great achievements, we have passed to the *search of little objectives* that apparently cannot affect the established order, which scatters the weakness of our abilities and projects;

> From the myth of the revolution that would change the people's destiny from night into day, we have passed over to *a sort of social kenosis* and to a painful struggle to gain concessions from the power-system that controls the world;

> From an ideological vision of politics we have passed over to a more *cultural vision,* through the growing re-discovery of the cultural identity of the races, of the minorities and of the native populations. This obliges us to a greater identification with the cultural values and historic struggles that we should make our own, without thinking that we can impose on the people our parameters and institutional values;

From an almost exclusively valuing the logos we have passed over to a still preliminary *recognition of eros;*

From the voluntarism of the *"instrumental reason"* (Habermas) we are moving toward a desire for the *"world of life,"* where there is ample space for creativity, for symbol, festival and beauty. As Maçaneiro says, in the religious spirituality that is arising at this turn-of-the-century "Eros becomes the place of the Spirit who educates our desires in the direction of the Good and of the Truth."[36]

From life conceived as our own conquest, we are passing over to *life as gift,* which is given in our interaction and in communion with all that is alive (ecology, holism, mystagogy, solidarity, tenderness, pilgrimage): justice through the intrinsic power of the good news, sown in patience and in hope;

From a locally oriented perception of the following of Jesus we are passing over to a holistic oriented view of our vocation as an evangelical commitment "ad omnes gentes."

A New Historical Image of Life/Liberation-Centered MRL

It is mainly the women theologians, not the men, who are developing among us the notion of life as a defining element of MRL in its concrete historic figure and mode of existence. Checking through the list of contents of the monthly review of the Conference of Religious of Brazil, I noted how frequent were the references to Life, but how rarely it is developed as a separate topic. When this does happen, it is always a woman who goes into the question at length. It would seem that the driving source of this theology of MRL consists in the actual experience of being consecrated women who seek to live as a community of disciples, concerned for the passing over of humankind from death into life.

The young Brazilian theologian Ivoni Fritzen goes even further. She attempts to broaden and systematize a bold but ambiguous phrase by the Korean theologian Chung Hyug Kyung, for whom "in the future, spirituality and theology will move from Christo-centric to Life-centrism." Fritzen wonders what would a *Life-centered* MRL be like, which she outlines as "the human being in his/her needs, desires and most practical relationships with other people, the struggle and belief, trying to survive-- since life is always under threat -- in the ambient world and in great sorrow (and subject to the power of death), living without bread and without support, without sharing and in exclusion from everything."

Here are some aspects which are surely lacking in the andro-centric formulations of a theology of mission and of MRL inspired by a one-sided view of the liberation process. Let's enumerate some features of this life/liberation-centered theology:

> Its concern is for the concrete conditions and methods of a life that is worthy and full for all, and not for feelings and abstractions. Therefore MRL does not stay silent in face of the exclusions caused by neo-liberalism, nor will it give in, in the face of violence in all its forms of death and neglect of the poor, to which mainline political life today seems indifferent;

> This theology tries to restore the dignity of the human body, since it is a temple of the Spirit, destined to rise in fullness. In the same line, it defends the body/soul unity in the diversity of races (anti-racism) and the relationship of the sexes (anti-machismo);

> This Liberation/Life-centered missionary theology ensures that each subject -- woman or man, individuals or groups-- can relate to others in conditions of full equality, each one with the right of speaking and recognizing each other as partners in building and defending life, as subjects of law both within and outside the church;

> The theology focused upon Life/Liberation insists that community life is for life and mission, freely and conscientiously chosen in order to generate and share new life--because life is only life when it is shared;

> It says its word on the basis of an openness to the Word of God, heard in the Bible and in life, from the viewpoint of the poor. This is the viewpoint that generates within us the

creative freedom of the children of God--and not as a testing
and exercise of power;

The theology based on Life/Liberation embraces and makes
its own the great Utopia of justice and freedom that pulses
in the heart of humankind and nature, though it is never
fully realized in history;

It is included in the line of "amorização" ("filling with
love") which moves all creation in the direction of Omega
point (Teilhard de Chardin), the goal of an creational
evolution which God planned from the first breath of
creation, and which will reach its fullness in the parousia;

It requires therefore a creaturely attitude of adoration and
of active expectation. It cultivates a lived dialogue with all
peoples and cultures, with all religions and philosophies;

A Life/Liberation-centered Theology is intrinsically
pneumaological and eschatological. It requires in itself an
attitude of contemplation-action and of attention to the
"provocations" of the Spirit (John Paul II) in history;

It asks for an ethical and political attitude oriented to the
building of a humanity reconciled with nature and the
cosmos, and so, more full with the life of God, hidden and
revealed in the mystery of the one and triune God, who
made us in God's own likeness.

Towards a New "Historic Form" of Missionary Religious Life

Looking at the limits of the renewal of Latin American MRL in
general during the last forty years, one basic difficulty is to discover the
causes of today's crossroad. Now the cause is probably the one-sided
emphasis on only one historical concrete figure with which the following of
Jesus was identified since the Middle Ages and even earlier. An historical
figure in the life of an institution can perdure meaningfully only in the
measure that it has a recognized visibility to others, through a series of
signals that configure his identity and render it recognizable. Historical
figures have a "soul," a content, a unifying principle that gives them meaning

and inspiration. It is a living message, and that is why others see them, understand them and respond to them.

The present official configuration of MRL is clearly the result of a certain convergence of historical factors that already have lost their social plausibility. With the loss of this plausibility, it suffers both the greatness and weakness of every figure in decline. It enters into a sociological crisis which brings an structural incapacity of responding to the appeals of reality; it is as though the Spirit were leaving the body. The expressions that made it a carrier of a living message have disappeared. The same can be said of its inner missionary force.

This is the process through which the current forms of MRL are passing. They are losing their social visibility and their capacity to attract. They are no longer able to render visible the experience of the Kingdom to the society. Up until a short while ago, they succeeded in doing so. But their capacity for this is worn out, to a large extent. The still-dominant missionary model of RL is unable to allow the vital synthesis of the experience of God and the apostolic mission to shine through. It is showing itself incapable of assimilating the "new" which shines out in so many current processes and in the need felt today for a real evangelical transparency. This "novum" is surprisingly irreducible to the kind of configuration with which we were so familiar. The tension is irreconcilable because the new paradigms, perspectives and presuppositions are so different.

As Carlos Palacio puts it tersely, "what is in play is not just this or that element in isolation, it is the project of life in its totality."[37] The solution, therefore is that experienced by Abraham, our father in faith, when he was called to sacrifice the son in whom all his hopes were invested, for the fulfillment of the promise made to him by God. The attitude that is needed now is both sacrificial and exodal: "leave your country and go … to the place that I will show you" (Gen 12:4).

We need to re-create, from the very roots, the old institutional forms still in use, and on which some authorities insist. These forms must be revitalized in their foundational elements: in the way of experiencing the God of Jesus Christ, in the perception and discernment of the challenges that lie at the heart of a "world of death," injustice and exclusion; in the option for ways and means that are apt to announce the Good News, in terms not only of modernity and post modernity, but specially of the cultures which don't belong to the western way of living and conceiving the mystery of God's presence and action in the world.

Former SVD Vice Superior General Joseph Connolly quotes Reinhold Neibuhr,[38] who says, "nothing that is worth doing is achieved in our life time; therefore we must be saved by hope. Nothing that is true and beautiful or good makes complete sense in any context of history; therefore we must be saved by faith. Nothing we do, however virtuous, can be accomplished alone; therefore we must be saved by love."

Let me conclude quoting Connolly himself,[39] who, speaking about the kind of missionary leadership the Divine Word Missionaries needs in the twenty-first century, says something important for MRL in Latin America at this crossroad of its history: "our formation and spirituality programs have stressed the importance of 'passing over' as a constitutive element of our missionary vocation. Equally important at this point of our history is the spirituality of 'handing over' and 'letting go.'"

My conclusion, after this analysis of the historical context and process of MRL in Latin America in the beginning of the twenty-first century, is that our most important missionary task in the future is to let ourselves and our institutions be modeled by the Spirit, at the desert or historic frontier to which God is leading us.

Notes

1. Eloy Bueno, *La Iglesia en la encrucijada de la misión* (Estella: Editorial Verbo Divino, 1999).

2. See Documents of the XV General Chapter SVD 2000, in *In Dialogue with the Word* #1 (Rome: SVD Publications, 2000), 16-23.

3. Walbert Bühlmann, *The Coming of the Third Church: An Analysis of the Present and Future of the Church* (Maryknoll, NY: Orbis Books, 1977).

4. Documents of the XV General Chapter SVD, 30-38.

5. Arnaiz, José Maria, "Fidelidade criativa: fio condutor de Vita Consecrata," in: VV.AA., *Fidelidade criativa. Um apelo à vida consagrada,* (São Paulo: CRB/Loyola, 1997), 25-46.

6. See Carlos Palacio, "O sacrifício de Israel: uma parábola da vida religiosa," *Convergência* (1992): 359-376.

7. See the two volumes of CEHILA: *História geral da Igreja na América Latina* (Petrópolis/São Paulo: Vozes/Paulinas, 1983). On Religious Life in Brazil in the past five hundred years of our history, an overview can be found in: Edênio Valle,

O século XX interpela a VR brasileira. Guia para uma reflexão histórica (Aparecida: Editora Santuário, 1999).

8. See for instance the concluding document of the Santo Domingo meeting of the Latin American Bishops' Conference, #244, in A. T. Hennelly, ed., *Santo Domingo and Beyond* (Maryknoll, NY: Orbis Books, 1993), 139.

9. Medellin, of course, is the name of a city in Colombia, the site of the Second Assembly of Latin American Bishops shortly after Vatican II (1968). The document of Medellin had a decisive role in the direction of our churches, especially between 1968 and 1985. After the beginning of the pontificate of John Paul II there was a backward motion in the direction inspired by Medellin, but that direction continued nevertheless in the two other Bishops' general assemblies in Puebla (1979) and Santo Domingo (1992).

10. I will not go into detail on this subject because it would bring us too far afield, but I consider this one of the main pillars of the refounding of MRL in Latin America. See E. Hoornaert, *A formação do catolicismo brasileiro (1550-1800)*, (Petrópolis: Vozes, 1991).

11. See the Santo Domingo Document, #16-21.

12. For a brief account see: Valle, 26-34.

13. See M. R. Fachini and R. M. G. Neves, "As reduções jesuíticas dos guaranís (1610-1768). Uma utopia evangelizadora," in: CEHILA, *História da Evangelização na América Latina* (São Paulo, Paulinas, 1988).

14. Over 600 Jesuits, for instance, were expelled from Brazil in the seventeenth century.

15. Brazil, for example, received ten female congregations in the last decade of the nineteenth century; between 1900 and 1920, thirty-four others arrived. Only in these thirty years we have a total of fifty-two new congregations (both of men and of women) coming from France (most of them), Italy, Germany, Spain, Belgium and Portugal. A very small number of them went to the indigenous areas of Brazil, where circa one million native Indians lived by that time. Also the SVD and SSpS did very little for the evangelization of those groups. We were more interested in the pastoral care of European immigrants and of the new cities, like Belo Horizonte, Juiz de Fora or Vitoria. The same happened with the SVDs in Argentina and Chile, with few exceptions. In Paraguay we tried to found a real work among "pagans" in the Monay River. Bishop Juan Bockwinkel, from Paraguay, has an interesting book on this subject. Small attempts were also made in the Brazilian states of Paraná and Minas Gerais. The SVD anthropologists were

interested in the Mapuchos of Chile, but for scientific reasons, it seems.

16. See Valle, 59-67.

17. As a matter of fact the missionary enthusiasm of the new religious congregations was relatively poor. In this matter we should avoid carefully both a triumphalistic as well as a pessimistic view of this time and model. The Salesians--men and women-- for instance were among the pioneers in the contact with the Indians of the central-west part of Brazil. Regarding the Afro-Brazilians (50% of the population), very little was done.

18. The SVDs arrived in Brazil in 1895 and the SSpS in 1902. See Joseph P. McGovern, *A fertilidade de Canãa. História da Congregação do Verbo Divino no Brasil*, 1975; José V. César, *História da SVD no Brasil* (Belo Horizonte, 1995); José M. Wisniewski, "História da Congregação do Verbo Divino no Brasil," in: VVAA, *Desafios missionários hoje*, Ano do Centenário, 1995, 9-30.

19. See CEHILA, *A mulher pobre na história da Igreja latino-americana* (São Paulo, Edições Paulinas, 1984).

20. See Vatican Council II, Decree on the Appropriate Renewal of Religious Life (*Perfectae Caritatis*--PC) 2 and 5, in Walter M. Abbot, ed., *The Documents of Vatican II* (New York: Herder and Herder / Association Press, 1966), 468-471.

21.Gerald   Arbuckle, *Out of Chaos: Refounding Religious Congregations* (Mahwah, NJ: Paulist Press, 1988).

22. Honestly speaking I see the influence of AG in our church as irrelevant. RM was influential only inside the church. EN gave an extraordinary impulse in the whole conception and organization of the evangelizational and pastoral work of our church.

23. It is important to say that in Brazil, for instance, more than 90% of the Bishops supported the work done by Religious Life. The controversy between CLAR (Latin American Religious Confederation) and CELAM (Latin American Bishops Counsel) involved more the presidency of CELAM and a small group of conservative Bishops. Two main issues were in the center of this discussion: the pastoral activity of MRL and the reading of the Bible from the viewpoint of the poor. Regarding this, see: Carlos Mesters and EdênioValle, "La lecture de la parole de Dieu à partir des pauvres. Le projet Parole et Vie," in Ignace Berten and René Luneau, eds., *Le rendez-vous de Saint Domingue. Les enjeux d'un anniversaire (1492 – 1992)* (Paris: Centurion, 1991), 149-177.

24. See Valle, 113-142.

25. The three levels of this situation are well described by the SVD Fifteenth General Chapter in its social, political, ecological, cultural and religious consequences. See: *Documents of the XV General Chapter SVD 2000*, 18-20.

26. In the 1990s the utopia of liberation lost part of its historic strength. The re-democratization which aroused such hopes in Brazil did not get very far. Modernization of the economy had led to the abandonment of the lower classes and the middle classes. Violence reached unimaginable levels, with the growth of organized gangs and drug-trafficking. The basic claims of the people regarding education, health, housing, work and land, and their desire for social and political participation remained unfulfilled. Most countries are flooded in a wave of corruption. There is frightful unemployment.

27. There is a new flowering of male vocations, though there is much debate about their missionary quality. Within the female MRL, the vocation problem has its special difficulties related probably to the complex question of women's role in society and church. Among consecrated women, the median age of the group continues to rise. In 1970 the professed religious women were 40,462; in 2000 they are 33,950. I see a difference between religious women who participate directly in civil life and those who work more within the church. The more church-oriented group seems to have less consciousness of the meaning of the present crossroad situation.

28.Edênio Valle, *Que futuro para a Vida religiosa? Reflexões em torno da virada do milênio* (Aparecida: Editora Santuário, 1997).

29. According to João Batista Libânio, there are presently four main scenarios in the Brazilian church. For the present all we can do is ask ourselves: what kind of scenario will prevail in RL in the future? The *institutional* model? Or will RL be modeled on the enthusiasm of the *charismatics,* for whom exaltation and subjective piety are the key elements of spirituality. Or again, will it flow from a *testimonial* and *kerygmatic* model? Or, finally, will the *liberation* model prevail, bringing the MRL to really identify itself with the joys and sufferings of the poor, so becoming a sign of life and of hope for them? See J. Batista Libânio, *Cenários de Igreja (* São Paulo: Loyola, 2000).

30. This was a word frequently used by Mons. Helder Câmara to express the feeling of urgency present among Christians in the 1960s. The milestones of this "Abrahamic" way are closely related to what we call the *Prayerful Reading of the Bible.* This is a densely-packed concept that would merit more detailed consideration than our space allows here. The CRB (Religious Conference of Brazil) has published eight interesting books as support of a nation-wide program of Bible reading for religious.

31. See CRB, Programação Religiosa 2001, 9.

32. To this list may be added a series of words current in the charismatic movement of the Catholic Church, where the semantic world is totally removed from matters of political and social concern. These are expressions that I imagine are current throughout the world, due to the Pentecostal influence with its metaphorical language and vertically focusing on praise, healing and thanksgiving.

33. This hymn was composed by a Brazilian SVD composer and is sung all over the country.

34. Nevertheless, the number of missionaries sent by the Latin American churches to other churches, including Africa and Asia, is increasing year after year. Brazil presently has more than 1800 religious and lay missionaries working outside the country.

35. Marcial, Maçaneiro, "Espiritualidade e novos paradigmas," *Convergência,* 32, 304 (1997): 365.

36. Ibid., 366.

37. Palacio, 375

38. Quoted in Joseph Connolly, "Leadership Today," in: *SVD Leadership: The Challenge of Tomorrow* (Techny: The Mission Center, 1998), 8.

39. Ibid.

MISSION FOR THE TWENTY-FIRST CENTURY IN NORTH AMERICA

Anthony J. Gittins, CSSP[*]

Prelude

At the end of his book *The Church in the Midst of Creation*, Vincent Donovan has a chapter entitled "Preaching the Gospel to America." His words provide us with a context:

> [We] must face the very real problem that is pressing in on us. We are confronted with the formidable task of the evangelization of America.
> Evangelization is not the same thing as convert-making. Evangelization is essentially related to a culture, to a community. Convert-making is geared to individuals. It would be impossible to *convert* [280] million individual Americans, [but] it is not only possible, it is essential to *evangelize* the American culture, or the many cultures that make up the American people. Evangelization means bringing the full force of the gospel to the American culture and letting the chips fall where they may, or where the Spirit lets them fall. Evangelization is essentially unpredictable. The outcome cannot be known ahead of time. The conversion, or *metanoia*, involved is a conversion of both the evangelist and the evangelized.

*Anthony J. Gittins is Bishop Francis X. Ford, M.M. Professor of Missiology at Catholic Theological Union, Chicago. Born in Britain, Fr. Gittins has served as a missionary in Sierra Leone, has taught and lectured throughout the world, and continues a missionary ministry with the homeless in Chicago. He is the author of several books, among which are **Reading the Clouds: Mission Spirituality for New Times** (1999), **A Presence that Disturbs: Christianity without Christendom** (2001), and **Gifts and Strangers: Meeting the Challenge of Inculturation** (second edition, 2001).*

If [the American people] accept the message, they must be free to understand it and to express it from the midst of their culture. One has to wonder if Americans have ever before been presented with that opportunity--white Americans, or black Americans or Native Americans.

We must speak the language of the people. Language includes more than just words. It has to contain the richness, power, and emotions these words convey. We have to understand the mentality of the people being evangelized, their fears, their dreams, their history.

It is difficult to stand back and look at [culture]. We are so at one with it that we are reluctant to think that it stands in need of evangelization and conversion.

We have to be like strangers, missionaries perhaps, who have never been in America, or have been away from it for a long time and are allowed to return to it. At that point we can begin to look on America with the restless eyes of a missionary.

If Christ comes to a culture in the process of evangelization, something will live and something will die. Christ comes to fulfill every culture and to prophesy against every culture.

The message itself will take on different emphases in different cultures. It will *sound* different. The preaching of the gospel in the United States will have an unmistakable American accent (Donovan 1989: 125-127).

Introduction

Our topic then, is mission for the twenty-first century, and our context is these United States of America. It is of course, both notoriously presumptuous to speak about the future in any detail, and frequently unhelpful to do so in generalities. Perhaps this is particularly so at this moment, when many of the most trustworthy sages confidently yet soberly predict, as virtually inevitable, a nuclear holocaust on some apocalyptic scale, whether by design or accident. Nevertheless, as W.S. Gilbert (of Gilbert and Sullivan) reminded us, "nothing venture, nothing win." So I will attempt to characterize some of the features of our contemporary world and suggest where some missionary challenges may lie.

There will be three sections. First, I identify four priorities for the American church; second, four facets of evangelization; and finally four pressing issues that cannot be legitimately avoided. But first, three introductory remarks.

With others, I am convinced that a critical mass of Christians must believe passionately and publicly that the *status quo* both of the church and of American society is unacceptable, and that greater faithfulness to God and commitment to God's people is imperative. We are gathered at an historic point in American political history, when, almost five weeks after the presidential elections, nobody knows who the next president will be, and fewer and fewer people seem much to care. They want an end to the process, but their expectations of the new president and for the next four years at home and abroad are inchoate to the point of non-existent. If the Christian community is as indecisive and unclear about its agenda as are contemporary politicians and would-be presidents, it is not surprising that the world at home and abroad does not appear to be holding its breath in expectation of a renewed and relevant Christianity.

Second, in the light of the three documents around which our symposium is crafted, it appears that we do not need a completely new set of programs for mission in the new century, but that we do need to identify a new set of priorities. As *Ad Gentes* (AG) stated thirty-five years ago, many things in the world have "utterly changed" in recent years (AG 6). And this is much more dramatically true as we look back over the final third of the twentieth century, and acknowledge that the pace of change has accelerated so much that we are indeed caught up in a runaway world.

The third remark is this: the church is a *sacrament* or sign. There are many signs vying for our attention as we speed down highways or through cities and towns. But some of them, due to defacement or delapidation, are illegible or irrelevant. They are, if anything, counter-signs rather than helpful indicators or bearers of information. As *Evangelii Nuntiandi* (EN) says, the church must be not simply a sign but a sign that carries a message: "simultaneously obscure and luminous" (EN 15) but certainly not meaningless. Because the church is a sign, it must be visible, audible, tangible: it must, in other words, "proclaim the faith and salvation which comes from Christ" (AG 5).

With these three points of reference as our starting point, let us look at the American church today.

Four Priorities for the American Church

A workshop can only hope to articulate and bring to discussion a limited number of issues, and our field is vast. The priorities identified here are all found in the documents under review.

A Preferential Option for the Poor and a Challenge to the Rich

The evangelization of cultures requires and produces an authentic engagement with real people (see the fourth point, below). It cannot be reduced to the production of good ideas or recommendations, but must become an incarnation, a new birth. Members of an individualistic culture may not take kindly to an invitation to move from the center to the margins, to go beyond a willingness to sit on committees or to provide "handouts" for the needy. But the church must be seen in the company of the poor and heard to irritate the comfortable. Jesus was unequivocal in calling the rich to a profound conversion, under pain of exclusion from the Kingdom or Realm of God. "Woe to you rich" is one of the most unequivocal and chilling phrases on his lips.

The preferential option for the poor, the actual choice God makes for the needy and brokenhearted (see Luke 4:18), is the basis for what we ourselves do. It is alluded to by Pope John Paul II, who says that "it is true that the 'option for the neediest' means that we should not overlook the most abandoned and isolated human groups" (RM 37). It is clearer still in the words of Pope Paul VI: "The world calls for and expects from us . . . charity towards all, especially towards the lowly and the poor" (EN 76).

We can identify in this country, three groups of "poor." There are forty million people struggling to survive below the poverty line, of whom-- on even the mildest night of the year--three quarters of a million are homeless. But that figure is the tip of a much bigger iceberg: the social fact of poverty and homelessness in this country is an obscenity.

But the poor are not only the homeless, and the homeless poor are not the only people who experience exclusion; our churches practice a form of Apartheid that effectively divides people who share a common baptism. Truly multicultural parishes are a rarity compared to the number of multicultural communities whose ethnically or socially diverse members have to find their own discrete parish communities. For parishioners to maintain that they are not segregated and that all are welcome, when the liturgy or expression of community blatantly favors one group and implicitly excludes others, is unChristian.

A third group of overlooked and needy Americans is "anyone who cannot cope," as Jean Vanier described "the poor" in this country. Those who acknowledge that--for whatever reason--they are unable to remain afloat and are slowly sinking, are among the neediest of this rapidly changing society. As Pope Paul VI said so forcefully, evangelization "includes the preaching of hope . . . of God's love . . . of brotherly love for all . . . of helping one's brother and sister, which . . . is the kernel of the Gospel" (EN 27).

As for "the rich," it is simply immoral for people to luxuriate in material well-being (EN 35); the gospel challenge to repentance is unequivocal (Lk 6:24). The church in the United States is required to confront the comfortable and call them *by example* to a truly missionary response: a turning of their lives *inside out* rather than a careful *outside-in* maintenance of their own self-sufficiency and privilege. The gospel does not only console like balm; it stings like an astringent on an open sore. The question must be asked: has the church in the United States--numerically strong, economically comfortable and ethnically much less representative of the general population--betrayed the gospel and overlooked many of those whom Jesus favored?

The Promotion of New Communities

Agricultural societies whose members live close to a subsistence level know that each annual harvest serves a double purpose: it will feed the community today, but some of it must be kept back to become the seed of next year's harvest. If the Christian gospel is to nurture the community in the U.S., it must not simply sustain the well-fed but provide seed for a wider scattering. It must be planted in new or abandoned fields and not simply be gathered into barns. A renewal of the life-bearing seeds of faith is urgently required if the United States is not to suffer a great famine.

Conventional parish structures may be like rusty machinery: once effective, but no longer so, due to wear and tear and changed times. Parishes are not "service stations" and Christians are not chauffeurs bringing automobiles for tune-ups. A service-station is of little help to an automobile that fails on the highway, and of even less to a chauffeur stricken by a heart attack at the wheel. Service-stations--or barns--are inadequate models for the church of tomorrow. If yesterday the people came to church, tomorrow the church must go to people. If not, not only will it continue to lose the people, it will lose its own soul. Tomorrow's church will need to be less institutional and more relational, less a dispenser of sacraments-on-schedule and more a community of faith-and-works. The church needs to be reinvented, and traditional parish-structures and ordained ministries are simply not adequate for the task.

Pope John Paul II reminded us that in times of uncertainty one must renew the central nucleus of one's faith: the issue is faith, not structures, whether bureaucratic or architectural. Still too many church buildings dot our landscape, while too few communities of support and encouragement are to be found. Catechisms, and catechetical knowledge, cannot substitute for faith; to know what Catholics believe is not to know how their faith underwrites their daily lives. We are called to put our belief into practice: to become people of faith. But to do that we need to rediscover ourselves as a people and not simply as individuals. The leadership of tomorrow's church faces a daunting task and may fall far short of what is needed.

Religious sociologist Rodney Stark spoke of "cost-effective Christianity." His thesis was that in the early centuries, to be a Christian was very costly or expensive. The religion was outlawed and the penalties were severe. Yet the community grew exponentially over the first three centuries. People could identify something worth living for, and even worth dying for; and the community was internally cohesive and externally active. In the U.S. today however, it is certainly not very costly to be a Christian: in fact, it is quite inexpensive. It is possible to be a Christian without conflict to patriotism or citizenship, and to assume that to be "a good American" and "a Good Christian" are compatible if not identical. To be an American might be both worth living for and worth dying for, but to be a Christian appears to require nothing more and to add nothing to that national identity. The Christian currency has become devalued and is effectively worthless. What was once very expensive and highly desirable is now--in the opinion of a growing number of people -- both unfashionable and trivial.

Centrifugal Christianity

Though it has been more than a third of a century since AG asserted that the church is missionary by nature (AG 2), this can hardly be said to be axiomatic among the faithful of this country. Many of our parishes are dying because they are turned in upon themselves, not because they lack for money; while those that are truly alive are invariably turned outward in a centrifugal or missionary posture, even though they often have unimpressive financial assets. There is a great need for Christians committed to mission rather than maintenance--but this in turn requires both missionary leadership and the practice of true subsidiarity. Missionary leadership is risk-taking and trusting. Not every leader needs to be young, ostentatious, or even dynamic. But every true leader needs to inspire and encourage and promote those with greater imagination and energy. Subsidiarity refers to a form of delegation or shared leadership, in which the person with greatest authority is not the general *factotum* but rather the one who practice mutuality, shared responsibility and genuine graciousness.

Sadly, the institutional church in the U.S. has become sclerotic and stratified, sometimes more *magisterial* than *ministerial*. Increasingly, as we have moved from a community-based and duty-driven society, to an individualistic and rights-based society, our effectiveness as God's people has been compromised. If the church in the dawning century is not to become a memory, individuals must discover that they can become community. Insular lives must experience the vitality that comes from wider encounters. Leaders must neither arrogate to themselves all the power and the glory nor refuse to encourage and build up the community of which they are an integral part. Moreover, a church marked more by nostalgia than imagination and by caution rather than enthusiasm must repent, be converted and discover the missionary call it heard in its youth.

Mission in Reverse

Since the church *is called* (AG 1) to be the sacrament of salvation (AG 5), it follows that the church should *respond.* But a response is very different from an initiative (the latter originating with the self, the former outside of the self). Thus we could image the process as God taking the church to the world rather than the church taking God. One of the implications of this is that no matter what the church or its missionaries have to give, they most emphatically have something to receive. The process whereby the one sent is in turn enriched and converted by the Spirit and the local people is known as *mission in reverse.* As Pope Paul said, "the church has constant need of *being evangelized"* (EN 15).

Who is to evangelize the evangelizers, other than God's own Spirit? Not only the virtuous and strong, the orthodox and the baptized, but also the skeptical, the cynical and the hurt: those who articulate criticism and challenge as much as affirmation and encouragement. The church in U.S. at this time must be seen to want to listen and to learn, as much as to talk and to teach. There are millions of disillusioned and dispirited people--including many former active Catholics--in this country today, and they cannot simply be dismissed as people of bad will. A listening church still has something to learn; a deaf church is forever closed to conversion.

We need to ask, urgently and seriously, whether the church--and ourselves, its members-- are muzzling the Spirit and taking quite illegitimate initiatives. To quote Pope Paul again, "all evangelizers, *whoever they may be* . . . let themselves prudently be guided by [the Spirit] as the decisive inspirer of their plans, their initiatives, and their evangelizing activity" (EN 75). This would be to practice mission in reverse, and even to re-establish the church's credibility and relevance among those who find it literally incredible and irrelevant.

Four Facets of Evangelization

Evangelization has a number of facets or faces. It is *integral* (EN 6; AG 3), affecting all aspects of the ministry of Jesus. It is integral too, inasmuch as it requires the integrated proclamation of both church and Kingdom or Realm of God (AG 6, 40). We would do well to examine some of the facets of evangelization as they are reflected in the missionary documents: and we begin with the ambiguous word *proclamation* itself.

Proclamation

During two millennia, evangelization has sometimes been effectively reduced to proclamation. But once we understand evangelization to refer to the total ministry of Jesus we see how distorted such a perspective would be. Jesus undertook much more than a didactic ministry; and Pope Paul VI is clear that proclamation includes the proclamation of Jesus as Savior, and of the Kingdom of God. Jesus himself proclaimed the Kingdom, even as he proclaimed himself its messenger. We too must proclaim Jesus, Kingdom, and church (RM 17-20), though "only the Kingdom is absolute, and it makes everything else relative" (EN 8). Though there will always be some tension between the imperative of proclaiming Jesus, Kingdom and church (EN 17; AG 15) in specific cases, nevertheless proclamation itself is not synonymous with evangelization and not to be equated with it. Proclamation is only one facet of evangelization.

Liberation

We are called to proclaim God's saving works which are also God's liberating works (EN 9; AG 12), as Jesus did constantly. And the evangelization we promote must be *integrated* rather than fragmented. Liberation refers to freeing people from anything that confines their human dignity or constrains their legitimate freedom. But it must also show itself as a presentation of life-giving alternatives to people whose lives are either over-controlled or overwhelmed by a plethora of competing opportunities. Authentic liberation transforms humanity (EN 18) destabilizing the complacent or irking the comfortable (EN 20). But though it should *relativize* lives (warning of the danger of idols and idolatry), it is primarily intended to *revitalize* them (inviting people to more abundant life). Liberation requires that Christians become *involved* in society and, while not becoming totally caught up in social services, responding generously and genuinely to all that militates against human dignity and well-being (EN 29-31).

Witness

Witness is described as the very first (RM 42), or foundational (EN 76) form of mission. It may be wordless (EN 21), must always be underwritten by a life of integrity (EN 41, 76), but nevertheless needs to be made explicit (EN 22). It was St. Francis of Assisi who urged Christians to proclaim the Gospel--and *if necessary* to use words. In the case of witness, the embodiment of love and salvation is given a certain precedence over formal, verbal proclamation; but in reality witness and proclamation are two sides of the same coin. Two things must be attended to: on the one hand it may be inappropriate to proclaim verbally at every moment; on the other, to shy away from explicit proclamation is not an option for those who minister in places where freedom of religion is supported. Good news wants to spread itself, and disciples are broadcasters.

Encounter

The fourth facet of evangelization is particularly strong in these documents. It bespeaks the relational rather than the doctrinaire or didactic nature of Christianity. Christianity seeks to relate people to God and to each other in a novel way: personal relationships with God are possible and desirable; every human person is one's neighbor and equal before God. H. Richard Niebuhr compared people's inner history with their outer history. The latter can be reduced to facts and figures *about* people: the former concerns actual life-shaping experiences and relationships. Jesus did not simply *know about* prostitutes and sinners, sick people and Samaritans: he numbered such actual people among his acquaintances and friends. We must aspire to a similar level of relationship with those we encounter and among whom we minister. Evangelization must therefore encounter actual people, and Pope Paul VI is particularly strong on this (EN 46, 47, 57, 63).

The impact of these four aspects of evangelization is to produce a Christianizing of American culture, and in turn an Americanization of Christianity. In other words, inculturation will only be mature when American culture bows the knee before Christ and produces its own unique fruits, and when Christianity as it exists elsewhere in the world is enriched by this new response to the gospel. Neither Christianity nor culture will escape from the encounter without insight and modification.

Four Pressing Issues

We come, finally, to a quartet of issues that are both significant in the contemporary American climate and find some echo or resonance in the magisterial documents under review.

The Split Between Gospel and Culture

This phrase in *Evangelii Nuntiandi* stands out like the tallest tree in a forest of phrases: "The split between the Gospel and culture is without doubt the drama of our time" (EN 20). Yet the language seems to create a false reification of both "the gospel" and "culture," treating them as objective realities and independent variables. In actuality, "the gospel" here refers to a way of life or living out of the Good News of Jesus Christ; and "culture" is not a concrete, empirical entity but is encountered in myriad subtle ways as a work in progress, or the process and evolution of behaviors and relationship.

Truly the gospel of Jesus Christ must be offered to the people of America in such a way that they can absorb it and make it their own rather than simply drape themselves with it as with fashion or frippery. And the absorption of the Gospel within a multicultural society must produce real inculturation without Balkanization, by respecting authentic cultural difference yet not isolating people of different ethnicities. If ethnicity has to do with *who people are*, while culture has more to do with *how people behave,* then multi-ethnic communities are not precluded from developing common cultures or common markers--including language, food, dress and worship. Cultural differences should not be erased, yet there is often considerable mutual intelligibility between different cultures as indeed between different languages.

A thorough study of various cultures is a *sine qua non* of effective evangelization and inculturation. To pay lip-service to separate development rather than to work for intercultural communication and common worship is to practice a veiled form of Christian apartheid: it is sinful. The interrelated issues of multiculturalism, racism and integral development need to be addressed as an urgent priority.

The Breakdown of Christendom: The Vulnerability of the Church

Many authors have recently drawn attention to the fact of post-Christendom Christianity. For some it is an unmitigated disaster and a sign of pervasive corruption and apostasy. For others is represents the best opportunity since Constantine in the fourth century for Christians to stand up and be counted, and for Christianity to rediscover or reinvent itself, sparer, more streamlined, and more cost-effective.

No longer can the church persuade people that it is the only way to salvation. No longer is salvation itself as highly prized as it once was. The bombast of the church fails to convince, and in a pluralistic world of multiple choice, most people look elsewhere for their priorities. The church is no longer a temporal power, and to many contemporary people not even a spiritual power of any substance. The Enlightenment, democracy, secularism and science have taken their toll on the religious plausibility structures of the past. If the church wishes to convince in future, it will be through service, dedication and vulnerability rather than censoriousness, diktat and invincibility.

A Paralyzing Divisiveness in the American Church

In the past three or four decades, as the *magisterium* has lost much of its sway, ecclesiastical neo-conservatism has served to polarize the church and produce a debilitating divide between the hierarchy (including some lower clergy) and the rest of the Christian community. This polarization is most visible when it opposes theologians and bishops, or laity and clergy. Patriarchy is alive in the church, as indeed are clericalism, sexism and racism, and other unsavory examples of ecclesiastical high-handedness, too well-known to need exemplifying.

The church in the United States is potentially creative, strong, and faith-filled; but its members are neither sheep to be meekly led, nor idiots to be disregarded. A divide has become increasingly evident and Christian charity requires that *all* members of the church commit themselves to unity in diversity, to loyalty to Jesus and lawful authorities, and to mutual respect and collaboration, for the building up of the Body of Christ and the long-term commitment to evangelization in the United States.

Catholics are sometimes contaminated with elements of contemporary culture that are incompatible with true Christianity. While all are called to conversion, it is nevertheless the case that loyal dissent has a place in the community, that fraternal correction works both ways, and that the sins of clericalism and patriarchy are no less serious than other sins. Trust is essential for mutual collaboration: it needs to be rebuilt painstakingly, in situations where it has become a casualty of recent interecclesial sparring.

Institutional Arrogance

This follows from the previous consideration. There is an overabundance of *magistry* and insufficient *ministry* in the church today. Jesus says that the master should be the servant, that the first should be the last, and that the insignificant would be first in the Realm of God. But not infrequently churchmen appear to curry privilege and power, to make themselves non-accountable, and to ride rough-shod over the sensibilities of the faithful. This is quite inconsistent with the attitude and teaching of Jesus. The church in our day would gain in credibility were some of its dignitaries and authorities to be more humble, more servant-like.

One expression of this would be a considerably greater willingness to trade bombast for a little diffidence, and assertion for an occasional apology. The credibility of the church is not served by posturing or denial in the face of unethical or unjust practices. As Vatican II stated so well, the church should "establish relationships of respect and love . . . uncover with gladness and respect those seeds of the word which lie hidden . . . and know and converse with those among whom [she lives], through sincere and patient dialogue. Christian charity is extended to all without distinction of race, social condition, or religion, and seeks neither gain nor gratitude" (AG 11,12). In this case we might say, charity really does begin at home.

The end point of evangelization is a new creation under the Spirit, where people worship in Spirit and in Truth according to the best of own cultural inheritance. It is not, and never has been a rigid conformity of discipline and doctrine. The Catechism can articulate the belief of Catholic Christianity, but it cannot bring to faith. Faith is very different from belief, and comes from a relationship with God. The church is called and authorized to help make communities of faith, not simply to enforce orthodoxy. To this end, the *Common Ground Initiative* of the late Cardinal Bernardin might very profitably be salvaged, before it is too late.

Coda

At the annual meeting of the Catholic Theological Society of America in 2000, Margaret Farley concluded her Presidential Address with these words:

> Embodying vulnerability in the expression of truth, never was the church more strong. Acknowledging not only mistakes but real evil, never was the church more prophetic in its commitment to justice. Respecting those who differ from the church--not only in belief but in policy, never were the church's own hopes for peace more clear.
>
> But whatever word is spoken, whatever action is taken, it needs to be formed with this same spirit: of humility, respect, and the deepest compassion. Only so will it be effective. Only so will it move us from scandal to prophetic witness (Farley 2000: 101).

AMEN!

References Cited

Donovan, Vincent.
> 1989   *The Church in the Midst of Creation.* Maryknoll, NY.: Orbis Books.

Farley, Margaret A.
> 2000   "The Church in the Public Forum: Scandal or Prophetic Witness?" *Presidential Address to the Catholic Theological Society of America. Proceedings of the Fifty-fifth Annual Convention* (Vol 55): 87-101.

Stark, Rodney.
> 1997   *The Rise Of Christianity.* San Francisco: HarperCollins.

A MISSIONARY VISION FOR ASIA
IN THE TWENTY-FIRST CENTURY

Jacob Kavunkal SVD*

Introduction

An essential point that we have to bear in mind while formulating our vision for mission in the twenty-first century, I would suggest, is that we are living in a multi-polar world. What we are encountering in the new century is not only a universe of globalization but also a pluriverse of faiths, cultures and contexts. In this situation we cannot hazard a common vision for mission without the risk of generalization. Hence I have narrowed down the theme to the Asian scene or even to the Indian context.

One wonders if, in the past, most of the Roman Documents did not confine themselves to a western perspective with regards to their world-view, ideology, language and expressions. True, the recent Apostolic Exhortation, *Ecclesia in Asia* endeavors to be more at home in the Asian world, though even here we can detect instances of the western concerns over-powering Asian priorities.

The Asian world in itself, and the nations in Asia, are experiencing the outcome of the multipolarity in different aspects of daily life, whether religious, social or political. In spite of this diversity of contexts, we can indicate certain broad trails that will configure a desirable pattern of mission in Asia. It is helpful also to remind ourselves that the New Testament is not a manual of a single missiology but it has an assortment of missiologies. Having said this I wish to present certain specific ingredients of an Asian Missiology.

The Salvific Motive

Beginning with the Constantinian era Christianity gradually made itself an idol by absolutizing itself, culminating in the Bellarminian theory of the church as the perfect society, having everything in itself. The church was

---

*Jacob Kavunkal is Professor at the Pontifical Seminary in Pune, India. He is the author and editor of many books and articles, including **To Gather Them Into One** (1985) and **Bible and Mission in India Today** (1993).

identified with the Kingdom. It had the monopoly over salvation and outside its boundaries there was only darkness, except when it grudgingly awarded salvation to those whom it judged had received the "baptism of desire."

Salvation, of which the church was the sole agent, was attained by Jesus Christ through his atoning death and resurrection. Thus Salvation began on Good Friday and it was entrusted to the church. This atonement theology made a clean jump from incarnation to the passion, eclipsing the entire ministry of Jesus Christ.

This claim of the church that it alone is salvific and other religions have no *de jure* right to exist, makes it ridiculous for the Asian religions some of which claim to be eternal (*sanatadharma*). Apart from the phenomenological consideration that the vast majority of Asian people have been finding their spiritual consolation in and through these religions, we have to ask also if their claims can be justified from a biblical point of view.

The biblical presentation of Incarnation is not that of a sudden irruption of the divine into the world but is part of an ongoing divine dealing with humankind. According to some New Testament texts like the Prologue of John (1:1-18), Col 1:15-20, Phil 2:6-11, etc., the Incarnate Word existed from the beginning with God and creation is in and through him. He enlightens everyone coming into the world (Jn 1:4,9). Similar texts can be found also in the Wisdom literature (Pro 3:7; 8:13, 22-26; Wis 6:19-20; 7:14, etc). Any knowledge of God is because of the Word (Jn 1:18). Since human beings are social and historical by nature, could we not say that the different religions are the social and historical expressions of the creative and enlightening process of the Word? If so they become also channels for the salvation effected by the activity of the Word. Wisdom/Word "is the theology of the redeemed man living in the world under God's rule" comments Graeme Goldswortrhy (1987:142).

This understanding does not go against the New Testament faith that Jesus Christ is the only mediator between God and humans. True, with regard to the name "Jesus Christ" there could be objections from the followers of other religions. Here again, could we not posit that what is important is the Person, Reality and not the name itself. The Word in itself is a Mystery, as we do not know all about the Word except what is revealed. St. Paul too speaks of the Mystery (Eph 3:4). Mystery would be acceptable also to the followers of other religions.

The Purpose of Incarnation

If Jn 1:1-5 describes the revealing work of the pre-existent Word, from 1:14 onwards John describes the revealing work of the Incarnate Word. The history of salvation moves from the pre-existence of the Word to the Incarnation and the ministry of the Word.

According to the gospels the death of Jesus is the outcome of his ministry. All the four gospels give the image of Jesus of Nazareth as one who relativized God in terms of the human beings because God as the intimate parent (*Abba*) was more concerned about others than God's own self. Accordingly even the Sabbath laws and the laws regarding ritual purity and pollution are secondary to the well being of human beings. This relativization of the religious laws, coupled with the attack on the temple and his claim to have the power to forgive sins, effected the arrest of Jesus. In fact the entire ministry of Jesus was the externalization of God's other-centeredness. Hence he can say, "those who have seen me have seen the Father" (Jn 14:9; 12:45).

The community of the disciples of Jesus Christ, the church, is sent to continue this mission of the Incarnate Word (Jn 20:19). They are to be his witnesses (Lk 24:48). They are to form communities of disciples in every culture (Mt 28:19), who would serve as the light, salt and leaven in the respective cultural block (Mt 5:13-15). It is interesting that the images Jesus used to describe the community, salt, light and leaven, are expendable and minority images and not all-displacing ones. Similarly St. Paul, the greatest of all evangelists, having given rise to communities in many leading places of the Roman empire, considers that he has evangelized the whole Roman empire (Rom 15:19). All these indicate that the church is not meant to be an all-comprising community, but a "little flock" (Lk 12:32), as the Lord himself characterized it. This must free us from the self-inflicted guilt feeling that Christianity has failed in Asia due to the small percentage of Christians in Asia and also from any design to convert the whole of Asia into Christianity.

On the other hand the ministry of Jesus himself was not a religious one in the sense of changing the religion of the people. In fact he was a Jew and died as a Jew. Similarly the earliest community even after Pentecost continued to be Jewish (Acts 3:1ff). The break from the parental body probably begins to occur when the new sect begins to admit Gentiles into itself without insisting on the Jewish practices (Acts 15). Our understanding of mission as targeted against the followers of other religions is a later development. For Jesus mission was all that he did and said as the sent one. For Jesus, mission derives its meaning from its source, i.e., as sent by the

Father, and not from the target groups. To realize God's reign was his passion. The major portion of his teaching is about this divine reign; his miracles are symbolic gestures of the realization of it; a major activity of Jesus, the Table Fellowship, is the anticipation and projection of this reign and he teaches his disciples to pray for the realization of it. Jesus is the revelation of the "Good News of the Kingdom" and brings it into being. In his ministry "only the Kingdom is absolute and it makes everything else relative" (EN 8).

The death of Jesus as we said above, was the logical result of his ministry of manifesting the other-centered God. However, neither the cross nor the tomb could contain him and his ministry. The God who sent him and affirmed him at the time of his baptism and later at the transfiguration, raised him up from the dead and thus affirmed his ministry.

The Church's Mission in Bold Humility

The foregoing reflections elucidate the point that Christian mission is neither a triumphant self-proclamation as the only true religion nor a self-assured beauty-contest among religions. Its role, as David Bosch has argued, rather, is a vulnerable one (1992). Fully conscious of how God's salvation reaches all people through their own religions because of the mediation of the Mystery of the Word, the community of the disciples of the Incarnate Word, the church, at the same time, is aware of the formidable demand on itself to re-present what took place in the ministry of its Lord. The awareness that the Lord to whom it witnesses is already present in other cultures and religions even before the church was constituted, makes it humble. On the other hand it has something that it has experienced in the Incarnate Word, which has a universal and definite significance. This makes it bold in witnessing to that experience. Though it is "the little flock," standing under the shadow of the cross, a symbol of weakness and inability to prove itself or force its way, it is sent in the power of the risen Lord (Jn 20:21).

The grammar of Incarnation is not a theory of a doctrinal claim but a praxis, an experience. It is a living relationship or relatedness and communion, without marginalization. The distinctiveness of Christianity is what it has learned from its Lord. He could not save himself, though he saved others. The cross was the sublime manifestation of his service. The missionary character of the cross is precisely because it is from there that Jesus Christ revealed the fundamental character of God: He came not to save himself! Far too long have we been brandishing the cross as the sign of uniqueness and superiority. We have wielded the cross as the sign of the only religion willed by God, thereby taunting the followers of other religions.

Asian Need for Prophets of Humanity

Jürgen Moltmann spoke of "the Crucified God." However, what is closer to the Asian experience is "the crucified people." In Asia people are condemned to suffer on the cross made for them by fellow human beings. This suffering consists of what liberation theology qualifies as "historical suffering" (Sobrino 1994:29), where people are despised, rejected, disrobed of the last thread of human dignity and become utterly defenseless, resulting in a slow death. What is involved in this suffering is the humanity of the human person.

In India nearly 25 per cent of an estimated one billion people have to cope up with the woes of caste and tribal discrimination. Some of them are condemned to carry night soil even to the present, while others are literally chained so that they may not flee from the greedy quarry owners (Prakash 2000:40). We come across cases where judges, supposed to be guardians of the Constitution of India, practicing untouchability to the extent of cleansing the entire court room including the furniture with the Ganga water to get rid of the pollution caused by his predecessor, reportedly hailing form the so-called lower caste (*Times* 2000: 8).

Today these unfortunate dregs of humanity are gradually becoming aware of their rights and have began to clamor for their share in the national resources and decision making. But this birth of enlightenment has added to their woes because it has often met with menacing attitude by the people who traditionally enjoyed the privileges at the expense of the dalits and tribals. It is common knowledge that even the recent attacks on Christians were largely motivated by socio-economic factors (Sarkar 1999: 1691). The rising number of private armies and militias of various hues, all converge on one target, destruction of human beings.

Another sector of anthropological discrimination in South Asia is that of women. Not only baby girls are done away with in some parts of India as soon as they are born by putting a few rice grains into their throats, but even unborn fetuses are not spared if they are found to be female in pre-natal tests. Reports of violence in one form or other against women, have become common feature. Even the state-owned Protection Homes for women sometimes become shelters of shame due to murder, rape and prostitution, making life in them a traumatic experience for the inmates (*Times* August 20, 2000:1).

Imposed poverty and exploitation have made life a hell for a sizable part of the Asian people. Often people with the right connections only can succeed in life. Others are reduced to a culture of silence and helplessness. The powerful keep the poor disenfranchised. The onslaught of globalization has only worsened their lot. Their cry for participation and equal opportunities go unheard.

It is disheartening to realize that in many instances, religions themselves have contributed to the existing woeful situation. Caste and gender discriminations are classical cases in this regard. Further South Asia has become a fertile ground for communal frenzy and religious violence. Mixed with political opportunism, communalism has played havoc in South Asia. Many instances of the ongoing destruction of human lives can be traced to religious bigotry.

With this background, mission in Asia, primarily, is neither an ecclesial question, nor an abstract soteriological one, but basically it is a human question. The need is to find the wholeness of the human person, rather than a new God or a new religion. Human beings are left on the roadside, half-dead, victims of exploitation, discrimination and dispossession. Theirs is a world of filth. It is the ugliest world and the smelliest as well. They spent their entire lives wallowing in filth. Five thousand years of institutionalized social inequality has ensured that certain categories of jobs belong to them. It is their meal ticket to survival. They live in fear: fear of the powerful, fear of hunger, fear of not finding a job for the next day, fear of repression, fear of being thrown out of the encroachment in which they live.

In short what we witness is the vandalization of their humanity beyond description. The greatest debt to be paid to them is the anthropological one. Their bodies are ill treated and their souls are defeated through the refusal to recognize them as human beings equal to the rest. It is in this Asian context that we suggest that the church in Asia has to be prophets of humans than prophets of a new religion or a new god. In fact Asia does not lack a sense of the divine, but a sense for the human! Such a prophetic mission would tie in with the ministry of Jesus which was a good news to the poor (Lk 4: 19).

In the elaborately structured Jewish society where purity-pollution played a leading role, there was a grading of persons according to which some were unfit for cult and to eat with (1 Qumran Sayings 2:3-9). For Jesus this hierarchical structuring of human persons was an evil to be eliminated. His "infamous" table fellowships, described repeatedly in the gospels was a clear challenge to this exclusion of human beings and a demonstration of their unconditional acceptance and inclusion. During one of these table fellowships he admonishes: "when you give a feast, invite the poor, the maimed, the lame, the blind and you will be blessed" (Lk 14:14). All these categories of people were debarred from a Jewish feast.

Commenting on Jesus' association with the outcasts Roger Haight points out: "It seems fairly certain that Jesus directed his attention to people who stood outside the margins of society, and that this was a disturbing factor in his ministry and message for the religiously upright" (1999:106). Through his association with sinners and tax collectors, Jesus became the externalization of the divine in rapport to the human. God's acting in history is primarily manifested through his involvement with those on the margins and the dehumanized.

Every religion has its own originary experience of the Transcendent. The Christian experience is Jesus' experience of God as his intimate parent (Abba) with its counter experience of other humans as brothers and sisters (neighbor). Recent research into biblical world has contoured a Christology of radical theo-centrism with strong feet in humanity. The core of Jesus' ministry is his concern for fellow human beings. Throughout his ministry Jesus manifests that when human beings are accepted and respected as they ought to be, especially those on the periphery, God is honored and God's reign realized (Lk 7: 22-23). Through his ministry Jesus demonstrates that we come to God only though our neighbor.

Jesus encounters God not primarily in temple, scripture or such other classical religious symbols but in human experiences. He begins concretely with the needy and the poor (Lk 4:16ff). He cannot remain indifferent to human suffering. He has come so that all will have life, justice and rights. His mission was a revolt against poverty and an exaltation of human dignity. Only from this perspective of the dignity of the poor can we understand his massage as a good news to the poor. His mission ushers in a family of God's children of free and equal persons.

Hence for the church in Asia the major reason for its existence is to be at the service of the poor and the victims of society so that they can experience the fruits of the arrival of the acceptable year of the Lord. Wherever and whenever artificial dependency is created in social, economic and even in religious fields, for the benefit of the powerful, it ferments dehumanization. If Jesus' main concern was saving people from alienation, marginalization and negation by restoring them to wholeness, church's route cannot be any different. Jesus needs followers for the mediation of God's compassionate love for all who suffer, all those who are oppressed, all those who are forced to the margins. Human suffering has to become the focus of church's mission today. What are to be dismantled today are not so much religious differences as much as the disgusting structures of dehumanization.

Crossing the Religious Borders

By considering itself as absolute, Christianity in the past had no need to cross the borders. When it did, it was only to teach, to give, to save and civilize the world. Church's crossing the borders was only to extend its borders. The church shared the common sentiment of most primal peoples: they were at the center of the world, not only geographically but in every other aspect as well. Each tribe considered itself to be the measure for all. Each group thought also that it was the most favored people of the deity enjoying its special protection and having a special relationship with the deity.

The awakening of the Afro-Asian religions and the resurgent vision of a coexisting peaceful world order, beckoned the church to come out of the self-imposed isolation to enter into dialogue with other religions. Pope Paul VI's *Ecclesiam Suam* was a trailblazer in this direction. Though recessionist forces still hold on to the hope of converting the whole world into the church, with the conviction that the church is the only God-intended religion, most Christians are challenged to a more open attitude to other religions. Theology today is looking for a more unifying human order as opposed to a fragmentative or atomizing one. "All peoples comprise a single community, and have a single origin . . . . One also is their final goal" (NA 1). This is an expansive and broadening view as opposed to a reductionistic one. This in turn enables us to cross the borders in confidence and trust leading to the teleological end of humanity, God's vision for humanity, communion of all.

Each religion must break forth from the prison of its reductionist identity and emerge as a decisive world force, as a manifestation of the Mystery, to meet similar manifestations. Just as the human nature, expressed differently in different cultures can benefit from mutual exposures, so too religions can benefit by crossing of borders of each other. This can lead to a true global religious renascence. What stands on the way to this crossing the borders is the self-imposed narrow sense of identity, either due to exclusivistic claims, or due to the failure to see other religions from a divine perspective. Such a myopic attitude is a sort of self-glorification resulting in paralysis. We have to look forward to a New World order in religions where each one is a receiver as well as a giver.

There should be a migratory space for each religion in the sense that each religion should have the room for encountering other religions and returning to itself enriched. In the macro-religious world where each individual religion stands as part of the unfolding of the Mystery, each one stands to profit by the migration to other similar manifestations of the Mystery. It is also possible that in this temporary migration one or the other decides to settle down permanently in the newfound religious space! This need not be looked up on as a perversion or a betrayal. What is important is the freedom for each one to choose his or her own religion. "No state or group has the right to control either directly or indirectly a person's religious conviction, nor can it justifiably claim the right to impose or impede the public profession and practice of religion or the respectful appeal of a particular religion to people's free conscience" (John Paul II 1999: 885).

The mind-boggling technological progress and the accompanying communication wonders have compressed space and time in such degrees that today we are said to be living in a globalized village. This globalization must facilitate a global encounter of religions, leading to mutual fecundation and mutual atonement of the various inter-religious wars and scars they have inscribed. Thus Pope John Paul II took the right step in asking pardon for the past sins of the Catholic church against other religions (2000:1). Only such encounter of religions can fulfil the roles of religions in the global village, in the converging global human family. Both eastern and western religions can learn from each other.

In fact this self-exposure, self-transcendence is constitutive to the self-realization of our radically interrelated world. David Tracy aptly describes the situation:

> The Christian focus on the event of Jesus Christ discloses the always-already, not-yet reality of grace. That grace, when reflected upon, unfolds its fuller meaning into the ordered relationships of the God who is love, the world that is beloved and a self gifted and commanded to become loving. With the self-respect of that self-identity, the Christian should be released to the self-transcendence of genuine other-regard by a willing self-exposure to and in the contemporary situation (1981:446).

Crossing the Borders and Intereligious Dialogue

The mono-logical character of the past theological paradigm based on the assumption that other religions have no salvific significance must give way to inter-faith dialogue leading to a sharing, "in the framework of complimentarity and harmony" (EA 6). Our very theology must evolve out of the context of crossing the religious borders. Vatican II initiated a truly positive evaluation of the world's religions. The Council spoke of the possibility of revelation (DV 3) and salvation (NA 1, GS 22) in other religions. Today the church is perceived as a threat to other religions. This is an abnormality in so far as every religion comes under the protection of the divine providence (Amos 9:7). The church's true vocation is the continuation of the work of Jesus of Nazareth, who was Emmanuel God with us. The church is the mystery of God's presence on earth (LG 5, 8).

In the New Testament, and more so in the fourth gospel, we come across three moments or dimensions of Christology. We have the pre-existent Word, the Incarnate Word and the exalted Lord. Though the Mystery is one and the same, the roles of each of these dimensions, like the persons in the Blessed Trinity, cannot be interchanged or confused. Nor does one delete or displace the other. The church realizes that while it is the continuation of the ministry of the Incarnate Word, other religions have their origin from the pre-existent Word. It is this faith that spurs the church to cross its borders for dialogue with the followers of other religions.

Interreligious dialogue is any activity in which we take the faith of the other seriously. Our commitment to Jesus Christ reminds us that our obligation is not just to Christianity but to God who reveals God's self in Christ through us. Being preoccupied only with Christianity is introvertedness. Hence we are challenged to enter into a new historical involvement through cooperation with the followers of other religions. Our ministry of witness among people of other faiths presupposes our presence with them with sensitivity to their deepest faith commitment and experience. It entails also our willingness to be their servants for Christ's sake, affirming what God has done and is doing among them. This is to be done with love for them. In this process of dialogue we witness to Jesus Christ. For as John Paul II said at Delhi, while addressing the religious leaders, "to wage war in the name of religions is a blatant contradiction. Religious leaders in particular have the duty to do everything possible to ensure that religion is what God intends it to be: a source of goodness, respect, harmony and peace" (1999:885).

Although we do not understand, nor approve of all what others think or say, we still hope that human conviviality makes sense, that we belong together and together we must strive. For, as GS puts it: "The joys and hopes, the griefs and the anxieties of the people of this age, especially those who are poor or in any way afflicted, these too are the joys and hopes, the griefs and anxieties of the followers of Christ. Indeed, nothing genuinely human fails to raise an echo in their hearts" (1).

Through dialogue Christians and the followers of other religions turn to each other in trust and openness, overcoming mutual prejudices. And together they turn to God. In this process there is room also for growth in the understanding and experience of the divine. This is described as the growth in Truth. However it has to be emphasized that this process of growth in Truth, is not aimed at a change of religion from either side, but together they turn to God with greater commitment and to each other with deeper acceptance and respect.

Interreligious dialogue, we said, is any activity where people of different faiths collaborate. Hence dialogue should not be interpreted as an activity pertaining to religious matters alone. It is to the merit of Aloysius Pieris to have pointed out that interreligious dialogue cannot remain imprisoned in the ivory towers of religious talks and religious experience alone, but must flow into human liberation. In the context of massive poverty and the religiosity of the masses, the Asian church must weave a new way of being church in Asia by a symbiosis of a two-fold praxis: i.e., liberation praxis with a praxis of inter religious dialogue (1980:75-95). Similarly Paul Knitter insists that inter religious dialogue must flow into dialogue with the suffering including the suffering of the earth. The religious other and the suffering other are the two partners with whom the church must carry on its mission of dialogue (1995:18).

Interreligious dialogue, seeking true communion, cannot be blind to the reality next door-- one of starvation, dehumanizing living conditions, injustice and ecological deterioration. In the context of Asia, I would suggest that what must bring the followers of different religions together, is this suffering rather than a God search. God is to be found in finding solutions to the suffering. Thus interreligious dialogue in Asia can be described as a search for the restoration of lost human dignity. A dialogue that is unconcerned about the suffering other, would be equivalent to cleaning our compound only to dump the dirt on the neighbor's compound. It will remain a hollow exercise.

Servant of the Kingdom

We have seen how the Kingdom, the reality of God's reign, was the core of Jesus ministry. In fact Jesus was not interested in God as such but in God's relation to humans and in the realization of God's will with regard to the human situation. Hence when the disciples of John the Baptist approach him asking if he were indeed the Messiah, he replies to them by asking them to go and tell John what they actually saw and heard: the divine reign has come in him (Mt 11:4-5). By actualizing the divine Reign Jesus becomes God-with us, Emmanuel. That was the purpose for which he was sent: "My food is to do the will of the Father who sent me and to accomplish his work" (Jn 4:34).

In so far as the church has experienced the Kingdom in the ministry of Jesus Christ and it has been constituted and sent to continue this ministry, the church is the servant of the Kingdom to the followers of other religions. However the effectiveness of this service depends on how far it is transparent to its vocation by being faithful to Jesus Christ. To the extent it is a human community it is not the fulfillment or fullness of the Kingdom. The fullness is an eschatological reality towards which the church pilgrimages along with the followers of other religions.

In this pilgrimage the church is conscious how the other religions, in so far as the Word is active in them, also share in the elements of the Kingdom. Through its faith Christianity perceives its relation to other religions and is duty bound to enter into rapport with them. Therefore the church must collaborate with them in its mission of realizing the Kingdom. The church can not only enrich other religions but can also learn from them in so far as the Word is operative in them.

Evangelization is not the same thing as convert-making. It is bringing the full force of the gospel to a particular culture and transforming it from within (EN 20). In the process it effects a conversion both of the evangelizer and the evangelized. It is serving the world by helping it to be conformed to the divine design for the world. Jesus' concern for the divine reign frequently brought him in conflict with the Jewish authorities for whom the blind observance of the law was all that mattered. Hence Jesus spoke of his message as that of a sword and fire (Mt 10:34). His prophetic mission was not one of submission to the existing dehumanizing values nor compromising with selfishness but confronting them to effect justice to the poor. The Incarnation is claiming the dignity of the human person and of the earth. Through his "self-emptying" the Word becomes flesh, thereby affirming the human person and matter. Hence Vatican II declares: "The proposals of this Council are intended for all people . . ., to make the world conform better to the surpassing dignity of humans, to strive for a more deeply rooted sense of universal brotherhood/sisterhood, and to meet the pressing appeals of our times with a generous and common effort of love" (GS 91).

From what has been said it should not be construed that the church in Asia is not interested in forming new communities of faith. In the ministry of Jesus, the message of the Kingdom is accompanied by the formation of a community (Mk 1:14ff), as the servant of the Kingdom. After the resurrection the disciples are sent to form communities of disciples in every *ethne* (Mt 28:19). Asia always had appreciation of Jesus Christ. Many will be attracted by our Christian life and they will desire to commit themselves fully to the Lord in the community. Such a mission takes place in the climate of good will and collaboration. Even when the church seeks new members, it is primarily for continuing the mission of Jesus Christ. The church is for mission, not mission for the church.

Concluding Remarks

The foregoing discussion enables us to look for a new focus of mission in Asia without denying the significance of the Pascal Mystery. In Asia we can return to the ministry of *Jesus of Nazareth,* a title used nineteen times in the New Testament, thus insisting on the historical character of his mission. What Asia likes in Jesus is his compassion. This compassion can make the church in Asia weak and powerless with those who are weak and powerless. But it is a compassion that stands against injustices and exploitation. It is a compassion that works to restore human wholeness.

Asian missiology evolves from the interpretation of the gospels in the light of the social, economic and religious context of Asia. Evangelization in Asia is not primarily a matter of geography and numbers but "affecting and upsetting through the power of the gospel (Asia's) criteria of judgement, determining values, points of interests, lines of thought, sources of inspiration and models of life, which are in contrast with the Word of God and the plan of salvation" (EN 19).

References

Bosch, David J.
   1992   "The Vulnerability of Mission," *Vidyajoyti*. 56: 577-596.
Goldsworthy, Graeme
   1987   *Gospel and Wisdom*. Lanver: Pater Noster.
Haight, Roger
   1999   *Jesus Symbol of God*. Maryknoll, NY: Orbis Books.
John Paul II
   1999   "Address to the Religious Leaders," *Vidyajyoti*. 63. 12: 885-
           86.
John Paul II
   2000   *L'Osservatore Romano* (English edition). March, 12: 1.
Knitter, Paul
   1995   *One Earth Many Religions*. Maryknoll, NY: Orbis Books.
Pieris, Aloysius
   1980   "Towards an Asian Theology of Liberation." In Virginia
           Fabella, ed. *Asia's Struggle for Full Humanity*. Maryknoll, NY:
           Orbis Books. Pp. 75-95.
Prakash, Soorya
   2000   "Life in Chains." *The Week* (July 9): 40-42.
Sarkar, Sunit
   1999   "Conversions and Politics of Hindu Right." *Economic &
           Political Weekly* (June 26): 1691-1700.
Sobrino Jon
   1994   *The Principle of Mercy*. Maryknoll, NY: Orbis Books.
Times of India
   2000   (September 18): 9.
Times of India
   2000   (August 20): 1.
Tracy David
   1981   *The Analogical Imagination*. London: SCM.

MISSIO AD GENTES:
An Asian Way of Mission Today

Leo Kleden, SVD*

"From the Depth I Cry To You"

It was early December 1997. I was invited to be a facilitator in a training session for human rights activists in East Timor. There were twenty-four participants. During the first three days the interaction process was very difficult. There was too much feeling of anger, resentment, suspicion and woundedness--all of which blocked the process. So one of my colleagues asked if I could lead a prayer service and sharing where the participants could express their traumatic feelings. In the evening we gathered in a small chapel. All of us sat on the floor in a circle. In the middle we lit a candle. It was an Advent candle. We read the beautiful text of Isaiah 35 which announced the coming of the Lord to save God's people. We also read Isaiah 65:17-25 about the new heavens and new earth. Then I asked the participants to share. Several of them talked and we listened. Then a woman, a very thin woman, stood up, walked to the middle, sat beside the candle and told us a long story of suffering. Her name was Alexandrina. We called her Adina.

When she was about 6 years old her parents were arrested by the Indonesian soldiers. Since then she had never seen them again. Some eyewitness said that they were shot in the forest. Adina was left behind with her elder brother who had joined the Fretelin freedom fighters struggling for the independence of East Timor. Some years later her brother was captured by the Indonesian soldiers.

Leo Kleden, SVD, from Indonesia, is a member of the General Council of the Society of the Divine Word.

*They tortured him, cut off his penis, and let him slowly die
a horrible death. Adina wept bitterly over the death of her
only brother, but she swore to herself to continue the
struggle. When Adina was in senior high school, the
military arrested her while she was giving food to a young
man who came to the village. They accused her of being a
collaborator of Fretelin. They tortured her until she was
half conscious, and then raped her.*

*At this point Adina could not continue her story.
Tears filled our eyes. There was a long silence in the
chapel. I do not know for how long, but it seemed like
ages. Then Adina gathered all her strength, see looked at
me and said in a faint voice: "Father, where is that
salvation promised by the Lord?" Again there was silence.
I could not answer her question. Tears flowed. Slowly I
raised my eyes and saw a wooden cross on the wall. I saw
it and understood the solidarity of the Crucified One, but
I could not utter a single word. Adina needed my
solidarity, not my word. For several years I have been
living with her question.*

Introduction

First of all I would like to thank the conveners for inviting me to
speak about *missio ad gentes* from an Asian perspective. Let me say from
the very beginning that I am not a missiologist by profession. I am a member
of a missionary congregation which is involved in missionary work and
reflection. The conveners could have invited some well-known missiologist
to give a better theological presentation. But they preferred instead to invite
somebody else to give information and reflection about mission from a less
known corner of the church, from Indonesia. Let me start by clarifying some
presuppositions implied in the title chosen for this presentation: *"Missio Ad
Gentes*: An Asian Way of Mission Today."

Mission

There are different paradigms used in speaking about mission. The
model used in this presentation is the paradigm of the Reign of God. Mission
is first of all *"missio Dei"* (RM 12-20). God's self-communication and
saving act which stretches from creation to new creation. The mission of the

church is a participation in this saving act of the Triune God, namely in the love of the Father made known in Christ Jesus through the power of the Holy Spirit (AG 2). Since Vatican II we have become more aware that the Reign of God is a reality deeper and more extensive than the church (LG 5). The church's mission is nothing else than giving witness to the Reign of God, to its universality and openness, which embraces all humanity i.e. all nations and cultures throughout the history. As a sacrament of salvation in God's hand the church can no longer claim that it monopolizes the whole truth and salvation as it once did. Once we acknowledge that the Reign of God is greater than the church, then we become more open to recognize what God has done to different peoples, in various cultures and religions. The first act of mission is, therefore, listening with full respect to what God has done to others. This kind of awareness will certainly influence and transform our way of mission.

"Ad Gentes"

When we speak about *"missio ad gentes"* in our time, who are supposed to be the *gentes*, the addressees of Church's mission today? At a certain period of history when the missionaries were urged by zeal and conviction that *"extra ecclesiam nulla salus,"* then *gentes* meant all those people who did not belong to the church, who were supposed to live in the darkness of sin and incredulity and who were therefore destined to perdition. But our understanding of mission has radically changed. We realize that God's saving act has been present and continuous to be present throughout history, in various cultures and religions of all peoples (RM 28-29).

Two things are implied in the proposition that the reality of God's Reign is deeper and greater than the church. On the one hand we believe that the Reign of God is actively present within the church but is not identical with the church. There are elements within the church which are contrary to the values of the God's Reign and therefore need purification and redemption. On the other hand we acknowledge that people of different faith communities, of different cultures and religions in one way or another have experienced the saving act of God. Of course they are also in need of full redemption and ultimate salvation. Mission is no longer a one-way traffic. We as Christians give witness to the Reign according to our faith-experience of God, but others too give witness to saving act of God in their midst.

With regard to the church can we still speak about her *missio ad gentes?* Yes, but with a significant qualification! *Gentes* are people who do not belong to the Christian community but they are not outside of God's loving embrace. As we Christians give witness and proclaim the Reign of God to the *gentes*, they also tell us about their own faith-experience of God. Understood in this way *missio ad gentes* is at the same time *missio de gentibus*. The Hindus, the Buddhists, the Moslems, the Confucians, the followers of Tao, the adherents of cosmic religions, the humanists and others can share with us their faith-experience of God and the fundamental values of their life. Mission requires as its prerequisite our readiness to listen to others and a sincere openness to share our faith with them. In the ideal cases where people of different faith communities work together in our common struggle for justice, peace, solidarity, reconciliation, love (to name some values of God's Reign) in order to build a greater communion of the scattered children of God (Jn 11:52), then *missio ad gentes* is *missio cum gentibus*.

Asia

Asia is a name for a pluralistic reality. It is home to nearly two third of the world's population with their different cultures, languages, customs, beliefs, traditions, social structures, political systems. It is impossible to characterize Asian peoples in general with the same cultural or social category. If, for instance, one describes Asian peoples using socio-cultural characteristics like "tolerance," "complementarity and harmony,"[1] another can easily contradict this statement by showing that the bloodiest ethnic and religious conflicts have been occurring all the time in different parts of Asia. The political panorama in Asia is also highly complex, ranging from democratic systems to military dictatorships, from secular models to theocratic governments. From the socio-economic point of view we find in this continent a whole range of social classes with an enormous gap between the poorest of the poor to the richest of the rich. Related to this social gap is the problem of population growth, urbanization, migration, the global market economy, malnutrition and hunger (to mention only a few). The reality of the poor in Asia remains a great challenge for humanity and a criticism to all our theology and ideology.

Asia is also the cradle of the world's major religions and spiritual traditions: Hinduism, Buddhism, Taoism, Confucianism, Judaism, Christianity, Islam, Shintoism, Zoroastrianism, Jainism, Sikhism. Christianity in Asia is a very tiny minority living among the people of other faith communities. With the exception of the Philippines, the church in Asia is the church in diaspora.[2] These small communities in diaspora have experienced many tensions, conflicts and persecutions, but they have also learned how to live peacefully with other faith communities, practicing a concrete "dialogue of life" with others for the common good of the whole society.

This sketchy picture should be enough to remind us that Asia is very pluralistic. And this pluralism is aggravated further by the contemporary post-modern condition, where, for some people at least : "Truth, humanitarianism, and justice now exist only in the plural. Therefore there is no longer a universal and definitively valid religion."[3] This is a great challenge for mission in Asia and indeed for the mission of the whole Church.

Given such a pluralistic situation, it is more reasonable that I start from the mission experience of the Catholic Church in my own country as part of the Asian experience and then refer from time to time to some similar experiences in other Asian countries.

Mission in Indonesia: A Short Historical Note [4]

When the Portuguese and Spanish sailors went to the East in the fifteenth and sixteenth centuries in search of spices, some Catholic missionaries came along with them. The most famous of them was St. Francis Xavier, who worked in India, Malaysia and Indonesia (in the Moluccas Islands) before sailing north to Japan. Portuguese missionaries established some Christian communities on the islands of Flores, Timor, and the Moluccas. In the early seventeenth century, however, Dutch colonialists took over the Indonesian archipelago from the Portuguese. They were Calvinists, and according to the reigning principle in Europe at that time, *"cuius regio, illius religio,"* they banned Catholicism for about two hundred years. Only Protestant missionaries were allowed to come in this period. After the declaration of religious freedom in Europe as one of the consequences of the French Revolution, Catholic missionaries were able to come again at the beginning of the nineteenth century. When these missionaries arrived on the island of Flores, they were astonished to discover that the Catholic faith was still alive. In a small town of Larantuka people continued to tell the stories from the Bible from generation to generation and they prayed the rosary in Portuguese. By telling biblical stories (with imaginative additions) and praying the rosary they managed to keep the Catholic faith alive.

In general, however, the Catholic communities in Indonesia were established only in the twentieth century. The Catholic Church, therefore, in Indonesia is still very young. Of the 210 million people of Indonesia at this time Catholics are about 3.5 per cent, Christians of various denominations 6.5 per cent, Islam 87 per cent (the largest Muslim population in the world). The rest are Hindus (in Bali), Buddhists, and Confucianists.

From 1850 onwards many Catholic missionaries came from Europe, worked, and even dedicated their whole lives for people in many islands of Indonesia. Their names remain alive in the heart of the people. In 1978, however, the Indonesian government took a drastic measure to ban foreign missionaries. Astonishingly, since then more and more young people, men and women, joined religious and missionary congregations. To give one example: In the missionary congregation of the Society of the Divine Word (SVD), whose members today are working in sixty-two countries, Indonesian members constitute about 22 per cent of the entire Congregation. Together with their confreres from India, Philippines, Japan, China, Vietnam, Asian SVD members constitute about 50 per cent. There are many vocations for other religious congregations as well. So it is almost a paradoxical situation that from Asia where Christianity is a tiny minority come so many religious vocations. Besides these missionaries who belong to religious congregations there are also many lay missionaries who work as catechists, teachers, social workers, and pastoral assistants.

If we now compare the situation of European missionary pioneers who came to Indonesia and contemporary Asian missionaries who are sent to work in other countries, including in Europe and Americas, we can see a significant difference. In general terms we may say that European missionaries came to Indonesia from a position of superiority. First of all, political superiority: they came from a colonizing country to a colonized country. This fact alone gave them a certain powerful status and authority. This authority was further assured by a special commission by the highest church hierarchy for "*plantatio ecclesiae*" in the colonized region. They also enjoyed protection and certain privileges granted to them by colonial government. This does not mean that they always supported or collaborated with the colonial government. On the contrary! In the case of Indonesia they often stood at the side of the local people, learned local languages and cultures, promoted education through schools, improved health care, and defended the rights of the indigenous people.

Secondly, cultural superiority. They came from a developed country to the so-called underdeveloped country. And as children of their epoch they assumed that the western model of modern civilization was the ideal model for humanity. For this reason they built schools, centers of training and education using the standard and curriculum of Europe. They were also financially supported by Christian communities in their home countries for many social projects.

Thirdly, religious superiority. The missionary pioneers from Europe knew very well that they were commissioned by the hierarchy in the name of the Lord in order to preach the Gospel, to baptize people and to make them members of the church, and thus bring salvation to those who lived in the darkness of sin and unbelief. Inspired by the conviction that there was no salvation outside the church, they dedicated their life to this missionary goal with vigor and militancy. Closely connected to this feeling of religious superiority was the monolithic model of theology in the Catholic Church, with the assumption that the truth of the Christian faith had been formulated once and for all in the dogmas taught by the magisterium. The missionaries then knew exactly what they had to preach to others. They learned the local language and culture in order to convey the Christian doctrine which had been formulated. Due to this conviction of religious superiority they tended to disregard and sometimes even destroyed mythic-religious elements of the traditional religions.

Now the mission situation has changed. In the last twenty years the former mission countries like India, Philippines, Indonesia have become mission-sending countries, while Europe has come to be seen as a new mission continent as well. Or to put it more exactly: The "locus" of mission nowadays is understood no longer so much in terms of geographical territory as in terms of specific missionary situations which can be found anywhere, in all the continents.[5] Can we imagine what happens when missionaries from the small island of Flores in Indonesia, from Bohol in the Philippines, or from Tamilnadu in India are sent to work in Europe or the Americas? What kind of superiority do they have? Nothing. They seem to go empty handed. And the situation has become much more difficult for them because we are now living in a pluralistic world where the monolithic model of theology has been abandoned. The very fact that they are sent empty handed is their weakness and their strength at the same time. Did not Jesus send his first disciples empty handed? This new situation characterizes the Asian way of mission.

An Asian Way of Mission

During the 14th General Chapter of the Divine Word Missionaries in Nemi, Rome, 1994, a European confrere raised the following question to the capitulars from the Asia-Pacific Zone: "As the majority of our membership is shifting from Europe to Asia, how do you give an Asian face and an Asian spirit to our mission?" This was an important question and it remains very significant. On many occasions we have been reflecting, sharing, discussing about this. What I am going to present here is the result of this common process of reflection among our missionaries in the Asia-Pacific zone and further in the SVD General Chapter.[6]

Dialogue As The Way of Mission

Christianity in Asia comprises about 3 per cent of the whole population. If we take out the Philippines as an exceptional case then Christians are only about 1.2 per cent. This is really a very small minority scattered among billions of people of other religions and convictions. This experience of living as tiny groups in diaspora cannot but teach Christians in Asia how to live with others. Many a time there have been conflicts, tensions, persecutions. And yet each time Christians learn how to survive, how to interact and to live side by side with other faith communities. More than that, they have also positive experience of meeting many good people of other faith, people with spiritual wisdom and authentic religiosity. This kind of encounter teaches them something about dialogue in a very concrete way. Long before the Federation of Asian Bishops' Conferences (FABC) began to speak officially about the threefold dialogue,[7] people had already learned how to dialogue through their actions and life.

Dialogue presupposes two things. On the subjective level it presupposes that I respect the other person as a subject with autonomy and freedom as myself. From this perspective dialogue is the basic attitude of respectful listening to others and of openness to communicate oneself to others. On the objective level it presupposes that every person and every human community has some valuable experience of the ultimate meaning of life which they can share with others. If I from my part am convinced that I can share my faith or my experience of the ultimate meaning of life in God with others, I must be prepared to listen to the others as well. The ultimate Truth is always greater than my own experience and knowledge, and no one, no institution, can claim to possess the whole truth. Understood as basic attitude of being open to others, dialogue is the only viable way of mission.

Two objections can be raised. (In fact these objections were already raised during an international meeting of missionaries). The first objection says that there is a priority of preaching the Good News. In other words, we have to *proclaim* the gospel first and *then* dialogue. It seems to me that this objection tends to reduce the meaning of dialogue to discussion. If, as we said, dialogue is the basic attitude of being open to others, then dialogue does not contradict the proclamation of the gospel at all. What is necessary is that we proclaim the Good News in a dialogical way, not primarily by words but by our life. As St. Francis of Assisi is credited with saying: "Preach always; if necessary use words." If God respects human freedom in response to the offer of salvation, how can we pretend to proclaim the Good News without respecting the others or without listening to their experience?

The second objection says: "You cannot dialogue with the oppressors." If this were true, what would be the alternative? Either you submit yourselves to the oppression (which is an immoral act) or you take arms to kill the oppressors, which means using violence against violence. I believe that we ought to dialogue even with the oppressors in order to break the circle of violence. In politics we have some shining examples of people like Mahatma Gandhi, Martin Luther King, Aung San Suu Kyi, Nelson Mandela. Their lives have become a prophetic affirmation that only dialogue can transform the vicious circle of violence into a virtuous circle of justice, forgiveness, reconciliation and peace. Dialogue is another name for the gospel message and appeal to love even your enemy.

The Christian attitude of dialogue in mission is more appropriately expressed in terms of "prophetic dialogue."[8] A prophet listens and proclaims the Word of God. In the proclamation of the Word, the prophet also criticizes injustice and evil elements in society which are contrary to the will of God, with the consequence that the prophet might undergo persecution and suffering. The same is true with dialogue in mission. What we are supposed to do is to listen, follow, witness and proclaim the Word of God. However, since we believe that God has spoken also to other peoples of other cultures and religions, mission means first of all listening to the Word of God coming to me through others. I let myself be addressed, be enriched, criticized and purified from my ideological and idolatrous attitude in the encounter with others. On the other hand, as far as I understand and am inspired by the Word of God coming to me through gospel within the Christian community, I share the richness of my faith-experience, I criticize the injustice and all evil elements in culture and society which enslave people, which are contrary to the will of God. At this point prophetic dialogue in mission has a risky side. It is possible that a missionary, like a prophet, has to undergo persecution and martyrdom because of his or her mission.

Who are the addressers and the addressees of mission dialogue? If the church is missionary by its nature, then every Christian community is the addresser of mission. However, within the Christian communities there are people who in a very special way dedicate themselves to mission and therefore are called missionaries. These people are sent in the name of the

Lord by the Christian communities and they in turn remind Christian communities of their missionary call. The missionaries are the addressers of mission par excellence. However, if mission is a dialogical process, then every addresser is at the same time an addressee and vice versa.

We need further to clarify the addressees or our partners in *missio ad gentes*. For many years FABC has spoken about the threefold dialogue, namely dialogue with people of other cultures, with people of different religions and with the poor. Recently, however, the Divine Word Missionaries added another aspect and so speak of a "fourfold prophetic dialogue."[9]

The first aspect is dialogue with faith seekers and people who have no faith community. In our contemporary world there are more and more people who do not belong to any faith community. In France, for instance, 47 per cent of the population describe themselves as a-religious or atheists; in Germany 38 per cent.[10] (I do not know the statistical data about the situation in Asia, but I presume that in Mainland China many people have been estranged from any faith community). In mission we reach out to all these people through our life and service, giving witness to the Reign of God's love. If they respond with interest, we welcome them to become members of our Christian communities and the followers of Jesus. We have to remember, however, that for missionaries from Asia working in Europe it is much more difficult to reach out to those new a-religious people in the post-Christian era. These people may criticize the Church and challenge us to live our faith more authentically. We need to listen to them because, as Ricoeùr has shown, even atheists can help to purify our faith if we take an appropriate attitude towards their criticism.[11]

The second aspect is dialogue with the poor and marginalized. In many parts of Asia Christians live among a great mass of very poor people. Mission among the poor means being in solidarity with them, participating in their life and their struggle for a more just and humane society. From their part the poor offer us an opportunity to undergo a radical conversion. As Pieris puts it: "The poor (the destitute, the dispossessed, the displaced and the discriminated) who form the bulk of Asian peoples, plus their specific brand of cosmic religiosity constitute a school where many Christian activists re-educate themselves in the art of speaking the language of God's reign, which is the language of liberation which God speaks through Jesus. Neither the academic nor the pastoral magisterium is conversant with this evangelical idiom."[12]

Third, there is dialogue with people of different cultures. The main issue in the dialogue with people of different cultures is the inculturation of the Gospel and the evangelization of culture, which are two aspects of the same missionary dialogue. For many centuries in the Catholic Church the universality (catholicity) of the church tended to be identified with the uniformity of doctrines (formulated in dogmas), of rites and laws. Only after the Vatican II has there been a great movement of inculturation in order to "incarnate" the gospel message into different languages and cultures. People now listen to the gospel in their own language, they sing and dance and celebrate their life of faith according to their own culture. The inculturation of theology is more difficult. It is a long-term project. Only from the authentic praxis of faith can follow a local and original theological reflection because theology is nothing else but a critical reflection on our life of faith.

How can we now envisage the relation between the particularity of the local church and the catholicity of the universal church? First of all, I assume that what we call "universal Church" is the *ecclesia ecclesiarum*, the communion of Christian communities in the Lord. I propose therefore to use the paradigm of art in order to better understand the relation between particularity and universality. In the case of art if somebody simply copies the work of another artist, he or she is not a real artist but an epigon. It is a paradoxical truth of art that the more unique and original a work of art is, the more universal value it has. I think the same thing can be said about the particularity and universality of the church. The more authentic and original the life of faith in the local churches, the more universal (catholic) value can it contribute to the communion of the church. If, however, the local church simply imitates what is done in Rome, then it is an imitation church, not yet an authentic church rooted in the local soil.

On the other hand, every culture contains the elements of alienation, the elements which enslave people and which do not promote the well-being of humanity. The message of the gospel is, therefore, a prophetic criticism and spiritual contribution to the life of a particular culture so that culture may become the celebration of human life before God.

Fourth and finally, we may speak of dialogue with people of other religions. All great religions teach about justice, peace, solidarity, compassion, love. And yet we have learned from history that there has been a lot of enmity, hatred, conflicts, and wars among people of different religions. Many factors (social, political, racial etc) may play their role in provoking such conflicts. But from religious point of view, the main reason is because the adherents of religion tend to absolutize it as if it possesses the whole truth and salvation. If we acknowledge that the Reign of God is greater than any religion and that other people in one way or another have experienced the love of God, then we would be more open to dialogue and collaboration.

Inter-religious dialogue can take various forms which together may constitute a "virtuous circle." The first form is dialogue of life where people of various religions live together in the same society with tolerance and respect for each other. Secondly, through dialogue of action they collaborate on some concrete projects such as helping the victims of natural disaster, promoting human rights, improving education for poor children and so on. Thirdly, people of different religions can also pray together and share their faith. To give one example: After the big riot in Jakarta, May 13-15, 1998, where 1190 people were killed, women activists of different religions (Islam, Christian, Hinduism, Buddhism) organized several prayer meetings where they openly denounced the act of violence and prayed together for justice, reconciliation and peace in a wounded nation. Finally there can be dialogue on the theological or doctrinal level. Here very often we have institutional obstacles. For this reason a group of Islamic, Christian, Hindu and Buddhist theologians in Indonesia formed a forum of interfaith dialogue, where each participant is supposed to speak from his or her own personal reflection without officially representing any institution.

Dialogue of life and action paves the way for theological dialogue. In its turn theological dialogue should enlighten and promote dialogue of life and action. Through creative inter-religious dialogue we may hope that people of various religious traditions can work together for a new spirituality which can inspire human beings in a post-modern world.

Mission from the Position of Weakness

In comparison to the former missionaries from Europe, the Asian missionaries today seem to be sent empty handed. This fact is their weakness and it should be their strength as well.

First of all, it is their weakness. Many of them come from a rural background with their cultural heritage in the pre-modern worldview. But very soon they enter into the modern world through education and schools. Now they are further confronted with the post-modern condition. They live in tensions between three worldviews which are not easy to harmonize. These missionaries need much more time than their predecessors not simply to learn another language and culture but also to orient themselves within the tensions and conflicts between those worldviews.

And what can they concretely do in their mission? We know that former missionaries preached the gospel, taught catechism, and baptized people; but they were also actively involved in education, health care, and in promoting social and economic development. All these were considered integral part of their mission. Today many of these jobs have been taken over by the state or secular institutions. When new missionaries are sent from Asia to Europe or America they cannot get involved in these fields. Even in teaching catechism or preaching many local people can do better than they.

From the religious perspective, former missionaries went to the countries where mythic-religious values were still predominant, whereas new missionaries are thrown into secularistic society. It is much more difficult to preach the gospel in the post-Christian situation.

On the other hand, this kind of weakness can and should be the strength of the new missionaries. Here is a golden opportunity to follow the example of the first disciples of Jesus who were sent empty handed but who were inspired by the Spirit of the Crucified and Risen Lord. The empty handed approach is therefore possible if their heart is full of faith, with the willingness to serve others as the Lord Jesus. Through the Spirit of the Lord human weakness (in socio-political sense) is transformed into evangelical *kenosis*. This approach becomes efficacious and fruitful on two preconditions. First, it presupposes that the missionaries believe in the people to whom they are sent. If you have nothing in your hand, and if you do not have any kind of superiority, then you have to rely on the people to whom you are sent. Missionaries are expected to work not simply for the people (from a position of superiority), but to work with the people. Above all, this approach presupposes that missionaries believe in the One who calls and sends them. "I am with you always to the end of time" (Mt 28:20).

Mission from a Contemplative Presence

The rabbis in Israel, the Gurus in Hindu and Buddhist traditions, the spiritual leaders in the Islamic *pesantren* in Indonesia, do not teach their disciples like modern teachers or professors in the classroom. They attract their followers by their life before inspiring them with their wisdom. Actually this is what happened with Jesus and his disciples and later with the spiritual and religious movements in the history of the church. Now if missionaries have nothing in their hands, then they have to carry out their mission from a contemplative presence. By contemplation we do not mean simply a method of prayer or meditation. Contemplation means living in intimate union with God. Since missionaries have to witness to the Reign and to proclaim the Word of God, they need first of all to experience the presence of God in their lives and listen to the Word addressed to them through the Bible and through others. Every authentic mission flows from contemplation, just as every poetic word is born out of silence. Mission without contemplation would be empty; contemplation without mission would be lame and mute.

Mission and contemplation are two fundamental aspects of Christian life. Hence those who live in the contemplative orders are called to be missionaries in silence like Theresa of Lisieux. Whereas missionaries who are actively working with people have to practice a *"contemplatio in via"* like Theresa of Calcutta.

Although what has been said is valid for all Christians, its urgency is felt all the more by those who are carrying their mission from the position of weakness.

We may express the same thing by using other terminologies, like "passing over" and "communion." Christian life is rooted in the communion with the Triune God and with our brothers and sisters within our small communities. Mission is passing-over to people of other cultures, other social classes, other religions and convictions in order to gather the scattered children of God into a greater and deeper communion.

Mission that Needs a Narrative Theology

Until now in many countries in Asia moral and religious values are told in myths and stories. The revelation of God's Word in the Bible is also given in a narrative. Of course there are many literary genres in the Bible. But all the commandments, prohibitions, laws, prayers and others are comprehensible only within the narrative of God's salvation.

For many centuries theology in the Catholic Church in the West has been formulated in dogmatic theology, that is a critical and systematic formulation of faith according to a certain philosophical framework. The advantage of dogmatic theology is that the content of our faith is formulated in a clear and rational way. The disadvantage is that people tend to identify the Word of God with dogmatic contents and thereby reduce the inexhaustible richness of the Word to a certain formulation.

Contemporary hermeneutics and exegesis tell us that the Word of God in the Bible is much richer than any dogmatic content that can be drawn from the biblical text. Christian message is first of all not a doctrine but a narrative of God's saving act, be it in the Exodus or in the story of life, death, and resurrection of Christ. All doctrines are to be understood in relation to the narrative. But every narrative is open to a multiple interpretation. It is in the process of interpretation that a story is decontextualized and recontextualized again and again. The living Word of

God is thus reincarnated every time a believing community reads the Bible, appropriates its meaning for itself and puts it into practice in everyday life.

Narrative is all the more important because, as Ricoeur and others have shown, the identity of a person and that of a human community is a narrative identity.[13] Christians read the story of the gospel and interpret their lives in the light of the gospel story, and then they weave the story of their life according to the model of the gospel.

Narrative has another advantage in comparison to dogmatic formulation. If dogmas tend to impose one theological framework on all and therefore is monolithic, narrative, on the contrary, tends to hold the creative tension between unity and plurality. The unity of the same story remains but every time it is understood in a different way, by a different people in a different context.

I started this presentation by telling the story of Adina. There is an endless number of stories of like this; the stories of the poor, the marginalized, and suffering people in Asia, Africa and else where. Missionaries have to listen to these stories, interpret them within the light of the gospel narrative, and help transform human tragedy into the Good News of salvation.

Liberation and Communion in the Reign of God

The mission of the church is a participation in the mission of God that goes from creation to new creation. God's saving act has always been present in history. We have experienced it already now and yet we are still hoping for its eschatological fulfillment, that is, the ultimate salvation in the Lord.

> Then I saw a new heaven and a new earth, the first heaven and the first earth had disappeared now, and there was no longer any sea. I saw the holy city, the new Jerusalem, coming down out of heaven from God, prepared as a bride dressed for her husband. Then I heard a loud voice call from the throne: 'Look, here God lives among human beings. He will make his home among them; they will be his people and he will be their God, God-with-them. He will wipe away all tears from their eyes; there will be no more death, and no more mourning or sadness or pain. The world of the past has gone'. The One sitting on the throne spoke: 'Look, I am making the whole creation new (Rev 21: 1-5).

Is this only an illusion? An empty utopia? If there is no sign at all of its concrete realization, then the Reign of God would be an illusion, and Christianity an opium of people. The Bible, however, offers some signs for discernment. We read for example in Is 65:17-18a; 19b-25.

" . . . For look, I am going to create new heavens and a new earth
and the past will not be remembered and will not come to mind.
Rather be joyful, be glad for ever at what I am creating...
No more will be the sound of weeping be heard there
nor the sound of a shriek;
never again will there be an infant there who lives only a few days
nor an old man who does not run his full course;
for the youngest will die at a hundred,
and at a hundred the sinner will be accursed.
They will build houses and live in them,
they will plant vineyards and eat their fruit.
They will not build for others to live in,
or plant for others to eat;
for the days of my people will be like the days of a tree,
And my chosen ones will themselves use what they have made.
They will not toil in vain,
nor bear children destined to disaster,
for they are the race of Yahweh's blessed ones
and so are their offspring.
Thus, before they call I shall answer,
before they stop speaking
I shall have heard.
The wolf and the young lamb will feed together,
the lion will eat hay like the ox
and dust be the serpent's food.
No hurt, no harm will be done
on all my holy mountain,"
Yahweh says.

This text shows how God's Reign has come in the signs of justice and peace (where children do not die, where the old are taken care of, where people build houses and live in them, they plant vineyards and eat their fruit; the wolf and lamb feed together).

If I may decipher the signs of God's salvation within the signs of our time, then I would like to indicate two great signs, namely the process of liberation and of communion in various realms of human life.

The Process of Liberation

After the Second World War there was a great movement of liberation. Many colonized countries in Asia and Africa declared their independence and became free nations. But political independence is only one step in the struggle for greater liberation. In the socio-economic field we can find an emerging process of empowering the poor and the marginalized in the struggle for a more just and humane society. Culturally there is a parallel movement of recognizing the intrinsic value of each culture, thus liberating it from the oppression of other dominating cultures. In the realm of religion there is a similar movement of liberating religion from a rigid and closed institution in order to rediscover it as "a fire of life," as a fundamental inspiration. Within the Catholic Church since Vatican II we find a movement of liberating both lay and clerics. It is a liberation of the lay, men and women, in order to reassume their rights and responsibility as full members of the church, as people of God. At the same time it is liberation of clerics from the hierarchic-pyramidal structure in order to reassume their vocation to be servants of God's people following the example of Jesus. Various movements of women can be situated within this process of liberation.

It is within this great movement of liberation that we have to decipher the presence of God who has revealed himself in the Bible as the One who liberates his people from all kinds of slavery. If this is true, then mission would mean reaching out to people of other cultures, religions and convictions, joining hands with them in the struggle for greater freedom.

But liberation for what? With this we pass to the second great process.

The Process of Communion

Our contemporary world is marked by globalization, a great process of transforming our world into a global village. But globalization often means domination of the powerful and the rich over those who are weak and poor. I prefer, therefore, to decipher God's saving act in a more positive sign which I call "communion." In politics we see how independent nations join the United Nations and other international associations, while acknowledging the Declaration of Human Rights as one important document of humanity.

Unfortunately in the socio-economic field we still have an enormous gap between rich and poor countries. Nevertheless, there is also a growing international awareness (among others through the network of NGO's) that if we let this gap widen and widen, we will end up in a catastrophe for all humanity. Through the ecological movement we have come to realize that we are all living in a very small planet called "Earth" where water, land, air, and all natural resources are limited. For this reason there has been more international collaboration for the preservation of the ecological system. There is also a greater communion in human knowledge, in scientific research, in all quest for truth and wisdom. Finally in religion we find a growing desire and increasing attempts for inter-religious dialogue and ecumenism, in spite of all contrary signs of fundamentalism and religious fanaticism.

In all these signs we may decipher the basic yearning of the human heart for communion and a sign of God's call to all of us. The Lord our God is a Triune God who calls us all into communion with him and with each other. Mission is reaching out to others beyond social, cultural, and religious boundaries for the sake of greater communion of all in the Lord.

Through both process of liberation and communion we discern the saving acts of God within our contemporary world. Liberation without communion tends to divide and scatter; communion without liberation tends to dominate and oppress. In concrete situations, however, these great signs should be deciphered and actualized more concretely in acts of solidarity, of defending the rights of marginalized, of helping the victims, of resolving the conflicts, of healing the wounds, of reconciliation and so on. Missionaries are participants in all these, illuminating them with the light of the gospel. They give witness that the Reign of God is actively present among us through all these signs and yet we are still hoping for its ultimate fulfillment when "God will be all in all" (1Cor 15:28). "Look, I am doing something new," says the Lord, "now it emerges; can you not see it?" (Is 43:19).

Notes

1. John Paul II, *Ecclesia in Asia* (http://www.vatican.va /holy_father/john_paul_ii/apost_exhortations/documents/hf_jp-ii_exh_06111999 _ecclesia-in-asia_en.html), 6.

2. Mangunwijaya, *Gereja Diaspora* (Yogyakarta: Kanisius, 1999).

3. Walter Kasper, "The Unicity and Universality of Jesus Christ," Address at the International Congress on Mission, Pontifical Urban University, October 15, 2000.

4. Sejera Muskens, *Gereja Katolik Indonesia*, 4 Vols. (Jakarta: KWI, 1973).

5. Documents of the XV General Chapter SVD 2000, in *In Dialogue with the Word* #1 (Rome: SVD Publications, 2000), 21.

6. Antonio Pernia, "Mission of the Twenty-First Century: An SVD Perspective," in this volume.

7. Gaudencio B. Rosales and Catalino G. Arévalo, eds., *For All the Peoples of Asia: FABC Documents from 1970-1991* (Quezon City: Claretian Publications; Maryknoll, NY: Orbis Books, 1992), 22-23; 42-43, *et passim*. Franz-Josef Eilers, ed., *For All the Peoples of Asia, Vol. 2: FABC Documents from 1992 to 1996* (Quezon City: Claretian Publications, 1997), 143-182; 193-205.

8. Documents of the XV General Chapter SVD 2000, 31.

9. Ibid., 30-36.

10. Peter Hünermann, "Evangelization of Europe?," Paper presented at the SEDOS Missionary Congress for the Jubilee Year, Rome April 3-8, 2000.

11. Paul Ricoeur, *The Conflict of Interpretations* (Evanston, IL: Northwestern University Press, 1974), 440-467.

12. Aloysius Pieris, "An Asian Paradigm: Inter-religious Dialogue and Theology of Religions," *Month* (April, 1993): 130.

13. Paul Ricoeur, *Time and Narrative*, Vol. 3 (Chicago: University of Chicago Press, 1988), 244-249.

STATEMENT OF THE CONSULTATION ON "MISSION FOR THE TWENTY-FIRST CENTURY"
Techny, IL – December 10-11, 2000

Introduction

On December 10 and 11, 2000, twenty-five missiologists and mission practitioners gathered at Techny, IL, the motherhouse of the Society of the Divine Word (SVD) in North America, to reflect together on the major directions that the church's mission will be taking in the opening years of this new century and new millennium. The consultation took place immediately following a symposium that was also entitled "Mission for the Twenty-first Century," in which plenum speakers and workshop leaders reflected on the future of mission both in the light of the twentieth century's three most important documents of the Roman Magisterium on mission (*Ad Gentes, Evangelii Nuntiandi,* and *Redemptoris Missio*), and of the Statement of the recently-concluded Fifteenth General Chapter of the Society of the Divine Word, entitled "Listening to the Spirit: Our Missionary Response Today" (*Listening*). The task of the participants in the consultation was to reflect further on the theme, particularly in view of the speakers and discussions of the symposium. Of the twenty-five present, eighteen were SVDs, one was a Mennonite, and one was a woman. The participants are working in fourteen countries worldwide, and represent fourteen ethnic groups or nationalities. Among the participants were Jozef Cardinal Tomko, Prefect of the Congregation for the Evangelization of Peoples, and Antonio M. Pernia, SVD, Superior General of the Society of the Divine Word.

In such a rich gathering of scholars and missionaries, discussion was lively, frank, and creative. The task of the consultation from the start was to produce a short document that would articulate the thinking of contemporary missiology and would set an agenda for the future, and this is what is expressed in the paragraphs that follow. The document has two major parts. The first part reflects what the twenty-five consultation participants consider to be the major points of content of missiology and mission theology today; the second part is a summary of a very lively discussion on the second day of the consultation, in which participants presented what they judged to be some of the major agenda for thinking about mission in the next one or two decades.

I. *Missiology and Mission Theology Today*

A. The Mission is First of All **God's** Mission (Missio Dei)

A.1 The Church's evangelizing mission is derived from, rooted in, and molded after the dialogic character of the inner mission of the Triune God. In the Trinity, the Father communicates his abundant life and love to the Son in the Holy Spirit.

A.2 This communication is continued in creation through the Word and in the Spirit, and in history where the Spirit is preparing "seeds of the Word" for the Gospel. Down through the ages, many people and nations have expressed a longing for that which is beyond. "This yearning itself is a sign of the Spirit's ceaseless invitation to humanity to become partners in the divine mission" (*Listening* 38). In the fullness of time, in the redemptive incarnation, that communication finds its fulfillment in the same Word who in his ministry, life, death, and resurrection, proclaimed and manifested this divine love.

A.3 To continue the same ministry 'till the end of time, the Son through the Spirit sends the church even as he himself was sent by the Father (cf. Jn 20:19-20). The church, conscious of being the agent of God's mission enters into dialogue with the world and its cultures and religions. The SVD, as a religious missionary congregation within the church, is particularly committed to this dialogue and finds special identity in enabling the church to carry on its missionary task.

B. "Deliver us from evil"

B.1 Participation in God's mission (*missio Dei*) leads us inexorably to God's gracious will (*optio Dei*) by which the Divine Word became flesh-- "made himself poor" (2Cor 8:9)--in the heart of the world for the sake of the world.

B.2 In looking at our world today, we recognize much that is good, yet we also come face to face with the mystery of evil (*mysterium iniquitatis*), in all its dimensions. There is, first, a cosmic dimension, referred to in the New Testament as the reign of sin, the realm of the principalities and powers. This cosmic dimension represents the anti-Reign, which Jesus calls in Luke's Gospel the realm of darkness.

B.3 There is a social dimension as well, with economic, political, and cultural dimensions. It manifests itself in the crushing poverty which most of the world's population experiences and in the destruction of the ecological balance. It stands behind the corruption that robs the poor of their resources, their dignity, and their future. Agents of the church, including ourselves, have sometimes been implicated in this. It is found in the indifference to disease and in the calculations of limited war. It converges in the experience of exclusion of the great mass of the human family from much of the world's political life and its economic prosperity.

B.4 There is, finally, the underlying personal dimension to this phenomenon of sin, where vice, the lack of virtue, and the refusal to assume responsibility result in scandalous actions which lead to dehumanization of some and the demonization of others.

B.5 These three dimensions of evil collude and interpenetrate one another to create a world of the "darkness of sin and the night of unbelief" (Arnold Janssen's prayer)which enslaves the human family and its future.

B.6 The Good News coming from God through Jesus Christ is the mystery of salvation (*mysterium salutis*), which confronts all three dimensions of evil's mysterious power. It confronts the personal dimension by allowing individuals to enter into the Paschal Mystery. Through baptism, we are liberated from sin by receiving forgiveness and embarking on a new way of life, and entering the church, the missionary community of the redeemed. This new life is continually strengthened by the Sacrament_ of Reconciliation and the Eucharist, leading to a strengthening of virtue and a formation of conscience.

B.7 The gospel confronts the social dimension by "proclaiming Good News to the poor" (Lk 4:18), a message of liberation, life, and morality, that manifests itself in effective action. Accepting this message leads us to liberation and the fullness of life, which finds expression in the pursuit of justice.

B.8 Finally, the gospel of "the light of the Word and the spirit of grace" (Arnold Janssen's prayer) is manifest in the cosmic reconciliation brought about by Christ, by which "God may be all in all (1 Cor 15:28)." We experience this fullness already as eschatological hope and joy, inspiring us in our missionary struggle against the three dimensions of evil; we anticipate it in our liturgical celebrations.

C. Diversity and Pluralism

C.1 God's mission today unfolds within a world that is changing at an unprecedented pace. This creates a process which gathers together peoples of diverse ethnicities, cultures, religions and ideologies, making the peoples of this earth--for the first time in history--truly "one world." This phenomenon has many positive and negative aspects. Positively, for example, the resulting diversity of cultures and religions holds the potential for mutual enrichment and respect, as well as a potential for an expanded world view and a less ethnocentric understanding of church. It calls the church in a way never before possible to the fullness of its catholicity. Negatively, however, while in no way denying the promise that such diversity holds for today's world, this rich diversity can be interpreted ideologically. Such an interpretation results in a kind of pluralism of thought and behavior that, on the one hand, makes it difficult to hold to any kind of absolute truth and, on the other, has led to a genuine crisis of meaning as women and men are simply overwhelmed by the multiplicity of information and possible choices. Perhaps even more disturbing, pluralism is used by the powerful to cloak with respectability what is really a naked hegemony over others. Often, therefore, there emerge reactions that either retreat into a narrow dogmatism or develop extreme and exclusive interpretations of cultural and religious traditions.

C.2 Within this context, choices must be made, and the church is challenged to witness to the gospel and to encounter all peoples in the name of Jesus. This salvific encounter calls people to a community of meaning, memory and hope.

C.3 In this pluralist society and evangelizing church, SVDs today are called to be unequivocal witnesses to the Word made flesh, who is the way, the truth and the life. We do this in particular by drawing on the positive experience of our internationality and our tradition of Trinitarian spirituality, both of which accent the validity and holiness of unity-in-diversity. Our commitment to the characteristic dimensions of the biblical apostolate and communication (see Listening 72-78) provides resources to respond positively to the world's burgeoning diversity, and to respond critically and constructively to this pluralist world.

D. Local Church

D.1 Within the church, diversity has been and continues to be a reality. Especially after Vatican II we have learned to think of the church as a communion of local churches which are not only distinct but diverse. The more each local church succeeds in inculturating itself, the more fully the richness of God's love and life is expressed.

D.2 We believe that one of the major aspects of the SVD missionary task is to cooperate in fostering a viable local church. This involves, among other things, the task of accompanying the local church in incarnating the gospel within the cultural and religious traditions of the people. It also entails mediating the dialogue among local churches themselves as well as serving as an advocate for concerns of local communities with local bishops and with the Holy See. Above all, the SVD mission in this regard is to enable the local churches to mature by helping them realize their unique participation to God's mission, both within and beyond their visible confines.

D.3 Today the SVD is called to do this by encouraging what it has discerned as a four-fold prophetic dialogue--with unbelievers and faith seekers, with the poor and the marginalized, , with people of different cultures, with people of other religious ways and secular ideologies--within this richly diverse world (Listening 58, 63, 66, 70). In this four-fold prophetic dialogue the SVD together with the local church need to seek out "the modern equivalents of the Areopagus" in which the gospel is to be proclaimed (see RM 37).

E. Missionary Spirituality

E.1 The presence of the missionary in today's world calls for a distinctive missionary spirituality. We come to mission as contemplatives, and as servants who witness and preach the gospel from a position of powerlessness and vulnerability. Amidst the increasing uncertainty and violence in our world, we encounter others by faithful presence, willing to "stay put," ready to suffer with the people--as shepherds, not hirelings (Jn 10).

E.2 Because prophetic dialogue is our mode of mission, the SVD missionary is called to cultivate a spirituality for which dialogue is at the core. Prophetic dialogue begins by listening, and only speaks when asked for the "reason for the hope" (see 1Pet 3:15-16). Nevertheless, dialogue also presumes a certain self-confidence and a strong sense of personal identity. A dialogical person has initiative and creativity, and willingly takes risks in reaching out and encountering the other--in "bold humility" as missiologist David Bosch says so well. Such a person draws inspiration not only from fellow Christians, but also from people of other faith traditions; he or she is willing to enunciate his or her faith to others, and willing as well to risk misunderstanding.

F. The Changing Face of Mission

Realizing that a majority of first appointments now come from Asia, the well-established structures of mission set up by, and for, western cross-cultural missionaries needs continual reappraisal. In addition, given that an increasing number of confreres are young--particularly those from Asia--their initiative and creativity should be fostered by encouraging them to come together to reflect upon their experience, to articulate their role more clearly, and to propose new ways of doing mission in fidelity to the missio Dei, God's saving presence and action in the world.

II. An Agenda for the Future

The following fourteen points were proposed by the participants as major agenda for missiologists and mission theologians--particularly SVDs--to think through in the future:

A.   Further reflection needs to be done regarding, on the one hand, the positive values of diversity, and, on the other, the negative values generated by an ideological approach to pluralism. Attention needs to be given to the fact that in some places (e.g. Asia) pluralism is looked upon as a positive idea.

B.   Further reflection also needs to be done in the area of understanding the mediating role of the SVD in regard to local churches. Can the SVD be advocates of local experiences over against the "institutional church"? Can it be a greater advocate of ecumenical concerns both within the local churches and in the worldwide communion of churches? Can it mediate to other local churches the voice of the poor?

C.   When we speak of "established structures of mission," we need to be more precise. Which structures are we talking about?

D.   When we speak about the four-fold prophetic dialogue, we need to be careful not simply to repeat the Chapter document.

E.   Further reflection on the roots of mission in God's mission (missio Dei) is called for. In the aftermath of Vatican Council II there may have been too much influence on the human dimension of missionary service (e.g. mission as development, mission as liberation, mission as accompaniment). Some theologies of the missio Dei (e.g. Hoekendijk) were also too humanistic in outlook. The challenge is to develop a theology of mission rooted in God's mission that emphasizes God's work, while at the same time emphasizing that God's work is indeed in this world, and committed to the integral salvation of this world.

F.   Inculturation will figure prominently in missiological discussions in the future. We will need to clarify the meaning and value of the experience of the local church; we will need to think in terms of newer understandings of culture that anthropologists are proposing today (e.g. culture as constructing an identity in a pluralist world); and we need to think of inculturation not only in terms of "culture," but also in terms of ethnicity, gender and generations.

G.   In the future, the relationship between "dialogue" and "proclamation" needs to be further clarified. While the Magisterium has been clear that there is a distinction, that distinction has not been sufficiently "teased out" as yet, and needs more reflection.

H.   More theological work will have to be done regarding the Holy Spirit and mission. How does the Holy Spirit accomplish its part in the Missio Dei? How is the Holy Spirit's work distinct, and yet linked to the work of Jesus Christ?

I.   There is need for interdisciplinary involvement in missiological issues. Philosophers in particular should be invited to join in missiological discussions, as well as systematic theologians, moral theologians, biblical scholars and experts in communication. The SVD should encourage meetings of groups of interdisciplinary reflection as well as groups of scholars in their discrete disciplines.

J.   The future should include closer collaboration with (particularly) the Holy Spirit Mission Sisters in SVD missiological reflection.

K.   In view of the fact that, increasingly, missionary work is being carried out in situations of violence, attention should be given to the practice and theory of reconciliation.

L.   The theory and practice of doing mission today should be used as a basis for rewriting the first chapter of SVD Constitutions.

M.   SVD mission scholars should work to inform all theological reflection with a missionary vision, emphasizing the fact that mission is a dimension of all theology.

N.   Reflection should be developed that plumbs the role of hope in today's world--this over against the lethargy caused by the seeming lack of alternatives to neoliberal capitalism, and in the light of the resurrection faith found in living the Paschal Mystery.

Conclusion

No document can capture the full flavor of the discussions that took place in the two days of the Consultation. What the participants hope, however, is that some of the enthusiasm, the honesty, the searching, and the struggle to move beyond well-worn platitudes that was experienced can be communicated in above paragraphs. The symposium that took place on the preceding days, and the consultation itself, concluded the year-long celebration of the one hundredth anniversary of the founding of Techny, and with the one hundred twenty-fifth anniversary of the Society of the Divine Word. As the participants looked back with gratitude on so many years of missionary service and missiological reflection, such a gathering confirmed their hope that the church's mission--or its participation in the mission that is God's--can and will continue to be renewed.

Gabriel Afagbegee, SVD
Thomas Ascheman, SVD
Ireneo Barreto, SVD
Heribert Bettscheider, SVD
Stephen Bevans, SVD
William R. Burrows
Philip Gibbs, SVD
Anthony J. Gittins, CSSP
Margaret Eletta Guider, OSF
Jacob Kavunkal, SVD
Robert Kisala, SVD
Lawrence Nemer, SVD
Peter Sam Nguyen, SVD
Antonio M. Pernia, SVD
    (*SVD Superior General*)

Peter C. Phan
John M. Prior, SVD
Gary Riebe-Estrella, SVD
Robert J. Schreiter, CPPS
Roger Schroeder, SVD
Wilbert R. Shenk
Arnold Sprenger, SVD
Christian Tauchner, SVD
Vincent Twoomey, SVD
Edenio Valle, SVD
+Jozef Cardinal Tomko
    (*Prefect, Congregation for the Evangelization of Peoples*)